NATIONAL SOCIALISM AND THE RELIGION
OF NATURE

NATIONAL SOCIALISM AND THE RELIGION OF NATURE

ROBERT A. POIS

CROOM HELM
London & Sydney

© 1986 Robert A. Pois
Croom Helm Ltd, Provident House, Burrell Row,
Beckenham, Kent BR3 1AT
Croom Helm Australia Pty Ltd, Suite 4, 6th Floor,
64–76 Kippax Street, Surry Hills, NSW 2010, Australia

British Library Cataloguing in Publication Data

Pois, Robert A.
    National socialism and the religion of nature.
    1. National socialism — Social aspects
    2. Religion and politics   3. Germany — Politics
    and government — 1933–1945
    I. Title
    306'.26   DD256.5
    ISBN 0-7099-4022-X

Filmset by Mayhew Typesetting, Bristol, England
Printed and bound in Great Britain
by Billing & Sons Limited, Worcester.

CONTENTS

For Anne Marie

FOREWORD AND ACKNOWLEDGEMENTS

This work is concerned with National Socialism and that religion of nature to which, in the eyes of those most important to the movement, it was supposed to approximate. It was a religion which was born of cultural, social, and psychological circumstances that have to be described as being largely 'German.' Yet, its vision — the appeal that it had for at least the fully-initiated — went so far beyond the concerns and demands that were largely responsible for the support it received from the German public, that the vital core of the National Socialist religion had always to remain secret. Except occasionally, this work will not be concerned with Nazi ritualism and ceremony. Enough attention already has been devoted to these themes. Rather, it will be focused on the 'vision'; a view of humankind as part and parcel of nature which allowed for a fusion of idealism and pragmatism absolutely singular in its nature and effectiveness. The religion informed by this vision could, and indeed had, to accommodate itself to the most banal of petty bourgeois usages. In fact, these had to be *sanctified* in the name of that higher purpose which, except for those who were viewed as embodying it, had to remain shrouded in mystery.

In dealing with this topic, the following organisation has been used. In the first chapter, the terms religion, ideology, and *Weltanschauung* are considered. Here, the author is not so much concerned with providing strict definitions of them. Such, at least with regard to their application to modern 'secular religiosity,' will always remain both elusive and illusive. Rather, the author provides a rough framework within which interrelationships and interactions in the context of National Socialist 'religiosity' can be described. A second chapter is concerned with the question of why it is crucial to appreciate the religious qualities of National Socialism; why, in fact, approaching it from any other perspective raises far more problems than it solves. In the next three chapters, we will focus upon the National Socialist religion of nature itself, the religion in power and the sanctification of national life that this entailed, and finally, the confrontation between self-proclaimed 'natural,' authentic human beings and so-called 'enemies of life.' Of crucial concern here is how easy it can be for individuals who believe that all actions undertaken by them — as self-proclaimed bearers of naturally-grounded truths — are *ipso facto* valid, to transform reality and thus bring it around to approximate their conceptions of it. At the same time, the vitiating weakness of a pragmatic/idealistic religion which, by its very nature, must justify itself through constant success, will be demonstrated.

The final two chapters deal with questions of an admittedly more hypothetical nature. In Chapter 6 the author considers the question of the 'terror of history,' as Mircea Eliade has described it. Here, we will be looking at National Socialism as both resulting from and embodying the search for what Eliade has called 'sacred time.' Of importance here is the extremely seductive nature of any faith which allows, in fact *demands*, that one step out of history. In the final chapter, the conclusion, the author deals with what he perceives to be the relevance of the National Socialist religion of nature for our own time. This chapter, written out of a sense of anger and frustration, is quite polemical in nature. It is, in large measure, a critique of modern nationalism, particularly that variety of it that has survived in the West, and the ideology of liberal capitalism that is inextricably intertwined with it. While not in full agreement with him, I owe much here to the analyses of Dr Richard Rubenstein. In the Appendix, we will be concerned with an issue that has been touched on in several places throughout the work, but never considered in any detail. This is the question of the relationship between the National Socialist religion of nature and the German people. Also, I will address the issue of whether such a relationship can ever be determined with any degree of precision.

In researching and completing this work, I am indebted to the University of Colorado Council on Research and Creative Work, which provided a Faculty Fellowship for the summer and fall of 1976, and a grant-in-aid for the spring of 1985, and to College of Arts and Sciences Dean Everly B. Fleischer who provided for my sabbatical leave for the spring, 1985. During my 1976 visits, the staffs of the *Bundesarchiv* in Koblenz and the *Institut für Zeitgeschichte* in Munich were always courteous and helpful. I am also indebted to the personnel of the UCLA library, where I did research while a visiting professor during the 1977-1978 academic year. The interlibrary loan office of the Norlin Library at Colorado University, Boulder, an office which, from time to time, I virtually haunted, was always patient and most helpful, and I am most grateful for the assistance of reference librarian Ms Ruth Friedman. In the spring of 1985, I visited the Wiener Library in London for the first time. I owe the people there a great deal, and in ways which go rather beyond the usual concerns and activities associated with archives. I will go into this a bit later in the Foreword. The encouragement and courtesy of the humanities editor of Croom Helm Ltd, Mr Richard Stoneman, have been

appreciated throughout, and his confidence in my work has been important in sustaining my own. I owe much to Alex McIntosh, copy-editor
sans pareil; readers of this work, probably even more. I am indebted
to Transaction Press, which gave me permission to utilise materials contained in *Political Symbolism and Modern Europe* (1982).

I know that the most influential person in my intellectual — and occasionally, even emotional — life has been my *Doktorvater* George L.
Mosse. Even beyond the immense support and encouragement he has
always provided for me, there has been the occasional challenge. For
example, his response to learning of my interest in psychohistory — 'You
must be kidding!' — will be long remembered and treasured, as will,
of course the very serious questions he raised about the psychohistorical
method. Above all, though, there is his example, and here the career
of a man who has written perceptively and well on topics ranging from
the Reformation to 19th Century sexuality, with ground-breaking contributions to our knowledge of the European radical right and political
symbolism along the way, must speak for itself — and for him.

I have benefited more than I can say, even in an extended essay, from
the friendship and support of Peter Loewenberg and George M. Kren.
Even before I got to know him personally, Peter Loewenberg's pioneering
work in psychohistory excited me to the point of learning all that I could
about it and, in fact, making use of the approach in my own work. I
am continually learning from him the potentialities contained within
psychohistory, and its limits as well, particularly for one without formal clinical training. In part, this is why the author has not utilised the
psychohistorical method in the present work. Getting to know Peter personally has been both meaningful and pleasurable for me. George M.
Kren, one of this country's most distinguished scholars of the Holocaust,
has offered a continual challenge to my, in part Freudian assumption,
that the triumph of reason over instinct will somehow crown the evolution of humanism. Also one who has made use of psychohistory, he has
been both a guide and sober analyst of the method's limitations. While
important, all of this takes second place to his friendship.

I owe much to David L. Gross, whose analytical abilities, particularly with regard to the vexed issues of cultural criticism, are second
to none. Boyd H. Hill, Jr. has offered much in the way of personal and
intellectual support during times of personal travail and great doubt.
Robert Schulzinger has shown both friendship and an interest in my work,
little realising that he would be called upon to read some of it. His suggestions and criticisms were of great value. As is the case with all
teachers, I owe much to a number of students whose comments,

criticisms, and original ideas on themes central to this work have been most helpful. Recognising the injustice involved, I can mention but a few — Frank Gordon, John Stovall, Tom Gordon, Jan Schweninger, David Harrison, Irene Gagel and, one 'from years back,' when some of the ideas contained herein were 'gleams in their father's eyes,' Tim Keck.

Ms. Sandy Marsh, departmental staff assistant, was of invaluable assistance in preparing this manuscript for publication. Without her hard work, and that of Ms Margaret Benshoff-Holler, Ms Veta Hartman, Mr Burt Rashbaum and Ms Patricia D Murphy (often under very trying conditions), there would have been no book at all. I owe them far more than the bottles that were passed out when the manuscript was completed.

When in London, I partook of the hospitality of Mrs Katherine Devey and Mr Stanley and Mrs Penny Lowry. I was, and am, very appreciative of this, and also of their providing delightful empirical evidence that some of my most cherished assumptions about British cuisine were wrong.

Earlier, I mentioned how much I owe, in a variety of ways, to the personnel of the Wiener Library. They were unfailingly helpful, offering suggestions about documents I did not even know existed. More than that, though, the director of the Library, Mrs Christa Wichmann, and her assistant, Mrs Alexandra Leas, provided an atmosphere of uncommon courtesy and consideration in which to work. I was both astounded and gratified at Mrs Leas' providing tea, at about 4.00 p.m. of course, for those working in the Library. At odd moments, in every sense of the word, I suppose, I would talk to Mrs Wichmann about some of my curious obsessions — steam locomotives and the creature up in Loch Ness. From that point on, Mrs Wichmann presented me, almost every day, with articles about steam trains she clipped from the newspapers. I knew that nothing unusual was occurring at Loch Ness for, no doubt, she would have told me of it. In an archive filled with documents produced by, or related to, the greatest horror of the twentieth century, these extraordinary people, one of whom had her own, very immediate experience of this horror, provided a warmth that I have never experienced in an academic setting and, for that matter, not all that many 'personal' settings either. Mrs Wichmann and Mrs Leas are wonderful people, and my expressions of gratitude must be meagre in comparison to what I owe them, in so many ways.

My wife Anne Marie, whose support has been indispensible, is now working on a doctoral dissertation concerning the Women's International League for Peace and Freedom. Long ago, the women of this organisation recognised that only with the elimination of murderous, obscene nationalism will war itself be abolished. Out of reason-informed compassion, these were, and are, the true students of *Realpolitik*. I hope that my work will help to shed some light on a sick past, awash in nationalist fantasies whose expression could only be murder. My wife's work will describe and analyse an organisation of women; the translation of *their* 'fantasy' into reality is our only hope.

Robert A Pois
Boulder, Colorado

INTRODUCTION

In recent years, a variety of individuals have expressed the fear that the National Socialist phenomenon and attendant events, often referred to collectively as 'The Holocaust', are in danger of being trivialised. Most assuredly, such already has occurred, at least to some degree. Terms such as 'genocide,' 'Nazi,' and even 'Holocaust' itself are increasingly used so loosely as to rob them of significance or even meaning and, only forty years after the end of World War II, gas chamber and crematoria jokes have taken their place alongside kindred ones concerned with throwing Christians to lions and enslaving blacks. This, of course, is a sure sign that the experience has been 'assimilated' at least in so far as its ability to prick the public conscience is in any way concerned. Indeed, outside of specialists and those with perhaps more personal interests in these subjects, the only souls seemingly concerned with the singularity of Nazism and related phenomena are the collectors of World War II German military medals, SS insignia, daggers, and other bits of memorabilia.

Trivialising of events is, of course, a very human tendency, and it is hardly confined to the question of Nazism — the primary victims of which were, after all, a minority group which has never been particularly well-liked — nor, for that matter, to the atrocities perpetrated upon the early Christians or black slaves. Some time ago, or so it now seems, ll November used to be designated as 'Armistice Day' and, at least in some American public schools, students would be required to stand and face east, towards France. This was done at 11.00 a.m. local time, supposedly the hour at which the armistice was signed, and the quite literal 'eleventh hour' aspect of it all was thus supposed to be impressed upon young still formative minds. As time went on, civic consciousness became impressed by the fact that another World War had supervened and this, plus Cold War adventures and the Korean conflict, were responsible for turning 'Armistice Day' into 'Veterans Day'. Of course, this was understandable and, perhaps in keeping with the symbolic usages attendant upon national memory, even necessary. Yet, the singularity of World War I which, for soldiers, remains as probably the most brutal, and brutalising, of all wars, has been lost. The same, of course, is occurring with regard to Nazism and the Holocaust, either as understandably anguished and indignant members of one or the other oppressed group

1

put forth claims that it has suffered a fate analogous to that of the Jews of Europe, or as distressed theologians of all persuasions turn the horrors of World War II into universal theological metaphor.

To a great extent, this work will be concerned with the 'singularity' of the Nazi phenomenon. In this regard, the author, while generally leaving 'theology' alone, will be concerned with National Socialism as a 'religion of nature,' and with how the leading representatives of this 'religion' sought to bring something that we can call 'objective reality' into conformity with its underlying precepts. While a general Western *malaise* regarding modernity and the conquest of nature provides the general background for it, a variety of traditions and circumstances which, taken together, can be described as 'German,' determined the basic ideational content of the National Socialist 'religion of nature' and why and when its rebellion against Judaeo-Christian usages took place. Singular with regard to time and place, German National Socialism was also such in the zeal, fanaticism if you wish, with which its leading exponents attempted to translate its leading precepts into reality or, as stated above, with which such individuals struggled — until the end, successfully in their own eyes — to bring reality into conformity with these precepts. The very significance of this enterprise necessitated that, even though National Socialism was a 'mass movement' and thus the product of mass concerns and/or pathologies, the ultimate goals of the 'religion,' i.e., what it in the end meant to accomplish and how it would bring this about, remain largely secret. While assuming that many Germans knew far more about what transpired during the Nazi period than they would later admit — or at least knew enough to determine that they could know no more — I believe that the fundamental concerns of at least the leadership were such that most Germans could not be allowed to know much of them. The individual German may have voted National Socialist or lent the movement support because such a person was afraid of the communists, anti-Semitic, alienated from the Republic, furiously revanchist, or simply disgusted with a moribund and chaotic *status quo*. As is well known, the Nazis were quite adept at appealing to a variety of groups and interests and were extraordinary political tacticians. Under certain circumstances, the movement or various of its representatives, could even appeal to established 'Christian' principles and institutions. Ultimately though, those who mattered in the movement were concerned with bringing into being a timeless reality, immune from the traumas of history; a reality within which biological mysteries would attain concrete expression. *Aspects* of this, of course had to be resonant with certain widely-held needs. The grandly hideous core, however, had to remain, at least for the present, the preserve of those whom a non-transcendent Providence had designated prophets of the new reality and of the 'new men' who would represent its highest forms.

It is always fashionable, I realise, while recognising the 'singular' aspects of National Socialism, to draw alarming parallels and analogies between at least elements of the movement and current phonemena. For those on the far left, this can be done almost naturally, that is, with a certain measure of ideological consistency. For that most harassed group of all, 'liberals,' there is a certain amount of masochistic satisfaction in it. Sometimes 'far left,' at least in an American context in which it is easy to be such, and more often than not 'liberal' (although hopefully not *masochistic*, at least politically), I must confess that I see certain parallels and analogies — although how 'alarming' they are is a matter of opinion — between elements of the National Socialist 'religion' and contemporary phenomena. The 'naturalism' of the former certainly has parallels with a sort of fuzzy nature-mysticism which can be observed throughout the West, perhaps, most prominently, in the United States. Thus, in its anti-Judaeo-Christian emphasis upon the sanctity of nature, 'National Socialism' has to be seen as symptomatic of a general, perhaps largely unconscious, discomfiture with the Judaeo-Christian tradition, something which attained *political* expression in Germany but can hardly be seen as confined to it. Of greater significance, though, are certain elements of National Socialism which must be seen as generic to modern nationalism in the West. These are (1) what can be called a 'flight from history,' or 'flight from transcendence'; (2) a sanctification of national life; and (3) the acceptance, and virtual sanctification, of a presumed 'natural order of things.' It is the author's contention that, while these elements may have been implicit in all nationalisms from their respective inceptions, they have attained articulation only in this century, and probably since World War I. In the concluding chapter, I will attempt to show how there can be *functional* analogies between current forms of political expression supposedly grounded in formal adherence to the Judaeo-Christian tradition and those of a movement which, both hypothetically and in practice, was proudly antithetical to the most humanistically meaningful aspects of this tradition. As can no doubt be anticipated, the shared 'rallying point' will be a rejection of humanism and transcendence.

At several points in this work, the author will bring up the question of psychohistory, and psychohistorical approaches to the National Socialist phenomenon. As a rule, although he has both defended and utilised this approach in the past, the author will only refer to it in this work. Further, he will point out what he perceives to be improper or problematical uses of this method. In so doing, he is not in any sense attempting to denigrate psychohistorical approaches, or even to play down their significance in offering new approaches to the National Socialist phenomenon. Indeed, as will become plain, he is of the opinion that probably the ultimately most satisfying explanations of why certain aspects of National Socialism were critical both in bringing the movement to power and holding it together in the face of the most hideous imaginable of self-imposed tasks will be offered by those able to bring to bear a considerable knowledge of psychology. The same would hold, and probably to an even greater degree, with regards to the extraordinary resonance that Hitler was able to have within the German people.

It is true that, particularly in recent years, Freudian psychoanalysis, for many the substructure of what they perceive to be the most penetrating and historically meaningful forms of psychohistory, has been under heavy attack. Of particular importance here have been attacks upon its theoretical underpinnings as a supposed 'scientific' enterprise. It is probably true that Freud and particularly many of those who followed him were much too sanguine about the presumed 'scientific' nature of their obviously subjective excursions into subjectivity. The manifestly subjective character of 'depth psychology' itself suggests that any variety of 'metapsychology,' and such, of course, is generic to the psychoanalytical enterprise, can often appear to be a contradiction in terms. Here, I think that a comparison with the Marxist method is apposite. In many respects, the philosophical foundations of Marxism as an 'ism', i.e., as an ideology, are weak and riven with contradiction. Thus, as a 'metahistorical' system of explanation, it often raises more problems than it solves. Yet, the questions posed by the Marxist method and the answers it can provide have proved to be of immense value, and the historical enterprise would be all the poorer without them. The same, I think, can be said of psychoanalysis in a clinical context, and the psychohistorical approaches informed by it. Its 'scientific' (or 'philosophical') foundations might be questionable, or even very shaky, and Freud himself, in his later years, became somewhat pessimistic as to its abilities to effect 'cures.' It is, however, as a humanistic endeavour, in its emphasis upon reason-informed empathetic understanding, that psychoanalysis has raised the most penetrating questions and offered the most meaningful answers. It is the humanism of psychoanalysis that has attracted historians. Empathetic understanding is of fundamental importance in attaining that synoptic knowledge which must be the goal of any meaningful historical enterprise. Whether or not psychoanalysis rests upon firm scientific foundations, it has provided, and will continue to provide, much of value with regard to human self-understanding. For history as a whole, a field which is never at its best when it purports to offer 'scientific' explanations, the psychohistorical approach has done, and will continue to do, the same.

Yet, while it is my belief that a general defence of psychohistory is in order, I have not utilised any sort of psychohistorical approach in this work. There are two reasons for this. First of all, I am at a point in my own historical education when, if further use is to be made of such an approach, it will be necessary for me to vastly increase my knowledge of psychoanalysis proper. This will necessitate formal training and with it some form of practical experience. In a word, without that requisite training as a 'lay analyst' I have gone about as far as I can with psychohistorical explanations. The second, less formally 'subjective' reason, for not utilising psychohistory in this work is that I think that it is absolutely crucial to understand what the National Socialist ideology 'meant' in the conscious realm of human affairs and fantasies. In a word, even if a psychohistorical approach can offer one or the other hypothesis as to the 'underlying' meaning of an ideology — or, more precisely, as we will be considering it, a variety of 'secular religion' — it behoves us to gain as great an understanding as possible of what historical actors thought that they were doing. Even if words must, in the end, be seen as attenuated metaphors or rationalisations for underlying concerns ultimately accessible only to some form of depth analysis, students of history cannot deprecate them as being 'merely' this. An underlying thesis of this work is that, as some have pointed out, human beings are always more 'religious' than they think they are. Even if religious quests are mere sublimations, they are often intensely powerful ones, and the 'ideas' which sustain or are generated by them, however abstract or absurd, can be as real, or more so, than economic indices, voting statistics, bomb-blasted landscapes, or piles of yellowed, desiccated corpses. Such is a crucial lesson bequeathed us by the National Socialist experience, a lesson continuously articulated in the alternately absurd or murderous religious quests that prevail in a variety of obsolete nationalisms. Unlike that couple hallowed by Christian *mythos*, the 'rough beast' which 'slouches towards Bethlehem to be born' has never lacked for shelter.

1 IDEOLOGY, *WELTANSCHAUUNG* AND RELIGION

German National Socialism was one of the most successful political movements of the twentieth century. With regard to the enthusiasm generated by it and the willingness of millions of people to put their lives on the line for National Socialist principles, it was a phenomenon which has no parallel in recent history. Explanations for the success enjoyed by Adolf Hitler have run the gamut from those favouring clever use of propaganda and mass manipulation to those which suggest that he was an embodiment of the devil himself, a veritable creature who was somehow able to tap a subterranean reservoir of diseased impulses and perversions. Psychohistorians have offered us tantalising hypotheses of how Hitler's own perversions were or came to be congruent with those of the German nation as a whole and, in so doing, they have performed a useful service in helping to obliterate the distinction between individuality and general forces that has plagued the historical profession ever since historicists raised the issue during the halcyon Rankean days of the nineteenth century.

It is the opinion of this writer that, in the final analysis, major historical — and, for that matter historiographical — problems such as those posed by the National Socialist phenomenon can best be explained by those historians who approach them armed with a fairly substantive knowledge of psychology. At the same time, though, one must appreciate the fact that, even if certain phylogenetic forces can be seen as being ultimately responsible for political and social actions, the actors of history, the so-called 'common people,' statesmen, generals, and political leaders, must assume that they are acting in terms of conscious motivation. Ideologies, religions, even mundane economic and political motives, might well be reducible to forces that the traditional instruments of the historical discipline cannot explicate. Nevertheless, people most certainly believe that they act in conformity with certain beliefs. Dedicated National Socialists represent excellent examples of this.

If we are to understand the historical significance of National Socialism, we cannot view it as being something demonic or, and this is of crucial importance, as being only the recrudescence of certain generally held prejudices and political viewpoints, although these certainly were crucial, particularly with regard to the relationship between the movement and the German people as a whole. In a word, we must press beyond the phrase 'National Socialism', in some respects an idea which had a well-established pedigree in German political theory, and determine just what it was the National Socialists themselves thought that they represented. Before proceeding further, however, it is necessary to provide, if not precise definitions, then at least regulative descriptions of three important terms: ideology, *Weltanschauung*, and religion.

According to Hannnah Arendt, an ideology 'is quite literally what its name indicates: it is the logic of an idea. Its subject matter is history, to which the 'idea' is applied; the result of this application is not a body of statements about something that *is*, but the unfolding of a process which is constant change.'[1] Most assuredly, I think, we can easily agree that an ideology is 'the logic of an idea.' The second portion of Arendt's definition must give us pause, particularly if we focus upon the *practical* aspect of the ideology, namely its role in day-to-day politics. In any case, while drawing of a well-defined line between being and becoming might have philosophical significance, its political purpose would put such a process under a cloud.

Otto Rank, although at times utilising the term ideology in a very loose way, e.g., referring, at one point in his writings, to an 'ideology of masochism,' has provided a remarkably concise and useful description of the term. For him, ideology was a 'genetic explanation of existing conditions, but at the same time a psychological interpretation of the same and an ideological indication as to their future reorganization.'[2] Most particularly with regards to that often obscure but none the less real point at which political, cultural, and social considerations meet and interpenetrate, this description is, I think, not only of heuristic value (a much overused term in an age of methodological uncertainties) but indeed *valid*.

The term *Weltanschauung* is a rather vexed one. German/English dictionaries offer 'ideology' as a translation of *Weltanschauung*, while various political commentators, several of whom we will consider in due course, consider *Weltanschauung* to be descriptive of a rather rough system of beliefs at some remove from those more finely developed ones which constitute a full-blown ideology. In a word, for many commentators, a *Weltanschauung* has to be seen as, quite literally, a 'world view,' i.e., *any* particular stance assumed by an individual or group of individuals towards the world. Arendt, whose view on ideology we already have considered, rather obfuscates the problem by at first talking about 'an ideology and its *Weltanschauung*', and then about 'The *Weltanschauungen* and ideologies of the nineteenth century'.[3] If we examine these statements closely, however, we can determine that, for Arendt, a *Weltanschauung* could serve as the point of departure for an ideology or it could remain somewhat less well-defined. Peter L. Berger has spoken of 'religious or quasi-religious *Weltanschauungen* . . . engaged in pluralistic competition in our society', thus suggesting that there can be a veritable manifold of 'world-views'.[4] For our purposes, I think that we can *relate Weltanschauung* to ideology in the following manner: the world-view of a figure or figures central to National Socialism could achieve full articulation only through establishment of an ideology, i.e., 'a genetic explanation of existing conditions'. *Mein Kampf* in large measure represented just such an attempt, while Alfred Rosenberg's tedious *Mythus des zwanzigsten Jahrhunderts* was a somewhat more stilted version of the effort. More often than not, National Socialism tended to prefer the term *Weltanschauung* as offering a greater degree of flexibility. At the same time, though, we must appreciate that for National Socialists, ideology and *Weltanschauung* were often used interchangeably, and, from time to time, we will be doing the same.

With the term 'religion,' we are confronted with a variety of problems, none of which can be satisfactorily resolved in a work of this nature. Dictionary definitions stretch the term between a rather formalised pole emphasising relationships between man and presumed deities and those concerns posed by mortality, and a more liberal — although scarcely more comforting one — emphasising dedication to various concerns or ideals. Peter Berger in his earlier work, *The Sacred Canopy*, defined religion as 'the human enterprise by which a sacred cosmos is established'.[5] In a general way, most concerned with the matter probably would accept this definition. In any case, however, psychologists, anthropologists and sociologists are not, and perhaps cannot, be satisfied by formalistic definitions of religion, particularly in view of the challenges posed by modern pluralistic pressures and by increased knowledge of non-Western cultures. Indeed, Professor Berger already has pointed out a problem one has to face when posing the concept of religion against another one, that of *Weltanschauung*. As we recall, he spoke of 'religious or quasi-religious *Weltanschauungen*'. Thus, there are religious 'world-views', and, seen from this angle, religion can be seen as the expression of a nexus of attitudes. Otto Rank presented us with *another* problem when he defined religion as 'the collective ideology par excellence, which can only spring from a powerful group-need and mass-consciousness, which itself springs from the need of the individual for dependence and implies his subjugation to higher forces'.[6] Now, religion is being viewed as a form of ideology. Particularly in view of the fact that common folk wisdom often declares ideology to be a sort of secularised religion, this statement by Rank — even when we bear in mind that he tended to use the term ideology rather loosely — must have a disquieting effect.

Religion, thus, can be many things. One can use the term to describe a formal institution, defined in terms of precept and organisation. Or religion can be viewed as being a particular form assumed by crucial psychic needs. Here it can be seen as embodying a given *Weltanschauung* or ideology. Of course, religion also can be all of these things at once. Perhaps not surprisingly, we appear to be dealing with a term which, over the years, has become increasingly difficult to pin down; certainly more so, in any case, than ideology or even *Weltanschauung*. None the less, there are *generalisations* we can make about it. First of all, as the anthropologist Mary Douglas has pointed out in her thought-provoking work, *Natural Symbols*, we can describe the role of religion as that of 'a technology for overcoming risk'.[7] Professor Douglas was firm in stating that the notion that even so-called 'primitive people' are inherently *deeply* religious is simply false.[8] However, the author went on to say, 'There is no person whose life does not need to unfold in a coherent symbolic system'.[9] Thus, what has emerged here is a description of religion as being some form of 'technology for overcoming risk' which necessarily expresses itself in a 'coherent symbolic system'. Each of the several 'technologies', to say nothing of the 'symbolic systems' has to be the product of, and responsive to, given, time-conditioned cultural needs and, throughout her work, Professor Douglas is careful not to fall back upon putative 'universal' religious demands of an aggressively specific nature. Yet, there are posited certain general needs which call forth solutions, or at least attitudes, which we can view as 'religious'. These can find expression in fully-articulated systems (so-called 'organised religions') or more loosely-defined and, at times, very loosely structured patterns of belief, patterns which none the less, constitute what Berger has called a 'sacred cosmos'.

When all is said and done, however, we find ourselves still confronting a term most elusive in nature. Accepting Professor Douglas's definition, or at least description, of religion as a 'technology for overcoming risk,' we can, at the same time, see that a well-developed *Weltanschauung* or ideology can perform the same function. Thus — we are driven back to the point raised by other commentators — namely, that religion can be seen as being a particular mode assumed by either of these two patterns of thought.

In this work, we will be concerned in part with the question of certain values which have been perceived as being of singular importance in the Judaeo-Christian religious tradition. These values have served, at least formally, to provide axiological if not ethical guidelines for Western civilisation and have been the unconscious legacy for millions whose devotion to the tradition has been limited. The greater portion of our analysis, however, will be devoted to analysing that National Socialist ideology — or *Weltanschauung* as it is usually described — which, in very crucial ways, challenged the Judaeo-Christian tradition. Thus far, we seem to have established that while some distinction can be made between ideology and *Weltanschauung*, matters become very much clouded when we pose religion against these two terms. What, then, are we talking about when we speak of a National Socialist challenge to a religious tradition?

First of all, we may recognize that one *can* have a religious *Weltanschauung* without having access to or accepting a fully-articulated religious tradition. In my opinion, Adolf Hitler and others of importance in the National Socialist movement had just such a 'world-view,' this despite the fact that many commentators on National Socialism have maintained that the movement was dominated exclusively by a sort of nihilistic biologism. As mentioned above, this writer also thinks that the aforementioned *Weltanschauung* had to express itself in the form of an ideology in order to find as full as possible articulation within a given cultural/political context. We will be talking, however, of a *National Socialist religion*, suggesting that there is, after all, a difference between religion and ideology; that, at a certain point, the 'need of the individual for . . . subjugation to higher forces' attains expression in an ideational form rather beyond those spanned even by Otto Rank's liberal definition of ideology.

Here, we must see that, according to Rank's aforementioned description of ideology, there was to be no recourse to mystery, no calling upon forces unknown. As Rank pointed out, however, in his 'Modern Education' essay, religion's greatest drawing card is the fact that it 'admits *the Unknown*, indeed, recognises it as the chief factor instead of pretending an omniscience that we do not possess'.[10] Thus, for Rank, probably of non-Marxists the most strident in identifying religion as a form of ideology, there was an ideational gap between the two which he never overcame. As I see it, while National Socialists either rejected or ignored supernaturalism — not mysticism, but the literal belief in some sort of deity *above* nature, as is characteristic of Judaeo-Christian thought — they were strong believers in a religion of nature *heavily* mystical in content. Here, we must bear in mind Peter Berger's definition of mysticism — 'any religious practice or doctrine that asserts the ultimate

unity of man and the divine'. [11] It was this mysticism which both complemented and reinforced the crude scientism which so often has been
singled out as being of central importance to National Socialist thought;
and, at the same time, it allowed for a fusion of this scientism (or
biologism, as it can be called) with perceived timeless mystery. Such
a fusion was necessary if certain avowed principles of the Judaeo-
Christian tradition, also grounded in mystery, were to be challenged.

The author believes that, if one takes the writings, speeches, and
memoranda of leading National Socialists seriously, the following relationship between *Weltanschauung* ideology and religion existed:
Weltanschauung, something which they saw as achieving increasing *articulation* in the form of ideology, embodied a set of principles religious
in nature. In a word, the National Socialist 'revolution of spirit,' to use
a phrase often, and accurately, associated with National Socialism, was
ultimately a true religious rebellion or, at the very least, assertion of
religious values antithetical to the Judaeo-Christian tradition.[12] Of course,
this interpretation of National Socialism is not entirely original. In the
opinion of the author, however, there has never been a *satisfactory*
analysis of this religion. This has not been done either because National
Socialism as a *religion of nature* has not been taken seriously, or because
investigation of such a religion could lead to extremely disquieting conclusions. As has been suggested earlier, the conclusion reached by this
writer is that National Socialism was a religion of nature, one that was
rooted in fundamental existential concerns of alienated, twentieth century man. Its content was German, but the form it assumed could well
prove to be congruent with the spiritual needs of all people who, rejecting Marxist solutions necessitating class-warfare, have been unable to
deal successfully with the necessarily alienating character of modern
society. In a word, National Socialism was *one* response to a general
problem which has haunted Western bourgeois culture during the industrial and, for that matter, post-industrial age.

It should be obvious that conclusions of this nature do not indicate
approval of National Socialism. In its claim to be rooted in fundamental
'laws of life,' and in its strident demand that all whom it saw as living
outside of such laws be exterminated, the National Socialist Movement
manifested an arrogance unequalled by any other modern mass political
movement. In the statements and writings of National Socialists'
ideologues, we can see that *hubris* so often characteristic of educated
barbarism. Nevertheless, the religious claim of National Socialism cannot be dismissed as ideological window dressing or reification. In it,
one can see longings and concerns that, as much as the Judaeo-Christian

tradition which National Socialism sought to supplant, have been the spiritual legacy of Wesern man. At the same time, though, these longings and concerns achieved an expression that was absolutely unique to National Socialism. Whether this will remain the case, of course, is for our and future generations to decide. This brief work is concerned with delineating certain problems and approaches which the author thinks are of value in determining why National Socialist leaders thought that their movement was able to speak to the needs of so many people.

Notes

1. Hannah Arendt, *The Origins of Totalitarianism* (New York, Harcourt Brace Jovanovich, 1973), p. 469. Emphasis is Arendt's.

2. Otto Rank, 'Modern Education' in Rank, *The Myth of the Birth of the Hero and Other Writings* (ed.) Philip Freund (New York, Vintage Books 1964), p. 248. Fred Weinstein, in his *The Dynamics of Nazism: Leadership, Ideology, and the Holocaust*, (New York, Academic Press 1980), has provided a definition somewhat similar to Rank's. 'Ideology is the structure and systematic form of high and low level (theoretical, philosophical, and common sense) language that people employ without reflection to explain all kinds of anticipated and unanticipated, favorable and unfavorable events'. (p. 119). For reasons of economy, I prefer Rank's definition.

3. Arendt, *The Origins of Totalitarianism*, p. 470

4. Peter L. Berger, *Facing up to Modernity* (New York, Basic Books 1977), p. 27.

5. Peter L. Berger, *The Sacred Canopy, Elements of the Sociological Theory of Religion* (New York, Doubleday 1967), p. 26.

6. From Rank, 'Art and Artist,' in *The Myth of the Birth of the Hero*, p. 122

7. Mary Douglas, *Natural Symbols: Explorations in Cosmology* (New York, Pantheon Books 1970) p. 126. In *The Sacred Canopy*, Berger has described the social use of religion as that of being 'a shield against terror'. (p. 22).

8. Ibid.

9. Ibid., p. 50.

10. Rank, 'Modern Education' in Rank, *The Myth of the Birth of the Hero*, p. 253. Emphasis is Rank's.

11. Peter L. Berger, *A Rumor of Angels: Modern Society and the Rediscovery of the Supernatural* (New York, Doubleday 1969), p. 111.

12. While a variety of scholars have dealt in varying degrees with religious elements in National Socialism, James M. Rhodes, in his *The Hitler Movement: A Modern Millenarian Revolution* (Stanford, Stanford University Press 1980), has presented us with perhaps the most thorough going work on this topic. Taking his point of departure from the writings of Norman Cohn and Eric Voegelin, he has emphasised millenarian aspects of National Socialism which he sees as being in the mainstream of those heretical offshoots of Christianity that can be traced back to third century Manichaeism. In the opinion of this writer (and others), there was a strong streak of millenarianism in National Socialism in general and Adolf Hitler's view of himself in particular. Nevertheless, it is his contention that those elements of 'Christianity' (heretical or otherwise) that one can discern in National Socialism were subsumed under or received their axiological content from a 'religion' *essentially* antithetical to the Judaeo-Christian tradition.

2 THE ROLE OF IDEOLOGY IN THE HISTORICAL ANALYSIS OF NATIONAL SOCIALISM AND THE QUESTION OF NAZI IDEOLOGY AS RELIGION

For many historians and political commentators, it has been and will continue to be extraordinarily difficult to believe that individuals and movements, perceived of as being evil, mean what they say. This stems from several obvious factors. First of all, it is perhaps easier to combat or condemn perceived dictatorial or totalitarian organisations and individuals if one can view tham as simply lying, i.e., as being stridently disingenuous in describing goals and purposes. Of probably greater importance, however, is the fact that those who, perhaps correctly, view themselves as being creatures of goodwill, find it inordinately difficult to accept the notion that such organisations and individuals seriously believed or believe in the necessity, even the moral correctness, of actions which are reprehensible in the eyes of rational human beings. In a world which, since the end of the Middle Ages, has been dominated by a nominalistic frame of mind, it is far easier to believe that dictators and organisations of a low repute are motivated more by concerns of personal gain and expediency rather than by commitments to perceived historical needs or ideals. To be sure, believers in everything from segregation to lycanthropy *are* often removed from ethical hooks through the warm-hearted assertion that: 'Well at least he means what he says. He is really an honest person after all.' At that point, however, at which belief has somehow been transformed into action, people tend to step back and begin casting about for ulterior motives — anything to preserve the implausible notion that evil-*doers* (if not necessarily evil-*thinkers*) are inherently dishonest mountebanks who were, as one *initially* suspected, really lying all along. Implied here, of course, is a massive gap between thought and action, one which inevitably is filled by ideologically-tinctured hypotheses.

The Nazi phenomenon, something which apparently will remain jammed in humanity's throat as a sort of perversely unassimilable bolus, lends itself to the sort of mental juggling thus described. After initially dismissing those who argue that the World War II Nazi atrocities never took place with the contempt that such souls roundly merit, we must deal with arguments which, for the historian, are far more crucial. While, as we will see, these arguments will take several forms, they all can

13

be reduced, in the final analysis, to the following fundamental assumption: the National Socialist ideology, as expressed by Hitler, various high National Socialist party officials, and the SS, was either a sham or, at most, a poorly-contrived rationalisation for motives rooted in economic self-interest, personal aggrandizement, or nihilistic drives towards self-destruction, essentially opaque to meaningful historical investigation.

The first systematic ideological investigation, undertaken by Hitler's former party-comrade, Hermann Rauschning, resulted in the conclusion that the Führer and his movement were essentially nihilistic in character.[1] After the conclusion of World War II, the ageing, albeit still respected, historian Friedrich Meinecke threw his weight behind this interpretation.[2] More recent interpreters, such as Martin Broszat, have continued to uphold this point of view. In Broszat's opinion, Hitler's ideology was 'an uncommitted fanaticism, without content, believing only in its own irresistible momentum'.[3] A more subtle and, I think, in part valid permutation of this argument has been offered by Aryeh Unger. In his well-argued work on totalitarian parties in the Soviet Union and Nazi Germany, he declared that 'The fundamental purpose of national socialism was to set the nation in motion', and that, bearing this goal in mind, the 'truth' of the National Socialist *Weltanschauung*, much less whether or not the population as a whole assimilated it, were matters of small importance.[4] 'On the whole . . .', Unger maintained, 'the ideological fervour of the Nazis was of a relatively low intensity'.[5] Indeed, totalitarian rulers in general were not concerned with bringing about 'widespread ideological sophistication' among their peoples. Rather, such ideologies were 'disbursed in small doses, to a limited group of people, and under conditions of maximum control'.[6] In view of the well-known caution exhibited by the National Socialist regime in dealing with the conventional state apparatus, organised religion and so on, it would appear that Unger's description has much to offer.

It can also be maintained that more recent psychohistorical interpretations of Hitler in particular are akin to those which view him and his movement as being essentially nihilistic, i.e., ahistorical, in character. Indeed, one of the most distinguished historians of the Nazi phenomenon, George L. Mosse has declared that to interpret Hitler's actions as being those of a psychopath provides 'a very facile explanation because if Hitler were a psychopath why don't we study psychoanalysis instead of politics?'[7] Here, a most important point with regard to so-called 'psychohistorical' explanations has been made; *viz.*, if one focuses upon the political leader and political action as being *au fond* informed by idiosyncratic psychopathology, then the very singularity of such phenomena would preclude any sort of meaningful historical investigation. Thus, explanations which are of immense phylogenetic significance to one imbued with the hypotheses and methodological approaches of psychoanalysis, can become, if utilised in too reductionist a manner, ahistorical ones for the historian, and nihilism once more has entered the picture. In this regard, it must be pointed out that it is the author's opinion that true 'psychohistorians' are *not* overly reductionist.

The 'personal aggrandisement' argument, one which informs the interpretations of historians such as Alan Bullock and Hugh Trevor-Roper, has within it that *tendency* towards viewing Hitler and ancillary phenomena as idiosyncratic in character.[8] Involved here is an unconscious but nevertheless quite real tendency towards radical historicism, i.e., an absolutising of the moment. In this process, emphasis is necessarily placed upon Hitler as demon, and the movement he headed as the product of someone singularly demonic in his efforts to attain aggrandizement no matter what the cost. It is obvious that here, too, questions of ideology become of secondary importance.

Approaches which emphasise the nihilistic or opportunistic character of Hitler and the National Socialist party or seek to explain these phenomena in terms of the Führer's personal psychopathology or simple power cravings are at that end of the spectrum — and often rather off it — of historical investigation that one can call individualising or, under certain circumstances, historicist. At the opposite end of this spectrum, at least hypothetically, there is that approach which seeks to explain Hitler and National Socialism as representing exponents of even greater forces, i.e., those of a large scale capitalism thrown on the defensive by crises grounded in internal systemic contradictions. According to this view, held largely, but by no means exclusively, by Marxists, Hitler came to power as the result of a panic-stricken bourgeoisie's efforts to save a system, bankrupt morally as well as ecomically, from total collapse.[9] In a word, Nazism, from this perspective, is seen as the creature of a degenerating and degenerative capitalism and its so-called 'ideology' must be viewed as being so much window-dressing for the desires of a class eager to assure its position — if necessary, through war and genocide. Recently, there have appeared somewhat more sophisticated versions of this argument.[10] Further, individuals like Wilhelm Reich and adherents to the so-called 'Frankfurt School' — at least by their own standards, Marxists all — have provided, in such works as *The Mass Psychology of Fascism* and *The Authoritarian Personality*, interpretations of the Nazi phenomenon in which the roles of symbol and myth, vital ingredients in the Nazi ideology, are emphasised.[11] Here, of course, the authors are concerned with demonstrating how perversions which they see as characteristic of bourgeois society — and not man's phylogenetic heritage, as Freud would have had us believe — are responsible for a singularly pernicious form of false consciousness apotheosised by the National Socialist ideology. In this context, obviously, a great deal of attention has been paid to the ideology. It is equally obvious, however, that, for such people as Reich and Theodor Adorno, ideology has to be, as for any Marxist, viewed as being a superstructural manifestation. To be sure, the usual, rather prosaic Marxist socio-economic substructure has been weighted down with a large consignment of Freudian ballast. Nevertheless, in the final analysis, Nazi ideology, for all of its singular symbolism and use of myth, must be seen as representing a variety of false consciousness in the traditional Marxist sense, albeit one honed against the whetstone of peculiarly twentieth century chiliastic drives.

From the point of view of Marxists, then — and, indeed, from that of any group of historians who choose to place primary emphasis upon the Nazi revolution as representing some sort of bourgeois counterrevolution — the role of ideology in National Socialism has to be seen as being of secondary interest. More recent Marxist writings on National Socialism and people like Reich and Adorno have proffered modifications of this approach; but, to remain within the Marxist fold, they can be only modifications.

Most historians, of course, are neither psychohistorians nor adherents to the Marxist interpretation(s) of why Hitler came to power or, more important for our purposes, what he wanted to do once he obtained it. Rather, their work tends to be informed by a sort of 'commonsense' approach to the problem; viz., the Nazi ideology was so bizarre in nature that, in the final analysis, one cannot take it all that seriously. Again in this context, we can observe the usual reaction of 'people of goodwill': Hitler was a madman or, at any rate, a rather singular individual. There was no doubt that he hated Jews and other perceived enemies. However, there cannot be, or perhaps even should not be, talk of his hateful beliefs constituting any sort of meaningful ideology. To be sure, he was able to get quite a few like-thinking individuals together, this in order to implement his ideas into actions but what held them together, essentially anti-Semitism, was no more ideological than a 'common obscenity'.[12] In the final analysis, then, the Nazi phenomenon has to be observed as representing a terrible balance between one man's personal pathology and certain social, economic, and political conditions which allowed him to translate this pathology into action. To take the ideology seriously would, in effect, be giving an obscene caricature of political thought far more credit than it deserves.

Yet we must appreciate the fact that, even if we accept a point of view, e.g., psychohistorical or Marxist, or the so-called 'commonsensical' one in which ideology's role is either made secondary or almost beside the point, we must appreciate the terrible fact that, whether or not they were enslaved by false consciousness or merely the unreflecting catspaws of unfathomable phylogenetic forces, millions of outwardly sane and, in many cases, personally decent (at least as they perceived themselves) human beings fought and died for a system of beliefs — an ideology or, as it was often referred to, a *Weltanschauung*. In other words, even if we are going to be thoroughly nominalistic about it, and declare that, at best, the Nazi ideology served only as some sort of rationalisation for actions undertaken in the service of more deep-seated underlying motives, this was a most powerful rationalisation indeed.

In fact, those who present cogent and, to some extent, persuasive arguments that ideology was of secondary importance in the Nazi movement and thus of secondary importance for those seeking to understand it, often find themselves in rather awkward positions in their attempts to discern reasons for the success of the National Socialist movement. As an example of this, we can consider Leonard Schapiro's extremely interesting observation that, in all totalitarian states, the role of ideology was to neutralise 'by ideological justifications the serious moral revulsion against the atrocities and brutalities perpetrated by the Leader'.[13] In this capacity, then, the ideology served to direct the hatred of people against certain classes or groups while at the same time justifying that terror 'upon which all arbitrary government relies for its survival and endurance'.[14] A few pages earlier, however, Schapiro made the following observations about the character of the National Socialist regime:

> If Fascism was a part enacted in public, National Socialism was necromancy; its reliance on symbolism, myth, mass hypnosis, and ritual was much greater.[15]

Hitler, Schapiro declared, used 'methods of necromancy to mobilise mass hysteria and to induce crowd hypnosis', successful to a degree unknown since 'the manifestations of religious dementia in the Middle Ages'.[16] At this point, we must ask ourselves what is meant by 'ideological justifications' and by 'necromancy'? Obviously, Professor Schapiro is utilising these terms in a manner to suggest that they were primarily agitational devices, deliberately designed to play upon the emotions of what would have to be referred to as 'the mob.' They were, so the argument must go, gimmicks, artifices, the use of which was to assure popular support for an 'arbitrary government' which was, in the final analysis, Hitler himself. This argument raises more questions than it answers.

First of all, is there a covering term which can be utilised to include such words as 'necromancy', 'symbolism', 'myth', 'mass hypnosis', and 'ritual'? In this regard, we must assume that the presumed agitational elements mentioned above were not selected at random, but, rather were congruent with certain perceived needs and fears. In a word, Hitler, Goebbels, *et al.* were providing an *emotional program* — an emotional program which, because it was concerned with the maintenance of and justification for, power, was, at the same time, a *political* one. It is obvious here that Professor Schapiro is referring to an ideology. Further, in order for an ideology to be effective, i.e., for it to *be* an ideology in any meaningful sense of the word, it 'must appeal to the deep instincts of the mass of the people, to their traditions, their emotions, their hatreds, fears and hopes'.[17] If a regime, e.g., Hitler's was *dependent* upon such a device — assuming, for sake of argument, that it was simply that — then we must ask ourselves whether such can be viewed as being merely one means, among others, of perpetuating its rule, or rather, whether the very success of the movement itself, at least in its own eyes, was contingent upon that ideology which somehow appealed 'to the deep instincts of the mass of the people'.

To all of this, the rejoinder could be made that the Nazi leadership itself did not take its symbolism, myth, ritual, etc., seriously. In this case, we would be confronted with an Orwellian situation in which the mass-supported campaigns of Oceania against the Eurasian enemy were merely devices to allow a regime to hold on to power. In the end, then, the ideology would be a weapon in the service of pervasive nihilism: If this were true then there could be no doubt that, for the leadership, 'National Socialism in Germany became the sinister embodiment of a dynamic nihilism devoid of ideological commitment'.[18] Here, though, we must remember what Unger maintained. While, unlike Schapiro, deprecating the notion that the regime was interested in imbuing the population as a whole with ideological fervour, he had suggested that, for a small group of people, the ideology was indeed important, so important that it *had* to be made available to the masses 'in small doses'. For Schapiro, there was an ideology for public consumption, this to maintain the Hitler regime in power. For Unger, while ideological proselytising was of secondary importance, there had to have been a hard core of true believers. Each of these two extremely perspicacious commentators upon totalitarian movements and institutions thus made ideology central to the National Socialist phenomenon, even though each 'placed' the ideology in a different position relative to the leadership of the movement.

The same problem seems to have haunted those who have maintained that, in National Socialist Germany, the naked will of the Führer was of central importance, while ideology was something that had been placed 'in the service of the will'.[19] As we shall see, there is a great deal that can be said on behalf of this viewpoint. For our present purposes, though, it is interesting to note that, in another work, Buchheim found it necessary to pose the following question: Why do men stick it out and do evil deeds if no real punishment threatens them and if they have not been disposed to do such things earlier?[20] There was, Buchheim maintained, a very human need for a person 'to prove himself in his social environment and correspond to its fundamental viewpoints and rules of conduct'.[21] Further, doubts or moral objections such an individual might have could be quashed through telling oneself that any abhorrence felt with regards to a particular action was based on a subjective lack of appreciation for and understanding of the doctrine involved.[22] In narrowing his discussion to focus upon the Nazi SS, Buchheim dilated further on the question of doctrine and ideology. People who entered the SS left the realm of state citizenship and entered the realm of ideology. '*All* declared ideological consent through their entrance and declared themselves ready to do more than their duty'.[23]

Thus, for this distinguished historian, one who adhered to the easily defendable notion that the Nazi ideology itself was subordinate to the will of the Führer, ideology provided at the very least substantive rationalisation for actions that otherwise would have to have been viewed as reprehensible by those undertaking them. To be absolutely fair about it, we have to note that Buchheim *never* maintained that the average SS-man or woman was an enthusiastic ideologue. Nevertheless, the ideology was there, providing at times vague, but none the less quite real, ideational and axiological purpose to the same extent that the average citizen in the Western world usually attempts to bring his behaviour into conformity with some dimly-sensed ten commandments.

For some observers, ideas were of central importance in grasping the significance of Hitler in particular and National Socialism in general. However, *ideology* was not, the claim here being that while certain substantive ideas were involved in National Socialist hypotheses and actions, they were never brought together into anything resembling a pattern. Students of the National Socialist phenomenon who take this point of view often draw a sharp distinction between *Weltanschauung* and ideology, pointing out correctly that Hitler himself usually utilised the former term whenever the subject of ideational content and purpose came under consideration. Here, Eberhard Jäckel wrote an extremely significant work devoted exclusively to determining the main elements of Hitler's *Weltanschauung*. At times, though, Professor Jäckel appeared to have been most uncertain as to the importance of even a *Weltanschauung* in determining the reasons for Hitler's effectiveness. By itself, Jäckel maintained, the fact that Hitler had a definite *Weltanschauung* tells us little since everybody, even the mentally ill, has a definite way of looking at the world.[24] Towards the conclusion of his work the author declared that, while his *Weltanschauung* was not the source of his effectiveness, an understanding of who Hitler was and what he did necessitated our bearing his *Weltanschauung* in mind.[25] Throughout his work, however, Jäckel presented points which, while not contradicting what he had to say as to the relative insignificance of Hitler's *Weltanschauung* taken by itself, nevertheless raised some questions. Probably the most important of these revolve around Jäckel's justifiable contention that, while Hitler's foreign policy concepts changed quite a bit, 'the racial-political [policy] remained astonishingly consistent'.[26] As early as 1921, the author pointed out, Hitler had suggested that Jews be thrown into concentration camps.[27] From beginning to end, Hitler saw the Jewish question as being the central aspect or mission of his general political task.[28] Thus, although Jäckel saw other factors such as terror and propaganda as being of decisive importance in determining Hitler's success, one would have to conclude that these mechanical elements served to provide the means by which a *Weltanschauung* was translated into action. Certainly *without* Hitler's *Weltanschauung*, the necessity for the existence of various party and state institutions would have been obviated.

Furthermore, even if we accept the notion that there is a meaningful difference between ideology and *Weltanschauung*, we can still raise the question of just how meaningful this difference was in so far as Hitler and National Socialism were concerned. A scholar who has studied Alfred Rosenberg pointed out that 'Unlike ideology which is usually applied to views held collectively, *Weltanschauung* in its primitive sense, need mean no more than the outlook of an individual on the world around him'.[29]. There can be no doubt that, as indicated earlier, Rosenberg and Hitler often confused these terms. At the same time, though, there can also be little doubt that they did attempt to impose their world view(s) on the world around them, albeit, in 'small doses'.[30] Further, Professor

Cecil maintained, the Nazis did attempt to *create* an ideology — accepting the fact that they did not have one before they came to power — and were concerned 'to unify, at least to some extent, the disparate *Weltanschauungen* of their followers. They never succeeded in doing so, any more than they succeeded in creating a fully totalitarian state; but that they aimed to do both can scarcely be in dispute'.[31]

We will have cause to question the Nazis' commitment to a so-called 'fully totalitarian state'. For the moment, however, we must see that Professor Cecil's reflections are suggestive of the following process: Hitler, Rosenberg, *inter alia* had definite world views which constituted a sort of core-structure of the Nazi ideational world. As time went on, they were driven to develop disparate *Weltanschauungen* into a more cohesive structure; in other words, they were driven to *construct* an ideology. For Cecil, this concern was absolutely central to the thinking of leading National Socialists. At any rate, even if we accept Professor Cecil's distinction between *Weltanschauung* and ideology (and, it must be emphasised again that *Weltanschauung* is often translated as ideology), the question at hand was largely *ideological* in nature, the concern being to develop what could have been construed as a singular, if not idiosyncratic, world view into an ideology.

We have considered viewpoints on the role and function of National Socialist ideology in order to establish two points, one of then rather obvious, the other perhaps less so. First of all, opinion on the role and function of ideology in the National Socialist movement is and no doubt will continue to be, quite varied. Secondly, even individuals who seem to deprecate such a role, or confine it to being of secondary importance, invariably reserve a place for ideology, furthermore, a place from which it appeared to exercise a great deal of influence and authority.

For the historian seeking to apply categories of critical understanding to the Nazi phenomenon, removal of ideology as a valid heuristic concept, or, at times, even relegating it to second place, can raise extremely severe problems. An implied gap between thought and action can allow ahistorical nihilism to insinuate itself into the process, thus obfuscating if not obliterating the role of historical analysis. Or, through overemphasis upon Hitler as being an individual singular in his demonic characteristics, we can lose sight of him as a historical creature, one whose historicity, even accepting its uniqueness, is of concern to us only as it was engaged in rationally deducible symbiosis with the larger historicity of his time and place.

For example, we may assume that psychohistorians are correct when they maintain that ultimately all ideologies are reducible to stereotyped patterns of displacement, sublimation, and projection. What makes psychohistorians *historians*, however, has to be their ability to see how, perhaps even why, a particular pattern of myth, ritual and symbolism which, taken together, we can refer to as manifestations of an ideology (or, perhaps even the ideology in itself). served as a vehicle for the expression of certain phylogenetic drives. In this regard, Richard A. Koenigsberg made a most interesting statement. In his study, *Hitler's Ideology: A Study in Psychoanalytic Sociology*, he is concerned with determining the psychological roots of Hitler's ideas. He is particularly interested in those statements of Hitler's which contained '*primary process imagery*', in other words, statements in which Hitler's perceptions of reality found concrete embodiment.[32] In considering this concern, Professor Koenigsberg states that 'In so far as we have focused upon Hitler's *perception of reality* rather than upon his *behavior*, the present work is not, essentially, an historical study'.[33] In a word, Professor Koenigsberg has made the rather obvious point that the historian's primary task is to study human behaviour, not from the point of view of a psychologist, who is eager to demonstrate how individual idiosyncracy somehow embodies or reflects metapsychological drives or pathologies, but from an angle useful for one concerned with individuals as political, cultural and economic actors, most important of all, with people acting within the context of a given time and place.

For the historian ideologies are points of departure for action and, when the bearers of an ideology seem to have translated its most important tenets into reality, the role of such an ideology must become of ever greater importance. Even if the historian accepts than an ideology, in order to be effective, must offer the individual '*a means whereby his fantasies might be expressed and discharged on the level of social reality*', he does so knowing that his or her task as an historian is to determine how particular myths, rituals and patterns of symbolism provided such means at a given time.[34] In a word, the question of 'primary process imagery' and related concerns must be left to the psychologist, even if, in a thoroughly reductionist manner, psychological causes are perceived as primary, or unmoved movers. The historian might have to accept that ideology provided the means for the '*expression and discharge*' of a fantasy shared by members of a culture.[35] The roots of the fantasy might well be sunk deeply into phylogenesis; but, for various reasons, people *need* ideologies, even if only to cloak their true motives, and the various time-conditioned forms these ideologies take and their relation(s) to conscious political and social action make them of singular importance in illuminating individuals as historical actors. For any historian

— perhaps most *especially* for the psychohistorian — ideology as a repository of time-conditioned myths and symbolic forms is of pivotal importance.

Going back to the beginning of this chapter, we recall that a primary reason why many observers of the Nazi phenomenon find it difficult to devote serious attention to the Hitlerian ideology is that somehow they do not wish to believe that the Hitlers, Rosenbergs and Himmlers often meant what they said and that, further, and most significantly, that what occurred during the twelve nightmare years 1933-45 in large measure resulted from the implementation of certain fundamental ideological principles. In some ways, it is far easier to fall back upon ahistorical arguments than to accept the fact that presumed 'men of bad will' were just as sincere in their commitment to principle as were their more admirable opponents.

Ultra-reductionist Marxist and psychological arguments — the latter potentially as ahistorical in nature as ones which fall back upon nihilism as representing the source and goal of National Socialism — can also serve the same purpose as those more 'commonsensical' arguments which reject ideology out of hand because it sounds far-fetched or absurd: they allow for the luxury of denying that people meant what they said or of assuming that even if they did mean it, such statements were in large measure irrelevant. People can thus be viewed as victimised by their consciousness or as having temporarily lost rational control over irrational longings and impulses. Never has the Enlightenment grounding of Marxist and Freudian social criticisms been so clearly revealed as in their approaches to National Socialism. For the historian, confronting a phenomenon whose central ideological precepts were never abandoned and which were indeed translated into reality once the movement attained power, it is absolutely necessary to accept the sombre fact that, even if committed Nazis did not in an ultimate sense say what they meant, they most assuredly meant what they said.

'I do not need the bourgeoisie', Hitler stated in a 1931 interview, 'the bourgeoisie needs me and my movement'. As he saw it, what allowed the NSDAP to attain spiritual ascendancy over traditional politically moribund German bourgeois circles was 'the totality of its ideology'.[36] There were substantial portions of the Twenty-Five Point Program of February, 1920 which were abandoned completely. In referring to ideology, however, Hitler was hardly referring to this. Rather, he was focusing upon certain core elements, the *ultimate* significance of which might well have been known only to him. In any case, Hitler was at least partially correct. As we will see, the Nazis came to power and exercised power successfully largely because of the pragmatic aspects of their ideology, elements which proved to be congruent with sensed social and cultural needs. Those deeper, underlying elements which were responsible for the birth of the *whole* ideology in the first place were reflected in its core, something which was believed in by the '*true* believers', even if it could not be fully articulated by the common people as a whole.

It has not been unusual, even for people who do not take the role of Nazi ideology in the rise of Hitler to power very seriously, to suggest that, in its rallies, ceremonies, and propaganda techniques, the National Socialists presented themselves as the bearers of a new *religion*. In this context Hitler is perceived as having either thought of himself — or wishing others to think of him — as the German messiah. An astute analyst of Nazi propaganda has described this in the following manner:

> The Führer was at once Father, Son and Holy Ghost. He was the Father because his essence was cosmic and he was sent to earth on a mission which was both of this world and beyond it. He rode the wave of the historical dialectic, which would culminate in the victory of Aryan man, and as the awakened Barbarossa he fulfilled the prophecies of the German right wing who longed for a 'great one come from above'. He was also the Son, the Son of Providence, who in his infinite Wisdom had created the Aryan Volk. As such it was Hitler's role to lead his people along the paths to greatness, a way fraught with danger and one which might demand that they perish in their own flame in the service of the higher ideal. The Nazi parallel to the Christian concept of the Holy Ghost was the spirit of Providence, reflected in the mystical source and life spirit of the *Volk*. Hitler was at once of this world and beyond. His flesh was the flesh of the Volk, and his spirit was their own life spirit.[37]

What has been described here is the so-called 'Führer cult', a phenomenon which often has been taken to constitute Nazism's substitute religion, i.e., the replacing of Judaeo-Christian forms by a sort of paganism necessarily swathed, or perhaps even embodied, in certain Christian usages. Here, emphasis has been placed not so much upon a Nazi *ideology*, i.e., system of beliefs, but rather upon Hitler's will. The Nazis thus 'made God manipulatable by equating him with man's 'inner voice' (the 'voice of the blood'); the Providence so often appealed to by Hitler was identified with his will'.[38] There can be no doubt that observers who have focused upon the phenomenon of the 'Hitler cult', particularly with regard to the question of mass appeal, have a most valid point, one with which any historian can scarcely take issue. In fact, later on in this book, we will be devoting considerable attention to the phenomenon of the 'Hitler cult'. It is certainly true that the success of Hitler and National Socialism can to some degree be viewed as having been due to a combination of a people's yearning for a saviour with clever, manipulative devices designed to persuade this people that one had indeed arrived. It is this writer's contention, however, that while National Socialism's ability to grab and hold on to power was in part due to factors attached to a 'Führer cult', its program of mass destruction, unparalleled in its wedding of idealism to brutality, did not stem from a blind worship of the Führer. Rather, one must look to a genuine overturning of religious values and symbolism of which the Führer cult was perhaps the most crucial part but, a part none the less. In focusing upon this, we must bear in mind a most cogent observation of Mosse's. Toward the end of his *The Nationalization of the Masses*, a book concerned with political symbolism, the following phrase appeared:

> We have been concerned with a cultural phenomenon which cannot be subsumed under the traditional canons of political theory. For it was not constructed as a logical and coherent system that could be understood through a rational analysis of philosophical writings. The phenomenon which has been our concern was a secular religion, the continuation from primitive and Christian times of viewing the world through myth and symbol, acting out one's hopes and fears within ceremonial and liturgical forms.[39]

James M. Rhodes, in his penetrating and thought-provoking work, *The Hitler Movement*, has picked up, as mentioned earlier, on the millenarian aspects of National Socialism and, while tying these into heretical *variants* of Christianity, nevertheless complements Mosse's approach through his term 'secular apocalyptic movement'.[40] Of importance here are such terms as 'secular religion', and 'secular apocalyptic movement', ones which often have been rather overused, most particularly in dealing with Marxism.[41] In this context, however, they point not only to the *form* of National Socialism, something which, as has been pointed out by Mosse and others, had at times to approximate traditional Christian modes, but to its content as well.

What Mosse has said is especially disturbing because it suggests that many of those elements which constituted the ideational substructure of National Socialism were part and parcel of modern efforts to retain a basic piety with regards to the world and one's role in it in the face of all those monstrous obstacles and challenges posed by an increasingly impersonal and deracinated modern civilization. Nazi ideology, then, cannot only be viewed as something which a radicalised few sought to impose upon a supine and morally anesthetised population. It was, rather, an expression of a pious quest for the natural and authentic. In the modern world, an ideology could articulate the concerns traditionally assigned to trascendentalism-bound religion, this due to the fact that 'popular piety and modern ideology are not so far removed from each other'.[42] In a word, we are concerned with something far more disturbing than some sort of idiosyncratic 'worship' of a Providentially-ordained Führer. We are concerned with a quest for religious verities which, in a time of increasing secularisation, had to articulate itself in ideological form. Thus, while National Socialism has to be viewed as fundamentally German in content, its form was, to a significant degree, determined by certain wellnigh universal human concerns.

The increasing sense of alienation in a burgeoning industrialised and urban society has been the subject of innumerable social and cultural studies. Accompanying this process was the continuous subjugation of nature by man. While, on the whole, humanity benefited materially from industrialisation and man's increasing mastery over nature, the price for such developments was high. An increasing sense of estrangement from nature, combined with a growing revulsion against technological, urbanised society, was responsible for a general reaction against modernity. This reaction was particularly strong in Germany, where industrialisation had occurred at an unusually frenetic pace, but the fear which subsisted at the base of this reaction could be observed, particularly in bourgeois circles, throughout the West.[43] The idea of mastery over nature had 'long been immersed in the darker side of the human psyche' and associated with 'evil, guilt, and fear'.[44] Ironically enough, that Faustian paganism which has been viewed as apotheosising man's desire to grasp the totality of the natural world can be traced back to the Judaeo-Christian tradition which, while imposing ethical obligations upon man with regard to his lordship over the earth, nevertheless placed the earth and all its natural resources and non-human inhabitants at his disposal.[45] In order for man to assert his authority over the earth, the Judaeo-Christian tradition had to in effect despiritualise nature, removing divinity from it through the establishment of a transcendental God.[46] In the sharp dualism between nature and spirit, a sense of magic seemed to have been removed from man's environment.

We cannot gainsay the fact that the Judaeo-Christian tradition has provided satisfactory solutions to the needs of millions for quite some time.

Beginning with modern times, however, that 'despiritualisation' of the world of nature had been implicit in this tradition became translated into reality and, in a world in which mystery seemed increasingly to be replaced by the mundane, those anti-transcendental elements that always had existed as alter ego to the mainstream of Western religious speculation came more and more to the fore. As the 'other-worldly' paradise posited by Judaeo-Christian speculation seemed to become increasingly irrelevant to human needs, it came to be replaced by the 'modern utopia . . . man-made paradise on earth'.[47] Particularly with the emergence of modern, mass society — the industrial age — humankind's perceived mastery over nature has been responsible for a variety of utopianism which emphasises the hallowed character of an assumed natural order. In this regard, some observations of Thorstein Veblen seem clearly apposite. Writing on the eve of World War I, this shrewd, at times infuriatingly provocative, critic of modern society remarked that the 'feeling of maladjustment and discomfort that he sensed as a response to the machine age, was often articulated in the call for a 'return to Nature'.[48] Further, he observed that harassed 'laymen' were 'seek[ing] respite in the fog of occult and esoteric faiths and cults'.[49]

While concerns about problems posed by humankind's increasing mastery over nature have increasingly been shared by ever larger groups of people embracing a plethora of ideologies, the most consistent 'pro-natural order' response found political embodiment on the radical right.[50] Virtually all Fascist groups placed a great deal of emphasis on dynamism, upon the emergence and cultivation of a sort of 'natural man' who, though objectively bourgeois in nature, would be liberated from the shackles of decadent bourgeois civilisation and would impose the stamp of his authentic will upon all of humanity. The 'blood and soil' motif was a fairly general one, early members of the Legion of the Archangel Michael, later the Rumanian Iron Guard, carrying this to logical, if perhaps sartorially discomfiting, conclusions by having bags of Transylvanian soil hung about their necks. However, German National Socialism was unique in a very crucial aspect: in it, the rebellion against the Judaeo-Christian concept of the role of man *vis à vis* nature achieved expression in a genuine religion of nature. This is not to deny that, in National Socialist ritual and ceremony, certain Christian forms were used and, in fact, *had* to have been used. Nevertheless, the content of the National Socialist ideology, an ideology which we will see must be viewed as religion articulated in secular, i.e., 'ideological', form, was anti-Judaeo-Christian in character. Of pivotal importance here was the National Socialist view of the natural world and man's role in it.

Before we continue any further, it is necessary to point out that many observers of so-called 'totalitarian systems' have maintained that all of these systems are characterised by the tendency to blur the distinction between religious and secular areas, with the ruler assuming the role of being a kind of substitute church.[51] Just as there were prayers to Hitler, so there were prayers to Stalin and, indeed, even after the death of Stalin, the Communist rulers of Russia have come to recognise that people needed quasi-religious ceremony and festival.[52] The Nazi religion, however, was singular in its effort to consciously supplant Judaeo-Christian forms, and to offer in their place a religion of nature congruent with the perceived needs of a people uprooted from nature. In the Soviet Union, attempts have periodically been made to constrain religious influences if not, at times, to abolish them.

It is of some importance to note, however, that the Marxist tradition, with its strongly humanistic overtones and its emphasis upon the singularity of the creative human spirit — to say nothing of its own permutation of chiliasm — was very much rooted in that Judaeo-Christian tradition which it has felt constrained to combat in the name of ideological purity. This sharply separates, always hypothetically and usually in practice, the Soviet Communist approach towards religion from that of the National Socialists. In sum, the Marxist approach to religion, hypothetically and in practice, must be seen as emerging dialectically from an ideational background itself Judaeo-Christian in character. Thus, the Marxist antipathy to religion cannot be viewed as representing a *rebellion* against it, even if one bears in mind such quasi-pagan absurdities as worship of Stalin and the placing on permanent display of an at least partially authentic Lenin. Nazism was most definitely a rebellion against the Judaeo-Christian tradition.

Whilst Hitler in due course felt secure enough to move against the Jews, the Nazi regime generally stayed away from formal doctrinal disputes with the Catholic and Lutheran Churches. Nevertheless, we will be able to see strong evidence that the eventual goal of National Socialism had to have been the extirpation of the entire Judaeo-Christian tradition, and that only pragmatic demands imposed by social, political and logistic realities prevented the regime from undertaking an anti-Christian *Kulturkampf* far more pervasive than anything Bismarck could have imagined. Also, and perhaps this is of primary importance, the National Socialist regime survived for but twelve years, hardly enough time to undertake, much less complete, a sustained campaign against Christianity. Thus, the average religious German continued to go to church and to pray to the traditional God of battles. Individual clergymen who spoke out against the National Socialist regime or, more rarely, actively sought to overthrow it, were imprisoned and in many cases killed. Despite this, however, open battle against Christianity was precluded by the various factors mentioned earlier. In fact, the churches remained strong enough to take the offensive occasionally, e.g., in publicly condemning the euthanasia program.[58]

In this work we will not be primarily concerned, except in the appendix, with the reaction of the vast mass of German citizenry to specific aspects of the National Socialist religion of nature, a religion which many Nazis sincerely believed would serve to liberate a putative 'Aryan man' from the shackles of a superannuated Judaeo-Christian tradition, one which was castigated as alienating and unnatural. Rather, we will be focusing primarily upon those who viewed themselves as the bearers of the new religion of nature, i.e., Hitler, Heinrich Himmler, Alfred Rosenberg, Robert Wagner, Ernst Krieck, Paul Josef Goebels and others; in a word, with those individuals who saw themselves as having to educate the German nation in particular and 'Aryan man' in general to the awesome historical and ethical tasks imposed upon them by nature expressing itself in the mysteries of the blood. The philosophical language of the religion of nature which provided the ideational background for the Nazi actions was German. In its frequent call for an 'embracing of life' strong, quasi-Nietzschean overtones are obvious, and in its emphasis on the supremacy of nature and in its expression in organic, *völkisch* forms, elements usually and correctly associated with German romanticism are in evidence. Furthermore, those forces of demoralisation and mass hysteria which swept the National Socialist movement into power were characteristic of a country in which liberal experimentation with constitutionalism and pluralism had not provided for the very real emotional needs of a people utterly unaccustomed to assuming political responsibility. Also, it is well to point out that the concept of 'national socialism,' if not necessarily the precise phrase, had played an important role in German political speculation for many years.[54] Hence, when we consider National Socialism *per se*, we will be examining a phenomenon which, at least in so far as ideational contents are concerned, could only have arisen in Germany.

We must not, however, lose sight of the fact that, in its concern that man, or at least Aryan man, regain his place in the natural order of things, National Socialism was simply, albeit in a more pointed fashion, expressing the wishes of a substantial portion of Western humanity. The 'return to nature,' a drive which is at least as strong in our time as it was in the 1920s and 1930s, can be understood in purely phylogenetic terms.[55] Nevertheless, even if we determine that it is due to a regression to a stage of 'primitive narcissism' brought about by socio-cultural pressures too strong for the self-consciously alienated individual to resist, the *conscious* politicalisation of this return was, at least in part, responsible for the triumph of a movement that, in the final analysis, provided solutions which a substantial number of people thought, or perhaps better, *felt* satisfying. After all, a community of human beings living at one with nature, healthy and wholesome, represented and, for many, still represents, a goal worthy of immense sacrifice, most particularly when the greatest burden of this sacrifice was to be borne by a group or groups singled out as being 'unnatural' or subsisting only at the lowest levels of life.

To be sure, as mentioned before, the German people as a whole did not and could not have known what the completed form of the Nazi religion of nature was to have been. Perhaps we can say that even most Nazis themselves did not know this. The people had to be only *gradually* introduced to that new religion which, to use a phrase much favoured by Nazi ideologues, 'in keeping with the laws of life' showed the way to a true utopia. As mentioned above, we will be concerned mainly with the 'official' efforts, arguments, and rationalisations which, taken together, constituted the National Socialist religion of nature as leading Nazis perceived it to have been. Yet we must acknowledge the disturbing fact that, although the German people were in ignorance of much of what their leaders had in mind, what they did know — or were allowed to know — of it seemed not to have distressed them very much. Part of this, of course, was due to the fact that years of cultural conditioning had to some extent prepared them for something like National Socialism. However, we must appreciate another fact; namely, that the National Socialist call for the establishment of a utopian community, the *Volksgemeinschaft*, rooted in a perceived natural order, an element of the 'religion' which *was* widely touted to the average people as a whole, reflected a certain extremely attractive dream historically very prominent in several forms of bourgeois ideology. The overcoming of alienation, not through some hideous form of class war, but rather through a revolution of consciousness, the result of which would be a new sense of rootedness and belonging, has constituted and will continue to constitute a substantial portion of the emotional legacy bequeathed to us as a result of the development of civilization. One can condemn so self-serving and essentially backward-looking a dream as being indicative of false consciousness. As Mosse put it, however, 'usually people have false rather than true consciousness . . . [and] history is still made by people based on people . . .'[56]

To cut through false consciousness we must initially come to appreciate the awesome power of those ideas and ideals through which it has obtained expression. In focusing upon National Socialism as the National Socialists themselves saw it, i.e., as a body of thought that, in the final analysis, would replace the Judaeo-Christian tradition, we will consider an, up to now, singular attempt to establish a nature-bound 'sacred cosmos'; a 'technology for overcoming risk' that could have arisen only in a technological age. In so doing, we will perhaps be better able to appreciate the dangers inherent in any sort of doctrine which attempts to grasp life in its wholeness and hence to end history.

Notes

1. This was the concern, of course, of his *The Revolution of Nihilism: A Warning to the West* (New York, Longmans Green and Co., 1939)
2. Friedrich Meinecke, 'Zusammenarbeit,' in *Politische Schriften und Reden*, Georg Kotowski, Herausgegeber, (Darmstadt, Toeche-Mittler, 1958) p. 488.
3. Martin Broszat, *German National Socialism 1919-1945*, translated from the German by Kurt Rosenbaum and Inge Pauli Boehm, (Santa Barbara, California, Clio Press, 1966), p. 59.
4. Aryeh L. Unger, *The Totalitarian Party: Party and People in Nazi Germany and Soviet Russia* (London, Cambridge University Press, 1974), p. 39.
5. Ibid., p. 41
6. Ibid., p. 43.
7. George L. Mosse, *Nazism: A Historical and Comparative Analysis of National Socialism* (New Brunswick, New Jersey, Transaction Press, 1978), p. 67.
8. Such an argument informs the still most valuable work of Bullock, *Hitler: A Study in Tyranny*, revised edition (New York, Harper and Row, 1964). In his introduction to *Hitler's Secret Conversations*, 1941-1944, Professor Trevor-Roper maintained that Hitler was concerned only with obtaining and holding onto power. He was, according to this view, a total materialist for whom ideals and moral values did not exist. See, Adolf Hitler, *Hitler's Secret Conversations, 1941-1944*, with an introductory essay on *The Mind of Adolf Hitler*, by H. R. Trevor-Roper, translated from the German by Norman Cameron and R. H. Stevens, (New York, Farrar, Strauss and Young, 1953), pp. xxviii-xxix.
9. An early example of a naive Marxist interpretation was Albert Norden, *Lehren deutscher Geschichte: Zur politischen Rolle des Finanzkapitals und der Junker* (Berlin, Dietz, 1947). A somewhat more sophisticated work is offered by Eberhard Czichon *Wer verhalf Hitler zur Macht? Zum Anteil der deutschen Industrie in der Zerstorung der Weimarer Republik* (Köln, Paul-Rugenstein, 1967). Also see Franz Neumann *Behemoth: The Structure and Practice of National Socialism* (New York, Harper and Row, 1942). For non-Marxist writers who essentially support the Marxist position on the role of capitalism in the rise of National Socialism to power, see George Hallgarten, *Hitler, Reichswehr and Industrie: Zur Geschichte der Jahre 1918-1933* (Frankfurt, Europaische Verlagsanstalt, 1955), and Arthur Schweitzer, *Big Business in the Third Reich* (Bloomington, Indiana, University of Indiana Press, 1964). Most Marxist arguments regarding the role of big buisness in the rise of Hitler have been effectively attacked by Henry Ashby Turner, Jr in his *Big Business and the Rise of Hitler* (New York, Oxford University Press, 1985).
10. See Anson G. Rabinbach, 'Toward a Marxist Theory of Fascism and National

Socialism: A Report on Developments in West Germany,' in *New German Critique*, 1974, *3*, Winter.

11. See Theodor Adorno *et al.*, *The Authoritarian Personality* (New York, Norton Library, 1950), and Wilheim Reich, *The Mass Psychology of Fascism*, translated from the German by Vincent R. Carfagno (New York, The Noonday Press, 1970).

12. This phrase appears in Peter H. Merkl's most interesting quantitative study, *Political Violence under the Swastika: 581 Early Nazis* (Princeton, New Jersey, Princeton University Press, 1975), p. 448.

13. Leonard Schapiro, *Totalitarianism* (New York and London, Praeger, 1972), p. 57.

14. Ibid., p. 58.

15. Ibid., p. 50.

16. Ibid., p. 53.

17. Ibid., p. 48.

18. Broszat, *German National Socialism*, p. 89.

19. Hans Buchheim, *Totalitarian Rule: Its Nature and Characteristics*, translated from the German by Ruth Hein, (Middletown, Connecticut, Wesleyan University Press, 1968), p. 19.

20. Hans Buchheim *et al.*, *Anatomie des SS- Staates*, Band 1., Hans Buchheim, *Die SS-das Herrschaftsinstrument, Befehl und Gehorsam.* (München, Deutscher Taschenbuch Verlag, 1967), p. 306.

21. Ibid.

22. Ibid., p. 307

23. Ibid., p. 312. Emphasis is Buchheim's.

24. Eberhard Jäckel, *Hitlers Weltanschauung* (Tübingen, R. Wünderlich, 1969).

25. Ibid., p. 159-60.

26. Ibid., p. 65.

27. Ibid.

28. Ibid., p. 67.

29. Robert Cecil, *The Myth of the Master Race: Alfred Rosenberg and Nazi Ideology* (London, B. T. Batsford, 1972), p. 61.

30. Ibid.

31. Ibid., p. 62.

32. Richard A. Koenigsberg, *Hitler's Ideology: A Study in Psychoanalytic Sociology* (New York, Library of Social Services, 1975), p. 3. The emphasis is Koenigsberg's.

33. Ibid., p. 4. The emphasis is Koenigsberg's.

34. Ibid., p. 85. The emphasis is Koenigsberg's.

35. Ibid., p. 86. The emphasis is Koenigsberg's.

36. Adolf Hitler, *Secret Conversations with Hitler: The Two Newly-Discovered 1931 Interviews*, edited by Edouard Calic, with a foreword by Golo Mann; translated from the German by Richard Berry, (New York, John Day Co., 1971), p. 22.

37. Jay W. Baird, *The Mythical World of Nazi War Propaganda: 1939-1945*, (Minneapolis, University of Minnesota Press, 1974), p. 10.

38. Buchheim, *Totalitarian Rule*, p. 20.

39. George L. Mosse, *The Nationalization of the Masses: Political Symbolism and Mass Movements in Germany from the Napoleonic Wars through the Third Reich* (New York, Howard Fertig, Inc., 1975), p. 214. Professor Mosse, in his *Towards the Final Solution*, has suggested that the much-utilised term 'metapolitics,' something which appeared after the writings of Gobineau became well-known, was suggestive of that process by which the political life of a nation becomes transformed into a 'secular religion'. See George L. Mosse, *Towards the Final Solution: A History of European Racism* (New York, Howard Fertig, Inc., 1978), p. 65.

40. James M. Rhodes, *The Hitler Movement: A Modern Millenarian Revolution* (Stanford, Stanford University Press, 1980), pp. 17-18, 30ff., 197-8.

41. Jean-Pierre Sironneau, in his *Sécularisation et religions politiques*, (The Hague, Paris, New York, Mouton, 1982), considers both Nazism and 'Leninism, Stalinism' in

religious terms. We will consider this work in another context.

42. Mosse, *Nazism*, p. 27.

43. The books on this subject are legion. Three of the most noteworthy are: Hans Kohn, *The Mind of Germany* (New York, Harper and Row, 1960), George L. Mosse, *The Crisis of German Ideology: Intellectual Origins of the Third Reich* (New York, Grosset and Dunlap, 1964), Fritz Stern, *The Politics of Cultural Despair* (New York, Doubleday, Anchor Books, 1965).

44. William Leiss, *The Domination Over Nature* (New York, S. Braziller, 1972), p. 44.

45. Ibid., p. 29, pp. 34-5.

46. Ibid., p. 181. Max Weber's phrase 'disenchantment of the world' has been used by Peter Berger in the *Sacred Canopy: Elements of a Sociological Theory of Religion*, (New York, Doubleday, 1967), p. 111. For another most interesting interpretation as to the effects attendant upon what he called the 'secularization' or 'disenchantment' of the world, see Richard L. Rubenstein, *The Cunning of History: Mass Death and the American Future* (New York, Harper and Row, 1975), pp. 27-8. This theme has been more fully developed in Richard L. Rubenstein, *The Age of Triage: Fear and Hope in an Overcrowded World* (Boston, Beacon Press, 1983).

47. Frank E. and Fritizie P. Manuel, 'Sketch for a Natural History of Paradise,' in Clifford Geertz (ed.) *Myth, Symbol, and Culture* (New York, Norton Library, 1972), p. 120.

48. Thorstein Veblen, *The Instinct of Workmanship and the State of the Industrial Arts* (New York, Macmillan Co., 1914), p. 319.

49. Ibid., p. 333.

50. Leiss has an interesting if somewhat general discussion of this phenomenon on page 172 of his *The Domination Over Nature*.

51. Schapiro, *Totalitarianism*, pp. 64-5.

52. Unger, *The Totalitarian Party*, pp. 188-91.

53. The Catholic Church in particular figured stongly in this fight. See Karl Dietrich Bracher, *The German Dictatorship*, translated from the German by Jean Steinberg, (New York, Praeger, 1972), p. 384.

54. The idea of a 'national socialist' *Volksgemeinschaft* can be found in rudimentary form in some of the writings of the German Idealist philosopher Johann Gottlieb Fichte. Ferdinand Lassalle's notion of state socialism approximated to this idea, while the National-Social Union of the German theologian and political speculator Friedrich Naumann was briefly prominent towards the end of the 19th Century. Many prominent German liberals, such as Max Weber, Theodor Heuss, and Freidrich Meinecke were greatly influenced by Naumann.

55. Leon Poliakov, *The Aryan Myth: A History of Racist and Nationalist Ideas in Europe*, translated from the French by Edmund Howard, (New York, Basic Books, 1974), p. 329.

56. Mosse, *Nazism*, p. 117.

3 MAN IN THE NATURAL WORLD: THE NATIONAL SOCIALIST RELIGION OF NATURE

How can you find any pleasure, Herr Kersten, in shooting behind cover at poor creatures browsing on the edge of a wood, innocent, defenceless and unsuspecting? Properly considered, it's pure murder . . . Nature is so marvellously beautiful and every animal has a right to live . . . You will find this respect for animals in all Indo-Germanic peoples. It was of extraordinary interest to me to hear recently that even today Buddhist monks, when they pass through a wood in the evening, carry a bell with them, to make any woodland animals they might meet keep away, so that no harm will come to them. But with us every slug is trampled on, every worm is destroyed.[1]

The romantic origins of much of what is considered to be central to National Socialist ideology have been obvious to historians and political analysts for quite some time. American observers in particular have tended, with considerable justification, to emphasize the politicalisation of romanticism as being, at least in degree, that singularly German phenomenon which constituted an important step in the direction of Hitler's coming to power in 1933.[2] In the opinion of this writer, there is very little reason to dispute the findings of these writers and each of them has made an important contribution to our understanding of how an apparently ingenuous permutation of mysticism could be developed in such a fashion as to provide justification for racism and mass-murder. It is also beyond dispute that, in so far as its ideational contents were concerned, Nazism was, in many ways, uniquely German — a product of German historical and psychological circumstances.

As we have seen in the previous chapter, it has not been unusual for historians to comment upon certain religious characteristics of the National Socialist movement. Here, the Führer cult, such things as Hitler's extraordinary charismatic appeal to the mob, the nature of the Nuremberg party rallies, and the neopaganism of Himmler and his SS have been emphasised.[3] From time to time, authors have pointed to an aspect of National Socialist religious thought which existed as a legacy of Nazism's romantic heritage, *viz.*, a pronounced interest in nature.[4] As a rule, however, this is a topic which has been touched upon rather lightly. Perhaps this should not be viewed as being particularly strange.

After all, in our largely nominalistic world, serious consideration of even the better-known (or perhaps better-*publicised*) aspects of Nazi ideology can be considered unusual, to say nothing of these more arcane elements which, either because of their ideational content or mundane circumstances, never attained implementation. Yet historians, particularly American historians, have been quick to pick up on any so-called 'red thread' which can be discerned throughout the history of National Socialism. This being the case, one wonders why so little attention has been paid to the most interesting view that the leading ideologues of Nazi Germany had with regard to humankind's place in the natural world. It is the opinion of this writer that, outside of the fact that, as mentioned earlier, some historians probably do not take this (or, in some cases *any*) aspect of Nazi ideology very seriously, there is another reason why Nazi concerns with a so-called 'natural' religion have not been considered to any significant degree. The reason is the following: in the character and *tone* of the Nazi approach one can readily apprehend — as we have already in part seen — elements which demonstrate that, in certain crucial aspects, National Socialism was very much in the mainstream not only of German but of *Western* philosophical and religious developments. Unconsciously, perhaps, people are a bit uncomfortable with this.

That, for one reason or another, man needs religion, even if the religion is an extremely loosely-organised symbolic or ritualistic system, is sometimes so widely accepted as to be almost bromidic. Like most bromides, of course, so blandly acceptable a statement is open to attack, and generations of Marxists and Freudians have done their best. However, Marx's drawing of a wellnigh ontological line between *Entstehungsgeschichte* and true 'human' history and Freud's occasional excursions into Comtean-like metahistorical speculations indicate the problems that confronted even these two seminal minds in attempting to adhere to their respective injunctions to dispense with the insidious 'opiate' or archaic 'illusion.' In any case, it would appear that up until now, and for the foreseeable future, people have needed and will continue to need some sort of recourse to a posited supermundane being or realm, however ill-defined it might be — this in order to provide existential and/or axiological content to existence. At the same time, though, it would be grossly erroneous to assume that Western man's need for such a recourse has been met or will be met in the future by adherence to that supposed foundation of Western civilization, the Judaeo-Christian tradition. For while it is true that this tradition has been at least nominally *the* tradition of the so-called 'West', it has within it certain fundamental characteristics with which human beings cannot be entirely comfortable, particularly during periods in which a sense of estrangement from nature and from one's fellow beings prevails. Of crucial importance for this essay are the following two: (1) The line drawn by this tradition between life and death (or earth and 'heaven'), and (2) the line drawn between man and nature.

As Ernst Cassirer has pointed out, primitive man, in the face of numberless challenges from an often hostile world, could not accept the reality of death. In fact, as Cassirer would have it, primitive religion, in its belief in the continuity of life is 'the strongest and most energetic affirmation of life that we find in human culture.[5]

We have seen that Mary Douglas rejected the notion that 'primitive people' are inherently *deeply* religious.[6] However, as we have also seen, the author went on to say, 'There is no person whose life does not need to unfold in a coherent symbolic system'.[7] In various circumstances, 'coherent symbolic system[s]' assume the forms of well-articulated religions. Naturally, *any given religion* has to be seen as the product of specific time-bound cultural and social needs. In this context, Douglas described the religion of a New Guinea tribe, the Garia, a people who had a very loose, pragmatic view of the universe and of religion, one which pretty much precluded the use of those moral restraints usually associated with religious beliefs. However, in a world in which, according to Cassirer, people strive to overcome death or, at the very least, deal with it in a manner which diminishes its impact, any pattern of religious beliefs, no matter how sketchy or ill-defined its symbolic content might be, must be a partial articulation of a primal urge to 'over[come] risk'. The gap posed by death, that cold, ultimately disquieting frontier between finite and infinite, was the primary challenge to which religions, even the most pragmatic and nonnormative of them, had to respond.

While it is true that at times more emphasis is placed on the hyphen than on either Judaeo or Christian, one cannot gainsay the fact that, for both Jews and Christians, an hiatus between finite man and an infinite God does exist and that this hiatus must necessarily be described by the term 'death'.[9] Of course, the Judaeo-Christian tradition, like many others, accepts the immortality of the soul and indeed life itself is in large measure rationalised through an assumed justification or condemnation of one's *particular* life that is to take place in some period or level of existence to come. There would appear to be, however, some psychic mechanism, that refuses to be comforted by such assumptions. Simply put — humankind seems to be unable to accept its finiteness, the ontological border of which is death.[10] If we accept Cassirer's contention that man originally 'became religious' precisely to avoid having to confront death (through denying its reality), then we must see that the Judaeo-Christian tradition does not satisfactorily deal with at times impalpable but, none the less, real psychic needs.

The line drawn between humankind and nature by the Judaeo-Christian tradition is due primarily to the influence of the Mosaic Code, something which caused Hegel (and quite a few others less kindly disposed towards Judaism) to condemn the Jewish faith as being too abstract and unnatural. However, orthodox Christianity has not — nor could it have — dispensed with this code, something by virtue of which human beings are elevated to the position of being, as the psalmist put it, 'little lower than the angels.' To be sure, humans have awesome responsibilities *to* nature. None of God's creatures can be taken for granted, and a substantial portion of orthodox Jewish family life has had to revolve around the stringent injunction that one must not eat a calf in its mother's milk. One cannot deny, however, that the general attitude towards nature central to Judaism — and through Judaism, to Christianity also, albeit to a somewhat lesser degree — is the one which sees it as being apart from God. Humankind, of course, is as well. Nevertheless, by being made in the image of the divine, humans must be seen as being ontologically superior to nature.[11] The responsibilities inherent in so elevated but uncomfortable a position, i.e., ensconced somewhere *between* the natural world and the Kingdom of God, must be great indeed and, as is to be expected, humans have rebelled against this demanding role. Indeed, according to some observers, such neo-pagan revivals as the search for Aryan roots and, most importantly, National Socialism, can be viewed as being in large measure rebellions of this nature.[12] It is no great secret that today, in most Western countries, many appear to be in full flight from the two rather stringent principles described above, *viz.*, the acceptance of there being a qualitative distinction between an infinite God and finite humans (and hence, acceptance of the reality of death), and avowal of man's divinely-determined separation from nature. This will be considered again later in this work. For now, we must turn to those aspects of the National Socialist religion germane to this discussion.

Of course, National Socialism did not survive long enough to implement some of the more thoroughgoing anti-Christian aspects of its ideology (or perhaps, to be doubly cautious, '*Weltanschauung*' ought to be utilised, even if most of the individuals whose writings and comments we will be considering often blurred the distinction between the two terms). None the less, there can be no doubt that the views to be examined were taken seriously, at times painfully so, by those National

Socialists who either created policy or were in positions to affect it. Furthermore, it is the contention of this writer that the National Socialist approach to religion was one which could and did serve to rationalise mass-murder.

In *Mein Kampf*, Hitler was not concerned with outlining any part of a National Socialist religion (at least not consciously so) to a major degree. Indeed, he often wallowed in a glutinous mixture of self-pity and cultural despair. However, a foreshadowing of what would become the National Socialist 'religion of nature' was certainly present. Of importance here was Hitler's deprecation of the role of humanity in a universe run according to pitiless natural laws. In decrying pacifism as being contrary to established natural laws of survival, Hitler made the following statement:

> At this point, someone or other may laugh, but this planet once moved through the ether for millions of years without human beings and it can do so again some day if men forget they owe their higher existence, not to the ideas of a few crazy ideologists, but to the knowledge and ruthless application of Nature's stern and rigid laws.[13]

Throughout Hitler's political career he would continually emphasise the importance of recognising nature's power over man. He scoffed at the notion of humans ever having the ability to 'control' or 'rule over' nature. In the *Secret Conversations*, the following statement — presumably made on the night of 11–12 July 1941 — appeared:

> At the end of the last century the progress of science and technique led liberalism astray into proclaiming man's mastery of nature and announcing that he would soon have dominion over space. But a simple storm is enough — and everything collapses like a pack of cards.[14]

In this statement, which obviously has more than a grain of truth in it, Hitler sounded remarkably like contemporary environmentalists who, with ample reason, proclaim that a sharp-tempered Mother Nature, weary of pitiful man's toying with her inflexible laws, will eventually avenge herself upon those who, at least since the onset of industrialisation, have tried her patience. In any case, a belief in certain fixed laws of nature, to which man must continuously render obedience, always remained an important aspect of Hitler's *Weltanschauung*. Man was part of nature, and there was nothing that suggested that there was any essence which elevated him above it. 'The earth continues to go round, whether it's the man who kills the tiger or the tiger who eats the man. The stronger asserts his will, it's the law of nature. The world doesn't change; its laws are eternal'.[15] In this context, Hitler found it extremely easy to supplant hoary religious axioms with a simple belief in putatively unchanging natural laws. For National Socialists, it was of no importance at all that one reflect upon the world to come. All that was necessary was that man 'conform to the laws of nature'.[16] Here, Hitler tempered the adherence to a romantic sort of *Lebensphilosophie* often associated with National Socialism by introducing a cold dose of nineteenth century scientism. In declaring that man must necessarily live in conformity with the laws of nature, formal religious worship was out of the question. The primary ambition of National Socialism was 'to construct a doctrine that is nothing more than a homage to reason'.[17] Further, 'The man who lives in communion with nature necessarily finds himself in opposition to the Churches. And that's why they're heading for ruin — for science is bound to win'.[18]

In these statements, one can observe several important elements: (1) a sanctification of nature (this despite Hitler's general opposition to 'worship,' at least in a *formal* religious context), and (2) an absolute belief in the supremacy of science over any form of religious belief. In a way, Hitler can be seen as being a sort of updated version of Turgenev's Bazaroff, i.e., a firm believer in the inviolability of natural laws, and a lover of those means collected under the rubric 'science' used to uncover them. Indeed, Hitler's apparent tendencies towards a sort of biologism have caused some analysers of National Socialism to suggest that Hitler had no ideology but rather was devoted to a crude nexus of naturalistic beliefs. For Hannah Arendt, the ultimate purpose of the Nazis was to turn men into beasts, while for Ernst Nolte, Hitler — here at one with Fascists as a whole — sought to guard against human development, i.e., transcendence, through embedding man in a thoroughgoing naturalism, devoid of spiritual content of any kind.[19] While National Socialism was fiercely anti-transcendental, this view is not entirely accurate. For underlying all of this 'scientific naturalism' was a belief in a variety of what one could call 'natural mysteries' and in the emergence of a new age, one to be ushered in by some sort of 'great world transformation' whose precise character eluded scientific observation and measurement.[20] There was soon to be a turning point in history, a belief which Rauschning saw as constituting the cornerstone of Hitler's 'biological mysticism'.[21] What Hitler had done was to wed a putatively scientific view of the universe to a form of pantheistic mysticism presumably congruent with adherence to 'natural laws'. In this, he bore a marked resemblence to such Darwinians as Ernst Haeckel who, as is well known, informed their scientific endeavours with large doses of romanticism (at the same time, as we shall see later, Hitler in particular and ideologically-concerned Nazis in general were opposed to Darwinian theories of evolution). Throughout the writings, not only of Hitler, but of most Nazi ideologues, one can discern a fundamental deprecation of human *vis-à-vis* nature, and, as a logical corollary to this, an attack upon human efforts to master nature. The formerly liberal then dedicated Nazi educator and ideologue Ernst Krieck best expressed this in attacking man's 'hubris and guilt' in seeking to master nature, an attempt which could only destroy the 'natural foundations of his life' as well as those of the community.[22]

The fact, however, that man as a whole has to stand in subservience to nature did not obviate the possibility that some men in general could emerge as superior. Indeed, Hitler firmly believed in the emergence of a new 'type' of man, one who, in conforming to the laws of nature in fact represented a sort of apotheosis of natural development. We will examine this phenomenon in detail later. For now, we must bear in mind that Hitler, who often expressed himself in savage, naturalistic attacks upon the very concept of humanity, nevertheless had to believe in the emergence of a new human type, development of which constituted a substantial portion of the Nazi ideology. Sounding — although accidentally so — quite Hegelian, Hitler could proclaim that, in the triumph of the new authentic man, one could see proof that 'Man is God in the making'.[23] In a very real sense Hitler and the National Socialist movement perceived themselves as being virtual mediators between man — or at least a group of men — and a savage natural world, understanding of which was absolutely fundamental to the preservation and advancement of the existence of the community. So profound a position allowed, in fact demanded, that the mediators make awesome and far-reaching decisions on behalf of this community.

It was Hitler's belief in (1) the existence of, as he expressed in *Mein Kampf*, 'stern and rigid' natural laws, and (2) the necessity for men to apply them to areas of human existence, which of course allowed him to declare that the preservation of inferior human races was against nature herself. 'Nature,' he said, '. . . usually makes certain corrective decisions with regard to the racial purity of earthly creatures. She has little love for bastards'.[24] A further, for Hitler perhaps more important, purpose was served. This was his ability to rationalise the emergence of the true political leader on the basis of a sort of crudely-apprehended 'natural selection'. As he put it: 'Natural development finally brought the best man to *the* place where he belonged. This will always be so and will eternally remain so, as it always has been so . . . the most powerful and swiftest . . . [will] be recognised, and will be the victor'.[25]

In these lines, Hitler was not talking about religion *per se*. However, he had virtually deified nature and he most assuredly identified God (or Providence) with it. In this, he was at one with Alfred Rosenberg whose works, *Der Mythus des 20. Jahrhunderts*, contained somewhat detailed descriptions of what the 'Nordic' religion was and, of equal importance, how it differed from the Judaeo-Christian religion conception. Before considering Rosenberg's views on the matter, perhaps one should come down heavily on the side of disclaimer. After all, as Joachim Fest has pointed out, few people seemed to take Rosenberg's at times ponderous musings very seriously, particularly after the Nazis came to power.[26] Hitler himself, who usually enjoyed posing as a sort of latter-day, Renaissance-man, admitted that he could read very little of the *Mythus*. Furthermore, it is of some interest to note that, at least at one point in his political career, Hitler was adamant in stating that Rosenberg's work should not be regarded 'as an expression of the official doctrine of the Party'.[27] The very term '*Mythus*' seems to have bothered him, particularly inasmuch as 'A National Socialist should affirm that to the myth of the nineteenth century he opposes the faith and science of our times'.[28] Nevertheless, Rosenberg's view of religion was one which, either because of or in spite of him, was *widely held* by most committed National Socialists.[29]

In the *Mythus*, Rosenberg sharply distinguished between the religion of the Jews (and, to the extent that much of it was carried over into the New Testament, orthodox Christianity as well) and what he liked to refer to as 'Nordic religion'. In this regard, he ridiculed belief in 'a remote and fearful God, enthroned over all', the Jahweh of the so-called Old Testament '. . . to whom one prays in fear and praises in trembling'.[30] Of importance for him was the rejection of what he called the 'monstrous principle' which declared that God created the world from nothing. This Jewish idea which, according to Rosenberg, constituted the foundation of Catholic beliefs as well, was rooted in a pernicious dualism. God created a world that was *separate* from Him. In Rosenberg's eyes, such a world was an unnatural one, since nature and her rules were being relegated to a secondary position. Belief in the Judaeo-Christian dualism could only lead to a situation in which the 'natural-grown Being of nature' would be crippled. 'These spiritual and racial cripples will then be collected under the Catholic roof'.[31] Rosenberg opposed to this an Aryan/Nordic race soul, whose basic religious tenets were rooted in India.

Of fundamental importance here was a *monistic* tradition in which an eternal 'order principle' struggled against chaos.

The ordering principle to which Rosenberg referred was, of course, nature itself, the form in which Providence found its only expression. In his view, Aryan man did not really *relate* to any sort of extrinsic or transcendental deity. Rather, as a creature of nature, the ordering principle of life lived within him, conferring upon him an at least racial immortality. '. . . Odin was and is dead', according to Rosenberg. 'However, the German mystic discovered this "strength from above" in his own soul. Divine Valhalla arose from the infinite, misty vastness buried in the human breast'.[32] For obvious reasons, the late-Medieval German mystic, Meister Eckhart, was a great favourite of Rosenberg.

Rosenberg differed from Hitler in that he was much more seriously concerned with *creating* (or, perhaps in his eyes, rediscovering) a *Mythus* which could serve those purposes normally assigned to orthodox religion. For Hitler, far more attuned to political realities than his more esoteric colleague, religious concerns were always tied to those of a practical nature. Hitler and Rosenberg were one, however, in their deification of nature and in the belief that adherence to certain natural qualities elevated some men above all others, indeed, served to make them 'immortal.' Rosenberg, in his sustained attacks on the Judaeo-Christian tradition, went somewhat further than Hitler in so far as theological issues were concerned. None the less, their respective emphases upon a sort of natural religion, in Rosenberg's case defined as being monistic in nature, were to receive substantive support over the years.

Of great importance for the National Socialist ideologues was the bringing together of so-called 'religious' and 'scientific' concerns. The important thing here was that aspect of the National Socialist *Weltanschauung* which, through its deification of nature itself, seemed to allow for a bridging of the gap between spirit and matter. According to a book concerned with biological instruction, the teaching of this subject had to place emphasis on the total view of things. 'The metabolic changes in a closed biotic community reveal a meaningful plan in the greater occurrences of nature.' Thus, it was possible to arrive 'at a concept of nature that does not conflict with religious experience, whereas this was necessarily the case with the former purely mechanistic attitude'.[33] The study of man, anthropology, had to take place within a biological context. Further, anthropocentric views in general had to be rejected. They would be valid only 'if it is assumed that nature has been created only for man. We decisively reject this attitude. According to our conception of nature, man is a link in the chain of living nature just as any other organism'.[34]

The 'chain of living nature' of which man was but a link was viewed as being congruent with the National Socialist *Weltanschauung*. This word received a fairly lucid definition in a term-handbook which was to be used in the well-known SS *Junkerschule* at Bad Tölz.[35] The definition was as follows: 'to observe all things in this life from a standpoint and to live according to it.'[36] After providing definitions for various terms — race, *Volk*, etc. — the general thrust of the work was revealed in a most interesting 'response' to the phrase 'humanity' (*'Menschheit'*): 'The concept of humanity is biological nonsense.' After all, in the natural world there was no *'Tierheit'*.[37]. Man, species-man, that is, and *not* humanity, was part of nature, a fact recognised by the National Socialist *Weltanschauung*. This *Weltanschauung* was a dynamic one that did not recognise *'Ruhe'* ('Rest'). 'In this regard', the pamphlet went on, 'nature gives us the best examples'. All of life was struggle and hence the National Socialist *Weltanschauung* was simply a recognition of natural laws.[38] Whether or not it was supposed to be a statement of SS policy or a sort of axiological charge to the Nordic world in general, the following statement is of some interest; 'Therefore the body must assimilate itself to the environment; certainly in wearing apparel, dress and temperature'.[39]

What was being emphasised here was the cruel struggle for existence, one in which the most natural of peoples would survive. Nature was merciless and showed no pity to those who could not respond to her, at times, seemingly overwhelming challenges. In such a struggle, there was no room for pity because 'pity obscures the principle of selection'.[40] At the same time, though, a traditional assumption of those who accepted fundamental Darwinian principles, i.e., descent from a common ancestor, had to be dispensed with. 'It is a completely false conception that man has descended from apes. Therefore, that man and apeman stem from a [common] source.'[41] So, as the Bad Tölz handbook envisioned it, life was a struggle between the several major races, the most 'natural' of which would win. In this context, the so-called 'Christian *Weltanschauung*' would appear to be singularly inappropriate, based as it was on a 'false division' between body and soul and also on the assumption that all bodies and all souls were somehow equal before God. 'We say that souls, bodies, and God belong together.'[42] Again, a form of immortality had been assumed.

Thus, as the National Socialist ideologue saw it, religion and science had been bound together in a *Weltanschauung* that was itself congruent with a nature of which it was the highest possible expression. This

Weltanschauung was neither overly-spiritual or overly-materialistic, but rather could be summed up in the engaging phrase ('Everything is Life') '*Alles ist Leben*' or, as was often more simply written, '*Natur*'. Spiritual, i.e. *overly* spiritual people captured by traditional religious beliefs, believed in the one God who created a world which He now ruled with caprice and harshness. Materialists were either coldly deistic or out-and-out atheists. However, the 'life-affirming' (to use a favourite phrase) National Socialists' *Weltanschauung* saw God's power and Nature's power as being one and the same thing. To ask for the source of life itself would be absurd. Its beginnings were unclear. But we do know, as the Bad Tölz document put it, that 'we are the bearers and shapers of eternal life'.[43] Since the gap between spiritual and mundane worlds has been bridged by the National Socialist *Weltanschauung*, and since a nature-bound people was, by definition, bound to the highest of spiritual principles then it indeed followed that the '*Volk* is the religion of our time'.[44]

Amidst the crudely pantheistic and proto-existentialist verbiage, one idea emerged with some clarity, *viz.*, that National Socialism was based upon a 'life-affirming' principle which was the principle of nature itself. The writings of Hitler and Rosenberg, and the Bad Tölz document itself, all point to this. This is seen in an address by Pg. (party comrade) Dr. Brachmann is seen at the *Religionswissenschaftliche Institut* at Halle. The topic of this lecture (the date for which, unfortunately, is not available, but it probably was given between 1934 and 1936) concerned the conflicting ideologies of East and West. Throughout the address, Brachmann attacked the 'other-worldliness' and legalisms that he saw as inherent in the Eastern, i.e., Judaeo-Christian tradition. Eastern religion was based on restrictions and fear. It was based on a spiritual condition which had lost the instinct for life (or perhaps, it had never had it in the first place).[45] Oriental religiosity, according to Brachmann, was, in all of its forms (but most particularly in Judaism and Pauline Christianity) based upon a 'denial of everything living'.[46] There was, withal, a virtual fear of life itself. Such a conception of life, one which seemed to emphasise its emptiness next to the almost opulent grandeur of God, was suitable for a nomadic people, unhappily rootless in the wastes of Asia. To this, Brachmann opposed the rooted, farming life, one which was responsible for a view of the world in which all so-called material elements — the soil, cattle, etc. — were seen as holy. In other words, according to Brachmann, what was holy for the rooted — and presumably, Nordic-European farmer — did not serve to separate men from nature.[47]

Unfortunately, through the triumph of the Judaeo-Christian tradition and thus of the Jewish God — a perniciously capricious one at that —

the European spirit had been enslaved by religious principles inherently foreign to it. The healthy 'peasant religion' was just now beginning to emerge. As an example of the sort of spirit that it would have to combat, Brachmann provided Moses who, before he could marry the daughter of Jethro, had to circumcise himself, i.e., sacrifice his manhood to a 'God of the wastes'.[48] Unfortunately, it was this type of God who, through John the Baptist, was brought into the New Testament itself. A religious *Weltanschauung* of this nature, i.e., one based on fear of a God of caprice, was necessarily dependent upon revelation. The Indo-Germanic religious *Weltanschauung*, however, took its point of departure from men and was apotheosised in that German sense of 'inwardness' which was responsible for, among other things, attempting to bring certain aspects of the Judaeo-Christian tradition back into harmony with nature through the Cult of the Virgin Mary. The robust glorification of mother and child, Brachmann stated, was hardly characteristic of the oriental world.[49] When we 'give thanks', it must be not to some capriciously tyrannical God of the wastes, but rather to that which demonstrates to us the congruity of 'man and life'.[50]

According to Alex Elbertzhagen, Nordic religiosity was in fact *embodied* in '*unreflective, joyful creation, and struggle*'. Confident in its '*right and strength*', it was '*the immediate experience of the immediate power of God*'.[51] It was this variety of religious experience, rooted in and reflective of life itself, which was responsible for the Nordic race's being the most creative on earth.[52] For such an experience necessarily called for heroic men who, confident of the power of God which surged within them, strove mightily against the seeming 'limits of humanity'.[53] Nordic religion was indeed a religion of 'God-men'. Naturally, Elbertzhagen was aware that such teachings were not exactly congruent with established Christian beliefs. Indeed, he maintained, the teaching of this 'Nordic religion' and of the values which flowed from it, could hardly be entrusted to the established clergy. Rather, he thought, such would have to be the task of school teachers educated for that purpose.[54]

The National Socialist *Weltanschauung* was celebrated as providing for a true 'religion of life'. The old dualisms could now be overthrown and, in their place, one could posit something for which such hoary precursors of National Socialism as Wilhelm Marr, Eugen Dühring, and Houston Stewart Chamberlain had argued — a religious belief congruent with those laws of nature in terms of which a true ('Folk Community') *Volksgemeinschaft* would develop to fruition. The liberation from Judaeo-Christian dogma would be apotheosised in the transcendence of — to use a phrase well-known at the time — 'life alien' usages. In an SS document of 1936, ('The Historical Development of the Essence of the German Reich') *Die geschichtliche Entwicklung der deutschen Reich-sein*, several songs to be sung at SS festivals were suggested. One of them captured the sense of liberation from the Judaeo-Christian tradition. In Asian wastes, i.e., the Holy Land,

> Verblutete deutsche Wehr
> Die Zeit verging, doch der Pfaffe blieb,
> Den Volk die Seele zu rauben,
> Und ob er es romisch, Lutherisch trieb,
> Er lehrte den jüdischen Glauben.[55]

> (German might has bled to death
> Time passed yet the priest remained
> to rob the people of its soul
> And whether he proselytised Roman or Lutheran
> He taught the Jewish faith)

A second song, entitled 'Juden raus, Papst Hinaus', (Jews out, away with the Pope') developed this theme a bit further:

> Nein, wir haben nicht geblutet namenlos und ohne Ruhm,
> Das der deutchen Art verjudet weiter durch der Christendum.

> (No, we have not bled anonymous and without fame,
> So that the German race will be Judaised through Christendom again)

Now, the German *Volk* had been liberated from Judaeo-Christian enslavement ('Wir sind frei von Berge Sinai'), and there was no further need for a church since German men and women would be living in accord with the laws of nature ('Sonnenrad führt uns allein')[56] (The Sun alone guides us').

At times, the Nazis seemed uncertain as to precisely which aspects of the Judaeo-Christian tradition they found most disturbing. Often, it was that 'Other-worldiness' so strongly attacked by Brachmann. At other times, though, the Nazis focused their attacks upon what they perceived to be the mundane and materialistic aspects of Judaism in particular, declaring, as expressed in a memorandum from Rosenberg's office, that what should be emphasised in ideological training was the 'oriental', mundane character of the Jewish dogma, something which, if believed in by enough people, had eventually to lead to Jewish political as well as spiritual domination.[57] Despite such apparent uncertainties, however, there can be little doubt that the Nazis were quite sincere in seeing themselves as rebels against the Judaeo-Christian tradition.

According to J. Spelter all 'established' world religions were characterised by emphases on *'cosmopolitanism'* or teachings of the *'equality of all men'*[58] Christianity, however, in which 'Jehovah's flaming hatred covered itself with the cloak of love,' was especially pernicious since it amounted to a triumph of Judaism, albeit in veiled form.[59]

The significance of the National Socialist theological revolution (for such it was) can perhaps be disputed. After all, despite the Bad Tölz documents, the rather simplistic, if not simple-minded, attacks on the Judaeo-Christian tradition, and the various *Hitler Jugend* sun and fire festivals, Germany remained nominally 'Christian' and the desires of some, such as Martin Bormann, that wars be declared on Christianity were never implemented, if only because there was not enough opportunity to do so. Moreover, as we will see, various Christian believers sought accommodation between Christian and National Socialist principles. It is obvious, however, that leading National Socialists *assumed* a fundamentally anti-Christian (to say nothing of *Judaeo*-Christian) stance and were able to rationalise many of their actions in terms of it. Hitler may have mocked Rosenberg for his garbled neologisms, and Bormann might well have despised minor party philosophers such as Brachmann, Krieck, and Wagner (to say nothing of the 'major' one, Rosenberg). All were united, however, in the belief that National Socialism represented a new *Lebensphilosophie* in which a fundamental understanding of the laws of life made it possible for science and religion to be brought together and the cleft between heaven and earth bridged.

We can get a good idea of this by considering some comments of Martin Bormann. In a 1942 piece on National Socialism and Christianity, he emphasised the incompatibility of 'National Socialist and Christian concepts'. National Socialism, Bormann declared, was based on 'scientific foundations', while Christianity's principles, laid down almost two thousand years ago, 'have increasingly stiffened into life-alien dogmas'.[60] National Socialism must always be guided by science and, instead of conceiving of God as being some sort of 'manlike being' sitting up somewhere in the heavens, the new *Weltanschauung* viewed it as some sort of force, one which governed heavenly spheres other than our 'unimportant earth'.[61]

> The assertion that this world-force can worry about the fate of every individual, every bacillus on earth, and that it can be influenced by so-called prayer or other astonishing things is based either on a suitable dose of naïveté or on outright commercial effrontery.[62]

The 'God' in which Bormann believes was (and is) the God of a fairly

substantial number of people. In part, Bormann's remarks were written
in the spirit of that agnosticism that has become the prevailing mood
of modern life. At the same time, though, Bormann was deprecating
the notion of the divinity of *man*, there being no 'manlike being' in whose
image he had been created. In place of divine humanity and a presumably
superannuated God, there was life itself, whose fundamental scientific
truths had been grasped in National Socialism. The somewhat more
mystically-inclined Heinrich Himmler persistently attacked Christianity for its notion that men should dominate the world. In place of this
he offered a presumably 'old German' belief in the interrelationship between macro- and microcosms. 'Man', Himmler maintained in a 9 June
1942 speech to SS chiefs in Berlin, 'is nothing special'. All that he was
was a piece of earth.[63]

Naturally, in all of this there was the implicit or explicit notion that
while '*man*' was nothing, some *men* were unto gods. These were those
humans fortunate enough to be endowed with a *Weltanschauung* rooted
in the laws of nature itself. Such people carried within themselves a life-
bound idealism. This notion came out quite strongly in a 17 February
1944 speech of the *Reich* Governor of Baden, Robert Wagner, at the
University of Strassburg. During the course of his address, Wagner posed
'the ideas and the idealism of the National Socialist *Weltanschauung*
against the suicidal struggle of the democratic historical era', an era
characterised, as he saw it, by materialistic self-seeking.[64] Men, Wagner
maintained, 'cannot build their concepts of life upon foundations of
egotistical wishes or abstract theories alien to life [*weltfremden*], but only
upon recognizable laws of nature'.[65] There had been the call 'back to
nature' and now this process had been completed by National Socialism
and by Adolf Hitler. National Socialism, then, was nothing else than
the grasping of natural laws through 'a spirit of genius' (Hitler's
presumably).[66] Again and again, Wagner came back to the theme that
the National Socialist *Weltanschauung* was 'nothing but,' or 'nothing
other' than 'authentic, true knowledge or, better said, knowledge of
nature'. In fact, so closely did the *Weltanschauung* of Hitler adhere to
the laws of life, that it was itself in a state of perpetual development.

> The Führer has consciously avoided allowing his National Socialism
> to develop into a stationary doctrine. It should and it must remain
> [a] revolutionary idea. Each doctrine leads all too easily to dogmatism
> and through that to alienation from the world [*Weltfremden*].[67]

In these lines, Pg. Wagner captured something that helps to explain the
extraordinary success of the National Socialist ideology, *viz.*, that

impressive balance between belief in posited eternal natural truths and a pragmatism which allowed for a great deal of flexibility in determining how such truths should be applied to the human world. Not since Thomas Müntzer espoused his belief in a 'continuous revelation' had so convenient a method of adjusting 'infinite laws' to finite conditions been adopted.

It is in this context that we can consider a most interesting phenomenon; the so called 'Hitler Cult,' for good reason viewed as being at the very heart of National Socialism. Here, Hitler's use of language is most instructive. As has often been pointed out, there often appeared to be a deliberate use of Christian imagery by Hitler, an imagery which conjured up ideas of his being a messiah. 'Thou art in me and I in thou', he proclaimed in a speech of 7 May 1933. 'So as I am yours, so you are mine. Just as I can have no other goal but to make Germany strong and free again, so must your will bind itself with mine'.[68] The impact of such imagery on youth could be particularly strong. Hence, in a 2 September 1933 speech to the *Hitler Jugend*, the following langauge must have made an immense impression: 'You, my young people, you are the living Germany of the future; not an empty idea, no pallid scheme, but you are blood of our blood, flesh of our flesh, spirit of our spirit — you are the regeneration of our people'.[69] Important throughout Hitler's speeches was the notion of redemption with, of course, party and Führer being the source of it. 'The guilt of our people is extinguished', he proclaimed in a 3 September 1933 speech to assembled SA and SS men; 'the desecration atoned for, the shame is conquered. The men of November are fallen and their power is past.'[70] There can be no question that, for those familiar with and respectful of, biblical langauge, the impact of such exhortations must have been enormous. Hitler himself was probably at least as deeply moved by them as anybody else. Yet, while certainly utilising biblical jeremiad and exhortation whenever he thought it to be of value, Hitler was always careful to draw a sharp line between the sort of spirituality which he saw as informing his movement and conventional, organised religion. This was most clearly expressed in a party day speech in Nuremberg, given on 6 September 1938. Perhaps because he was in the middle of the Sudeten crisis, this address was most stringent in tone. After declaring that Germany must be cleansed of all parasites and that, in the process of the struggle against 'the international Jewish world enemy', 'eternal values of blood and soil' had to be elevated to be the 'ruling laws of our life', Hitler proceeded to draw a line between National Socialism and Christianity.[71]

In this regard, Hitler spoke of the mystery of Christianity, a faith which throve in dark buildings filled with shadows. He did not want to fill the German people 'with a mysticism which lies outside the purpose and goal of our teaching'.[72] National Socialism, Hitler declared, was to be a '*Volksbewegung*', but 'under no conditions a *Kultbewegung*'. Under no circumstances was a mystery cult for the German people to be created.[73] The National Socialist movement preserved God's work and carried out the will of God not in the twilight world of the cult 'but before the open countenance of the Master'.[74] These are very revealing words. Hitler was in fact telling his audience that there were to be no more 'mysteries' in the Christian sense (although timeless 'mysteries of the blood' would remain, of course). Rather, in the National Socialist movement, one in which the 'principle of life', attained continuous affirmation, secular and spiritual worlds had been fused. There was really no need to appeal to any external force. Providence would be revealed in those actions undertaken by the movement; a movement which, embodying within itself laws of life revealed in nature, was in fact *acting as Providence*. Hence, any acts committed by the National Socialist movement in general or by Hitler in particular were justified by the very fact of their being committed in the first place. While the Nazis never proclaimed themselves, as Italian Fascists often did, as being pragmatists, there was a strong pragmatic core that subsisted at the centre of their ideology.

J. P. Stern has talked of 'a situation of total immanence' in which everyone 'including Hitler himself, fully believed in the image they have created'.[75] Here, in referring to the colour and pageantry of Nazi ceremonies, such as that described in the previous chapter, Stern has a most cogent point to make. Of immense importance here is the author's suggestion that in Nazi ceremonies image became reality, a necessary component of any *religious* ceremony. We must, however, suggest that Stern really did not go far enough. In its revolution against the Judaeo-Christian tradition, National Socialism, regardless of its calling upon religious imagery essentially Christian in character, had to reject the traditional notions of God and messiah. In this regard, I think it is of importance to bear in mind Professor Rhodes' injunction that in order to understand what the Nazis were about we must take their conceptions of themselves and their mission seriously.[76] If one does that, it becomes plain, for this writer, that the millenarian concerns which Rhodes, quite understandably, views as being of ultimate importance with regard to the ideational content of National Socialism, served *facilitatory* purposes within the context of an *anti*-Christian religion, a religion of nature. *Adherence* to such could only have conjured forth dualistic images of a movement striving to follow some sort of divinely prescribed program. Being 'rooted in life itself,' there was no need to do so and the symbol, the image, or however one wishes to describe the several aspects of National Socialistic ideology, had to be real; as real as the brick and concrete crematoria which were its technological expression. In a word, while ceremonial occasions obviously brought forth symbol and imagery in concentrated form — while at the same time transforming them into reality — all public activities of the National Socialists were informed by this process. In the pursuit of *Lebensraum* in the East and the final solution we can clearly see this process — myth, expressed in archetypal imagery, had become real.

Naturally, in all of this, the role of Hitler was central. As far as the German people are concerned, the impact he had as an orator was immense, and need not be discussed here. Furthermore, for many Germans, he became increasingly identified with the Fatherland even as they rejected a party increasingly viewed as incompetent and/or corrupt. For our purposes, though, it was Hitler's place within the symbolic structure of the National Socialist Religion that is crucial. For example, in the SS *Namensweihe* ceremony (baptism), something which in form was similar to its Christian counterpart but in content amply reflected the blood-and-soil *Mythus* of Himmler's organisation, a picture of Hitler as the new Christ stood in the middle of an altar decorated with swastikas.[77] Bearing this extraordinary image in mind, it is not at all surprising that Himmler and others in high SS circles saw Hitler as in fact taking the place of Christ. Here, the *Führer Mythus* had indeed become a 'Führer Cult', and Himmler himself often referred to Hitler as a '*Gottmensch*'.[78] Hitler's reaction to all of this preternatural adoration was humbly to deny that he was a messiah. 'To those . . . who, in their enthusiasm for the regeneration of our nation, go too far and hail me as a Prophet, a second Mahommed or a second Messiah, I can only retort that I can find no trace of any resemblance in myself to a Messiah.'[79] Whether Hitler was being genuinely or falsely modest must remain uncertain. In any case, the point can be made that, bearing in mind the character of the National Socialist religion of nature, the notion of a 'messiah' had become superfluous. With the overcoming, as they saw it, of the dualism between natural and supernatural, the Nazis had provided for a sanctification of the mundane, e.g., military campaigns, mechanical-like slaughter of 'natural enemies', which allowed for the most coldly technological methods to serve the needs of a community awash in naturalistic, petty bourgeois bathos. In such a situation, the need for a messiah serving the 'traditional' role of mediating between man and God had been obviated. There was no need for Himmler's '*Gottmensch*' to die on the cross for Germany's sins despite Hitler's own occasional use of biblical imagery.

Yet there can be no doubt that, as indicated earlier, for many ordinary Germans, Hitler *was* Germany and whatever positive they saw in National Socialism was identified with him. Certainly, in 'crisis' situations such as those posed by war, this would be of crucial importance.[80] Furthermore, within the ranks of the party faithful (in every sense of the word) the adulation of Hitler could attain proportions so extraordinary that, to explain it, the historian has to surrender a substantial portion of his 'territory' to the psychiatrist, or, better, psychohistorian. At the very least, the power of Hitler's personality was such as to compel those around him to accept 'his definition of reality, of the sources and purposes of struggle, of his definition of the enemy and how the enemy was to be treated'.[81] Moreover, while it is true that Hitler was not responsible for every element that would attach itself to the National Socialist religion, it is also true that nothing in the contributions of Rosenberg, Darre or Himmler contradicted the guiding principles of Hitler's own *Weltanschauung*.[82] In all events, the extraordinary ability of Hitler to define not merely ideological reality, but reality as a whole, for all who were in his presence, has caused one author to describe this ability as follows: 'We are very much in the presence of a total invasion of the personality by a consecrated object . . .'[83] There can be no doubt that, besides serving purposes of social control, the prayers *to* Hitler created, especially for German youth, by National Socialist religious zealots, expressed that genuine sense of awe which many felt for their *Führer*, at the very least a forerunner of that 'new man' who would emerge as both the bearer and product of National Socialist religiosity.[84] Thus could Himmler, who was much impressed by the Eastern religions, draw upon a description of the 'redeemer' found in the Bhagavad-Gita, in making the following extraordinary statement:

> This passage is absolutely made for the Führer . . . He rose up out of our deepest need, when the German people had come to a dead end . . . It has been ordained by Karma of the Germanic world that he should wage war against the East [!] and save the Germanic peoples — a figure of the greatest brilliance has become incarnate in his person.[85]

While Himmler's panegyrics might have been atypical, there can be no doubt that Hitler's singularity was believed in by all convinced National Socialists. This was certainly reflected in National Socialist art where Hitler, unlike the Stalin depicted in Soviet Socialist Realist works, was *always* pictured either alone, or as the central figure. Emphasis was always placed not upon certain disarming (in every sense of the word) avuncular qualities, as was the case with Stalin, but upon a sort of 'impersonal' '(*unpersönlich*) aspect which rendered him spiritually inaccessible.[86]

While there can be no question as to the significance of a 'Hitler Cult', nor as to its importance in the Nazi ideology, we must not allow ourselves to be totally absorbed by its more idiosyncratic and bizarre aspects. The 'cult' itself must be seen as representing only an aspect — albeit a most important one — of the National Socialist concept of the natural religion. 'Cult', after all, brings to mind visions of obscure rites and arcane rituals. Hitler, in distinguishing between National Socialism and traditional religion, was rather to the point. While the German people were not viewed as being politically mature enough to have precise knowledge of such events as the 'Final Solution', although they had been prepared for it to the greatest degree possible, Nazi pronouncements and policies were supposed to be interpreted as being in strict conformity with the laws of life. As Hitler and others saw it, living according to such laws was not easy. Human beings seemed to be perversely determined to rebel against them. Even with regard to diet, where men seemed to be determined to destroy themselves by eating meat, human beings 'alone among the living creatures, try to deny the laws of nature'.[87] However, when such laws are discovered, and if people are determined to live according to them, then everything can fall into place with relative ease.

This was, as Hitler saw it, particularly the case with regard to the 'natural' role of women. 'The phrase of women-emancipation is a phrase discovered only by the Jewish intellect, and its content is stamped by the same spirit', Hitler proclaimed in a 8 September 1934 speech to the *NS Frauenschaft*.[88] The German woman did not have to emancipate herself from German life. After all, nature had provided for her in that capacity.[89] Hitler, mostly privately, but occasionally publicly, admitted that he detested women in politics. At the same time, though, there was that sphere of activity, sanctified by nature, that was woman's. 'With each child which she brings into the world for the nation, she is fighting her struggle for the nation.'[90] To be sure, the man must represent his people, but the woman did the same for the family, and her equality was assured because 'she, in those areas of life determined for her by nature, [should] receive every deep respect due to her'.[91] Despite Hitler's well-known contempt for them as being socially uncreative, irrational creatures, there is little doubt that he was sincere in his belief that nature (the 'laws of life') had provided for a sanctified area of activity for women. In the following chapter, we will consider this issue at greater length.

Opposition to pronouncements such as those mentioned above could only reveal, as Alfred Rosenberg put it in a speech of 3 March 1938, an obstinacy indicative of a desire to 'reverse nature,' since the new 'laws of life' (*Lebensgesetze*) of the German nation were grounded in a recognition of general 'laws of life'.[92] Leading National Socialists were particularly critical of scholars who, ensconced in their respective specialities, refused to participate whole-heartedly in the National Socialist revolution. They were accused of 'drawing back from life', of dealing with specialised and distant things 'without an inner participation in the great struggles of the German *Volk*'.[93] The highest praise that Robert Ley could assign Hitler was that 'He affirms life', and, in so doing brought out the best in all of his people.[94] The philosophy of National Socialism, as represented by its Führer, had to be true and could not be contrary to any variety of scientific knowledge because, as Ernst Krieck put it, it stemmed from 'simple elemental truths and elemental conceptions constructed on foundations given by nature'. Indeed, the biological *Weltanschauung* of the National Socialist movement 'embrace[d] [the] concept of 'life' in its total width and depth'.[95]

In all of this, one must not assume that there was an absolutely monolithic National Socialist ideology, consistent in all details and adhered to in lock-step fashion by all National Socialists. While, as mentioned before, no ideologue deviated to any significant degree from the major principle of Hitler's *Weltanschauung*, there were disagreements on various points and, quite often, downright petty quarreling between leading exponents. As is well known, Rosenberg and Goebbels often disagreed and the former was often quite critical of Ernst Krieck's approaches to philosophy and science. All National Socialists, however, agreed on one fundamental principle: in their philosophy of 'life', certain perceived weaknesses, 'unnatural' in character, of the Judaeo-Christian tradition had been overthrown. How this could affect social attitudes was revealed in an extraordinary article, written by SS *Untersturmführer* Prof. Eckhardt, that appeared in the journal of the SS, *Das Schwarze Korps*, on 22 May 1935. In this article, Eckhardt pointed out that, in pre-Christian times, Nordic man had recognised that homosexuality and cowardice went together. As a consequence of this realisation, homosexuals had been executed. Only with the coming of Christianity which killed men because of sins against God *rather than* sins against the race, did the Nordic race lose sight of ancient customs rooted in nature.[96]

In this extremely important statement, the true meaning of the Nazi religion of nature is revealed. 'Unnatural' attitudes towards perceived unnatural acts had to have resulted when one believes in and prays to the distant Christian God. The 'true' God — and Himmler insisted that every SS man believe in Him — lived within a race-bound nation thus sanctified by nature itself.[97] If the SS, which was, after all, the elite of nature-bound Nordic man, decided that certain practices and attitudes were 'unnatural,' then such had to be the case or so far-reaching a decision could not have been made. While obviously the Jews were the target of greatest importance, the 'unnatural' quality of Christianity, a religion which Himmler described as 'a perverse *Weltanschauung* estranged from life', and 'the greatest pestilence in history which has befallen us', is something which Nazi ideologues emphasised over and over again.[98] Only when so inherently degenerate and unnatural a religion prevailed, could homosexuals, 'a danger to the national health', be tolerated, and not be drowned in bogs, as healthy Nordic ancestors once had dealt with them.[99]

The 'Hitler cult' played a crucial role in the ideology. We must appreciate, however, the fact that, while Hitler as head of the National Socialist party no doubt encouraged the emergence of a series of basic attitudes necessarily at least congruent with his own, he did not demand that flood of literature extolling the new, natural religion which appeared during the Nazi reign of power. The writings of such people as Bormann, Rosenberg, Krieck and many other lesser-known ideologues, point to certain basic and deep-seated concerns of which Hitler's own influential beliefs were but a part.

As we have thus far considered it, the National Socialist 'religion' emphasised two fundamental points: (1) the necessity of overcoming the gap between worldly and other-worldly (and hence, between the traditional realms of 'science' and 'religion') and (2) the necessity of seeing man as being part of nature, and thus subject to the pitiless judgement of natural law. In the first instance, the National Socialist *Weltanschauung* emphasised a very crude sort of Hegelianism, *viz.*, man's seeking of infinitude within his own breast. Where the National Socialists differed from Hegel, of course, was in their insistence that not all men could do this, since some, indeed, *most* of them, adhered to *weltfremden* doctrines, e.g., the Judaeo-Christian tradition, which in turn pointed to a lack of soulish, i.e., *natural*, qualities. Thus, point (2), the emphasis upon man's role in and *of* nature, was, at least in the eyes of National Socialists, inextricably intertwined with point (1). Having produced, as they saw it, a *Weltanschauung* that allowed two of the most disturbing dualisms in human existence to be overcome, i.e., the gaps between body and spirit and man and nature, it is not surprising that Nazi ideologists took their beliefs extremely seriously.

Under these circumstances, it can be easily understood why a September 1940 quarrel, originating in the *Gräberfürsorge* ('Graves Welfare') office of the SS — a dispute over whether the graves of fallen SS men should be marked with a so-called 'Tyr-rune' or a 'Man-rune' — eventually ended up involving the attention of Himmler himself.[100] One can also appreciate why, at a time when the war was all but lost — 15 December 1944 — Rosenberg could still be so deeply concerned over the correct appreciation of the significance of the National Socialist *Weltanschauung*, that he would send a 12-page *Schulungsbrief* on the subject to the SD (Security Service) office.[101] No doubt for the individual German soldier, by 1944 fighting desperately against impossible odds, the *Weltanschauung* issue might well have appeared to be a somewhat irrelevant one. But, from the point of view of those who mattered, i.e., the National Socialist leadership, it could not have been for, *au fond*, the war that they had chosen to bring upon Europe was in large measure concerned with the triumph of a *Weltanschauung* which embodied the hopes and ambitions of *some* of those estranged from Judaeo-Christian tenets.

It has been customary to view the National Socialist movement as crowning a series of trends and events which marked Germany's 'rebellion' against the West.[102] To an extent, such an opinion is supportable, particularly if one bears in mind that, at least until after World War II, Germany although contributing far more than her share to Western culture, was in some respects — economic, social and political — not really a West European nation at all. Furthermore, Nazism, as in large measure the result of a form of political romanticism that self-consciously defined itself against prevailing Western traditions, was something that could have arisen only in Germany. However, if by 'rebellion against the West' we mean 'rebellion against the Judaeo-Christian tradition', then we must see that the National Socialist *Weltanschauung* embodied within it elements that have existed as Western civilisation's alter ego from time to time.

Joachim of Fiore was only one representative, albeit perhaps the most intellectually respectable, of a chiliastic tradition which, while not consciously anti-Christian (indeed, those prominent in it often claimed to be the *true* Christians), nevertheless was most uncomfortable with the orthodox Christian view of eschatology and life eternal. A succession of false messiahs and embodiments of the Holy Ghost, from Montanus of Phrygia to the pseudo-Baldwin of Flanders, sought to demonstrate that the Kingdom of Death could be transcended in the here-and-now and spiritual truth realised through violent social action. The Manichean tradition, never completely reconciled to the delicate and, at times, seemingly artificial balance, between body and spirit proffered by the Judaeo-Christian tradition, denounced it altogether in favour of a permutation of Gnosticism, something that had to occasion the barbaric Albigensian Crusade of the 13th Century.[103] Theosophical societies, spiritualists, and purveyors of various forms of Eastern mysticism are as prominent as ever before throughout the West and in some places, e.g., the United States, probably *more* so than previously. The Judaeo-Christian tradition remains as the 'official' tradition of Western Civilisation, but for many its hold has come to be rather tenuous.

Hitler, while despising the renewal of old Germanic customs suggested by such people as Rosenberg and, contrary to popular belief, no great believer in astrology, most assuredly believed in the transcendence of the body/soul dichotomy through capturing a 'world-affirming' life source, a possibility for Aryans if for nobody else.[104] This belief was shared by all of those in the National Socialist movement who were prominent in ideological concerns. While specifically German historical circumstances and conditions were responsible for bringing the National Socialists to power, that element of the National Socialist *Weltanschauung* which rejected the Judaeo-Christian separation between finite and infinite — and hence implicitly rejected the reality of death — had a long pedigree in the history of Western Civilisation. That there could be such a tradition should not be particularly startling if one accepts Cassirer's contention that the rejection of death constituted the primary motive for primitive man's turning to religion in the first place.

From the point of view of those living in the last decades of the twentieth century, the second element of the National Socialist *Weltanschauung* which we have considered — emphasis upon man's role in and *of* nature — is perhaps of greater importance. Here too, the Nazi ideologists were drawing upon a long and well-established tradition. The dichotomy between a human world, inherently divine due to man's being made in God's image, and a natural world, over which man presumably has some degree of control, has never been a particularly comfortable one with which to live. First of all, as we have seen, the axiological charge to man, as a *singularly* divine creature, situated somewhere between heaven and earth, is an immense one. Secondly, the notion that humans, having certain powers *over* nature, are themselves *responsible* for it in some way (rather than simply adjusting to certain 'natural laws' beyond their control), places a great burden upon them. It has been, and is, a far easier choice to see man as not being apart from nature, much less above it, but *of* nature. This approach is one that has not been confined to woebegone romantics in full flight from modernity. Indeed, as Leon Poliakov has pointed out, the stripping of man of his divinity began with the crude scientism of the Enlightenment.[105]

Of course, for such thinkers as Linnaeus, Buffon, Voltaire, Meiners, and Kant there was a natural order of men just as there was of animals and things. In other words, while all men were part of nature, some were higher up on the developmental ladder than others. With the rise of modern nationalism and its partial reinforcement through the development of the Aryan myth, something for which the Frenchman Gobineau was to some extent responsible, the crude scientism of eighteenth century phylogenetic speculation was in part replaced by more baldly ethnocentric concerns. In all of this, the New World made no mean contribution of its own. Gobineau's writings, at first not taken terribly seriously in France, were translated into English in order to justify the existence of slavery, and the American war against Mexico, 1846-48, was to a great extent rationalized in racial terms.[106] By the end of the nineteenth century, the 'scientific' explanations of Enlightment thinkers were supplanted by those provided by proto-anthropologists, geographical determinists, theosophists, and phrenologists. While the Western peoples remained officially committed to the Judaeo-Christian tradition, and indeed, often rationalised imperialism in its name, the Mosaic code central to this tradition was being strenuously attacked from all sides. Vulgar interpretations of the Darwinian tradition were useful, of course, in these efforts though, as we have seen, the submergence of man in the world of nature antedated these to a great extent.

Though for the most part eschewing notions of race and racial supremacy, modern environmental concerns are in part rooted in this general tradition. As we have seen, National Socialist ideologues were in no small way concerned that man, or at least some men, live in harmony with the environment and, appreciating the fact that this is obviously necessary, we must recognise that just because something happens to have been emphasised by people as despicable as the Nazis does not make it wrong. Man is, at least in part, rooted in the natural world, a world too often viewed as being a simple object for exploitation. In their own version of the 'natural religion;' however, i.e., their *Lebensphilosphie*, the National Socialists exemplified a pernicious tendency that must be of special concern for anyone who chooses to see man as a product of some deified nature, and nothing more than that.

It is only with the reduction of men to being simple products of nature or, in Himmler's eyes, pieces of earth, that the following description of a people could have been offered:

> From all this it follows that Judaism is part of the organism of mankind just as, let us say, certain bacteria are part of man's body, and indeed the Jews are as necessary as bacteria . . . mankind needs the Jewish strain in order to preserve its vitality until its earthly mission is fulfilled. . . . It will collapse only when all mankind is redeemed.[107]

Only with the overthrow of the Mosaic code could Goebbels have described a people in the following manner: '*Judentum*', he said, was not just a nation, 'it is a singular, social-parasitic phenomenon', a poisoner of other cultures.[108] In the end, of course, 'social-parasitic' phenomena could only be dealt with in extremely radical ways. This being the case, the presumed bearers of life had to become purveyors of death, and the most idealistic of them wore the death's head as a sort of absolving talisman. Finite beings can never, of course, 'embrace life'; but, they can fetishise death, and the successful wedding of the most banal of pretty bourgeois attitudes and usages to a morbidity which, even today, excites awe, if not occasionally admiration, was no small achievement. Justifiably, the ultimate expression of that negativity which was the core of National Socialist 'life-bound' nationalism, is viewed as policies of extermination. Yet, at all times, it would seem that the most important of the 'life-affirming' bearers of National Socialist religious principles were always at their best in the valley of the shadow.[109]

Notes

1. Felix Kersten, *The Kersten Memoirs 1940–1945*, with an Introduction by H.R. Trevor-Roper, translated from the German by Constantine Fitzgibbon and James Oliver (London, Macmillan Co., 1956; New York, 1957), pp. 115–7.

2. See, among others, Peter Viereck, *Metapolitics: The Roots of the Nazi Mind*, (New York, Capricorn, 1961); Hans Kohn, *The Mind of Germany* (New York, Harper and Row, 1960); Fritz Stern, *The Politics of Cultural Despair* (New York, Doubleday, Anchor Books, 1965); and George L. Mosse, *The Crisis of German Ideology* (New York, Grosset and Dunlap, 1964). In his excellent psychohistorical study, *The Psychopathic God: Adolf Hitler*, Robert G.L. Waite has recently (Basic Books, 1977) reemphasised romanticism as constituting a major portion of the intellectual background both for National Socialism in general and for Hitler's very personal sublimations.

3. With regard to the questions of mass symbolism and the National Socialist religion, the following works are of importance. An excellent description of Hitler's impact on the mob is to be found in William L. Shirer's *Berlin Diary: The Journal of a Foreign Correspondent 1934–1941* (New York, Penguin, 1941), pp. 14–16. An important discussion

of Hitler's mass appeal can be found in Walter C. Langer, *The Mind of Adolf Hitler* (New York, Basic Books, 1973), see especially pp. 206–10. Albert Speer's memoirs, *Inside the Third Reich*, translated from the German by Richard and Clara Winston (New York, Macmillan Co., 1970), are still probably the best source for anyone interested in investigating the planning and actual staging of the Nuremberg rallies; see pp. 27–8 and 58–9 in particular. On Himmler's religious concerns, Josef Ackerman, *Heinrich Himmler als Ideologe* (Göttingen, Musterschmidt, 1970), offers numerous observations and insights. Also see Willi Frischauer, *Himmler, The Evil Genius of the Third Reich* (Boston, Beacon Press, 1953), pp. 40–2 in particular; Roger Manvell and Heinrich Fraenkel, *Heinrich Himmler* (London, New English Library, 1965), especially the discussions on pp. 46–9 and 177–8; Heinz Höhne, *The Order of the Death's Head: The Story of Hitler's SS*, translated from the German by Richard Berry (New York, Ballantine Books, 1970), in particular pp. 144–5, 153–5; *Reichsführer! Briefe an und von Himmler*, herausgegeben von Helmut Heiber (Stuttgart, Deutsche Verlagsanstalt, 1968), particularly pp. 11–12 of Heiber's excellent introduction. George L. Mosse, *The Nationalization of the Masses* (New York, Howard Fertig, Inc., 1975), is a most interesting study of the background for National Socialist symbolism. See also his *Towards the Final Solution: A History of European Racism* (New York, Howard Fertig, Inc., 1978). J.P. Stern, *Hitler: The Führer and the People* (Berkeley, University of California Press, 1974), has much to say about the religious appeal of Hitler. Friedrich Heer's *Der Glaube des Adolf Hitler: Anatomie einen Politischen Religiosität* (München, Bechtle, 1968), does much with Hitler's use of Christian symbolism. Robert G.L. Waite, in his *The Psychopathic God: Adolf Hitler* (New York, Basic Books, 1977), makes ample use of Heer's interpretations. As mentioned before, the most systematic study thus far of National Socialism as a religion is James M. Rhodes, *The Hitler Movement: A Modern Millenarian Revolution* (Stanford, Stanford University Press, 1980). Jean-Pierre Sironneau, *Sécularisation et religions politiques* (The Hague, Paris, New York, Mouton, 1982) allows the reader to compare Nazism to 'Leninism-Stalinism'. Fred Weinstein, *The Dynamics of Nazism, Leadership, Ideology, and the Holocaust* (New York, Academic Press, 1980), applies social-psychological approaches to the question of secular religion and the Hitler cult.

4. As an example of this, see Frischauer, *The Evil Genius*, p. 26.

5. Ernst Cassirer, *An Essay on Man: An Introduction to a Philosophy of Human Culture* (New York, Doubleday, 1953), p. 112.

6. Mary Douglas, *Natural Symbols: Explorations in Cosmology* (New York, Pantheon Books, 1970), p.x.

7. Ibid., p. 50.

8. Ibid., p. 126.

9. Of course, in the Christian tradition, Christ is God-as-Man, i.e., the infinite becoming finite in order to suffer for the accumulated sins of humanity. However, orthodox Christianity does not, and indeed cannot, see this as pointing to a *substantial* identification of man and God. Both Joachim of Fiore (1145–1202) and G.W.F. Hegel are often pointed out as having done this. But Hegel was talking about man's discovering infinitude in the species while Joachim, through his 'Age of the Spirit', which presumably would usher in the millenium, found it relatively easy to dispense with Christ, and hence, of course, with the orthodox Christian tradition, altogether. For a brief but pithy consideration of some of the problems raised by Joachim of Fiore's flirtations with chiliastic thinking see Norman Cohn, *The Pursuit of the Millenium* (New York, Harper and Row, 1961), pp. 98–101.

10. The classic, modern study of this problem is Sigmund Freud's, 'Thoughts for the Times on War and Death', Standard Edition of the *Complete Psychological Works*, volume XIV, edited by James Strachey (London, The Hogarth Press, 1957). Freud's contention that man simply cannot envision his own death except by observing it as a spectator (and hence not being really dead) has been modified to some extent by Robert Jay Lifton in his *History of Human Survival* (New York, Random House, 1971). See particularly his discussion on pp. 172–3. In this regard it is interesting, and perhaps instructive, to

consider that at least one psychoanalytic interpreter of Hitler's ideology has suggested that, in his efforts to preserve the nation and hold it together, Hitler was attempting to nullify the death instinct and, in fact, to render it *'inoperative'*. See Richard A. Koenigsberg, *Hitler's Ideology: A Study in Psychoanalytic Sociology* (New York, Library of Social Sciences, 1975), p. 12. Emphasis is Koenigsberg's.

11. The Old Testament distinction between men and animals is very well demonstrated in the Book of Judges, 7, where Gideon has been enjoined by God to employ a most interesting test in determining who was to be selected to fight the Midianites. Ten thousand men were taken to the banks of a river and told to drink from it. The three hundred who used their hands to bring water to their mouths were chosen. The nine thousand seven hundred others, who bent down and, with their tongues, lapped up the water 'as a dog', were not selected. Obviously, to drink water 'as a dog' was to suggest that one did not really view oneself as human and hence was a potential candidate for slavery.

12. As an example of this see Leon Poliakov, *The Aryan Myth*, translated from the French by Edmond Howard (New York, Basic Books, 1974), pp. 329–30. On the problems created by the Jewish 'God of conscience', who demanded control over 'natural' instincts and was opposed to somewhat more pliable gods of nature, see Bernhard Berliner's essay 'On Some Religious Motives of Anti-Semitism' in Ernst Simmel (ed.), *Anti-Semitism: A Social Disease* (New York, International Universities Press, 1946), pp. 79–84.

13. Adolf Hitler, *Mein Kampf*, translated from the German by Ralph Manheim (Boston, Houghton Mifflin, 1943), p. 288.

14. Adolf Hitler, *Secret Conversations, 1941–1944*. With an introductory essay on *The Mind of Adolf Hitler*, by H.R. Trevor-Roper, translated by Norman Cameron and R.H. Stevens (New York, Farrar, Straus and Young, 1953), p. 5.

15. Ibid., p. 33, conversation of 12 September 1941.

16. Ibid.

17. Ibid.

18. Ibid., p. 51, conversation of 14 October 1941.

19. Hannah Arendt, *The Origins of Totalitarianism* (New York, Harcourt, Brace, Jovanovich, 1973), pp. 178–80. Ernst Nolte, *Three Faces of Fascism* translated from the German by Leile Vennewitz (New York, New American Library, 1969), pp. 527–32.

20. Hermann Rauschning, *Hitler Speaks: A Series of Political Conversations with Adolph Hitler on His Real Aims* (London, Heinemann, 1939), p. 114.

21. Ibid., p. 240.

22. Ernst Krieck, *Völkische-Politische Anthropologie*, Band II — *Das Handeln und die Ordnungen* (Leipzig, Armanen Verlag, 1937), p. 147.

23. Rauschning, *Hitler Speaks*, p. 242. James P. Rhodes, in *The Hitler Movement*, has used the notion of man as 'God in the making' to emphasise National Socialism's link to millenarianism. See Rhodes, p. 77. Hitler once mentioned to Speer that he thought that either the Muslim or Shinto faith would have been more suitable for what he had in mind for Germany. See Speer, *Inside the Third Reich*, p. 114.

24. Ibid., p. 400.

25. Ibid., p. 512. Emphasis is Hitler's.

26. Joachim Fest, *The Face of the Third Reich: Portraits of the Nazi Leadership*, translated from the German by Michael Bullock (New York, Pantheon Books, 1970), pp. 165–70, p. 174.

27. Hitler, *Secret Conversations*, conversation of 11 April 1942, p. 342.

28. Ibid.

29. By 'committed National Socialists', one means those who fundamentally accepted the Nazi ideology or *Weltanschauung* to the point of utilising it at the very least to rationalise the activities undertaken by the National Socialist Party and the state which served as its vehicle. A quantitative study which has called into question some of the basic assumptions regarding National Socialism nevertheless has confirmed that the most fundamental aspect of the Nazi *Weltanschauung*, political anti-Semitism, was the most

important conscious motivating factor for those of *prominence* in the movement. See Peter H. Merkl, *Political Violence Under the Swastika*: *581 Early Nazis* (Princeton, Princeton University Press, 1975), pp. 503–4, 628.

30. Alfred Rosenberg, *Selected Writings*, translated and edited by R. Pois (London, Jonathan Cape, 1970), p. 114.

31. Ibid., p. 117.

32. Ibid., p. 119.

33. Paul Brohmer, *Biologieunterricht und völkische Erziehung* (Frankfurt, n.p.,1933) as quoted in George L. Mosse (ed.), *Nazi Culture* (New York, Grosset and Dunlap, 1965), pp. 83–4.

34. Ibid., p. 87. For another example of the National Socialist effort to root man firmly within the natural world, see Alfred Baeumler's 1939 lecture in which the nineteenth century 'racial scientist' Ludwig Woltmann was extolled for recognising that man 'must be understood *as a part of nature*'. Institut für Zeitgeschichte, reel no. MA 608, frame 55871. Emphasis is Baeumler's.

35. This school was established in 1932. From 1935 on, units that would become part of the *Waffen SS* were trained there. The date of this handbook is not known, but, internal evidence would suggest 1936.

36. Untitled material concerning *Weltanschauliche Erziehung*, Institute für Zeitgeschichte, reel no. MA 332, frame 2656648.

37. Ibid.

38. Ibid., 2656651.

39. Ibid., 2656652.

40. Ibid., 2656653.

41. Ibid., 2656652. Obviously, if one believed or believes in the superiority of a given race, the common ancestor theory had to be combatted. It is a weakness of Daniel Gasman's *The Scientific Origins of National Socialism* (New York and London, MacDonald and American Elsevier, 1971), which is concerned with trying to establish links between Ernst Haeckel's Monist League and National Socialism, that the author never really considers this problem in depth. For a sensitive treatment of the issue, see Günter Altner, *Weltanschauliche Hintergründe der Rassenlehre des Dritten Reichs. Zum Problem einer umfassenden Anthropologie* (Zurich, EVZ Verlag, 1968), pp. 23–5.

42. Ibid., 2656652.

43. Ibid., 2656673. At least one author has tried to establish a link between the 'Life Worship' of the National Socialists and German tribal worship of the 'Earth Mother'. See Sironneau, *Secularisation et religions politiques*, p. 535.

44. Ibid.

45. Institut für Zeitgeschichte, reel no. MA 45 1172, 250-c-10/5, pp. 3–4.

46. Ibid., 6.

47. Ibid., 8.

48. Ibid., 9.

49. Ibid., 13.

50. Ibid., 16.

51. Alex Elbertzhagen, *Kampf um Gott in der religiösen Erziehung* (Leipzig, Armanan Verlag, 1934), p. 21. Emphasis is Elbertzhagen's.

52. Ibid., p. 22.

53. Ibid., pp. 22–3

54. Ibid., p. 25.

55. Bundesarchiv, Sammlung-Schumacher, Gruppe XIV, Nr. 447.

56. Ibid. Of course, various forms of sun and fire worship had been of some significance in earlier youth and *völkisch* movements. See George L. Mosse, *The Crisis of German Ideology* (New York, Grosset and Dunlop, 1964), and Walter Laqueur, *Young Germany* (New York, Basic Books, 1962).

57. Institut für Zeitgeschichte, *Mitteilungen zur Weltanschaulichen Lage*, 2 Okt., 1936,

reel no. MA 603, frames 20474–20476.

58. Dr J. Spelter, *Der deutsche Erzieher als Lehrer der Rassenkunde* (Landsberg, Verlag Pfeiffer and Co., 1937), p. 32.

59. Ibid. See also, pp. 40–1. Emphasis is Spelter's.

60. Martin Bormann, from *Kirchliches Jahrbuch für die evangelische Kirche im Deutschland, 1933–44*, herausgeben von Joachim Beckmann (Gütersloh, n.p., 1948), as quoted in Mosse, *Nazi Culture*, p. 244.

61. Ibid., pp. 244–5.

62. Ibid., p. 245.

63. Heinrich Himmler, *Himmler: Geheimreden: 1933 bis 1945*, herausgegeben von Bradley F. Smith und Agnes F. Peterson (Frankfurt/M, Berlin, Propyläen Verlag, 1974), p. 160.

64. Institut für Zeitgeschichte, reel no. MA 138/1, frame 301767.

65. Ibid.

66. Ibid., 301768.

67. Ibid., 301789.

68. Max Domarus, *Hitler: Reden und Proklamationen 1932–1945*, Band I, Erster Halbband 1932–34 (München, Suddeutsche Verlag, 1965), p. 266.

69. Ibid., p. 298.

70. Ibid., p. 299. For an interesting treatment of Hitler's use of Christian imagery and of his interest in the structure and discipline of the Catholic Church, see Friedrich Heer, *Der Glaube des Adolf Hitler*. In the opinion of this writer, Professor Heer takes Hitler's interest in Christian usages far too seriously. Rhodes, in his above-mentioned work, places emphasis on the role of revelation, particularly with regards to Hitler's view of himself. See Rhodes, *The Hitler Movement*, p. 38ff.

71. Domarus Zweiter Halbband 1934–38, p. 890.

72. Ibid., p. 893.

73. Ibid.

74. Ibid., p. 894.

75. J. P. Stern, *Hitler, The Führer and the People* (Berkeley, University of California Press, 1974), p. 89.

76. Rhodes, *The Hitler Movement*, p. 14.

77. An excellent description of the ceremony is to be found in Josef Ackerman, *Heinrich Himmler als Ideologe* (Göttingen, Musterschmidt, 1970), pp. 85–7.

78. Ibid., p. 78.

79. Hitler, *Secret Conversations*, conversation of May 1942, p. 375.

80. Ian Kershaw's *Der Hitler-Mythos: Volksmeinung und Propaganda im Dritten Reich* (Stuttgart, Deutsche Verlag-Amstalt, 1980), which is focused primarily on Bavaria, offers an interesting treatment of this issue. We will be making further use of this work later on in the book.

81. Weinstein, *The Dynamics of Nazism*, p. 131.

82. Sironneau, *Secularisation et religions politiques*, p. 270. Some have maintained that the role of Hitler with regard to the National Socialist ideology has been overemphasised. See John Hiden and John Farquharson, *Explaining Hitler's Germany* (Totowa, New Jersey, Barnes and Noble, 1983), p. 33.

83. Sironneau, p. 249.

84. An example of such prayers is to be found in ibid., p. 330.

85. Kersten, *The Kersten Memoirs*, p. 152.

86. Joachim Petsch, *Kunst in Dritten Reich, Architektur, Plastic, Malerei* (Köln, Vista Point Verlag, 1983), p. 10.

87. Hitler, *Secret Conversations*, conversation of night of 28th–29th December 1941, p. 125.

88. Domarus, *Hitler, Einster Halbband*, p. 450.

89. Ibid.

90. Ibid.

91. Ibid.

92. Institut für Zeitgeschichte, reel number MA 603, frame 20197, *Staat und Partei zur Weltanschaulichen Lage*, 11.3.1938.

93. Alfred Rosenberg, 'Alfred Rosenberg über die Aufgaben der nationalsozialistischen Lehrens', in *Völkischer Beobachter*, Berliner Ausgabe, Nr. 301, 51.Jahrgang, 28 Oktober 1938, S.I.

94. Robert Ley, 'Der Führer', in ibid., Nr. 295, 51.Jahrgang, 22 Oktober 1938, S.2.

95. Ernst Krieck, *Völkische-Politische Anthropologie*, Band I, *Die Wirklichkeit* (Leipzig, 1938), p. v.

96. Professor Eckhardt, 'Widernatürliche Unzucht ist Todeswürdig,' in *Das Schwarze Korps*, 12. Folge, 2. Jahrgang, 22 Mai 1935, in Helmut Heiber and Hildegard von Kotze, *Facsimile Querschnitt durch das Schwarze Korps* (München, Scherz, 1968), pp. 60–1.

97. Kersten, *Kersten Memoirs*, p. 150.

98. Ackerman, *Heinrich Himmler, p. 92.*

99. Kersten, *Kersten Memoirs*, p. 57.

100. After an exchange of communications between an apparent expert in this area, a man named Willigut, and R. Brandt of Himmler's office, Himmler decided that SS graves should be marked either with a traditional cross or with a 'Man rune'. The reason for choosing the latter was that it was a '*Lebens-rune*', suggestive of immortal life for those fallen for the Fatherland. The '*Tyre-rune*', while suggestive of an eternal '*Kreislauf*', did not convey so optimistic a prospect for the individual soldier. See Bundesarchiv, Sammlung-Schumacher, Gruppe XIV, Nr. 447.

101. Institut für Zeitgeschichte, Reel no. MA 558, frames 9380476–9380488. To put this in some perspective, we can recall that this letter was dispatched just one day before the ill-fated Ardennes counter offensive was launched.

102. The number of authors and historians who have adhered to this viewpoint is legion. A.J.P. Taylor, William L. Shirer, Hermann Rauschning, Peter Viereck, Hans Kohn and Louis Snyder are perhaps the best known of them.

103. As mentioned above, Professor Rhodes, in his *The Hitler Movement*, attempted to tie National Socialism *directly* into this Millenial tradition. Large numbers of occultists who seek to explain Nazism in terms of various uncouth, supernatural forces believe that there is a connection between Hitler and the Albigensians. As an example of this, see Jean-Michel Angebert's *The Occult and the Third Reich*, translated by Lewis A. M. Swinberg (New York, Macmillan, 1974).

104. On Hitler's dislikes regarding old Germanic customs, see George L. Mosse, *The Nationalization of the Masses*, p. 183. Hitler's belief in life-forces is discussed on pp. 197–9 of this book. On Hitler's rejection of astrology, see page 473 of his *Secret Conversations*, one recorded on 19 July 1942, where he denounced 'The horoscope in which Anglo-Saxons in particular have great faith' as a 'swindle'. Also, Waite's *The Psychopathic God*, p. 435. Apparently, the National Socialist party as a whole was concerned with suppressing some of the occultism that seemed to have gained new strength with the coming to power of the movement. In an unsigned article in the *Völkischer Beobachter*, it was claimed that the ancient German view of the heavens, inherently dynamic as it was, did not allow for a belief in astrology. See 'Astrologie war den Germanen Fremd', in *Völkischer Beobachter*, Berliner Ausgabe, Nr.19. 52.Jahrgang, 19 Januar 1939, S.5.

105. Poliakov, *The Aryan Myth*, Chapter 8.

106. Gobineau had been somewhat pessimistic about the survival of the Aryan race. However, defenders of American slavery, as one might imagine, preferred happy endings. Hence, Gobineau's writings were edited by Holz, his translator, in such a fashion as to create one. As is well known, slavery's defenders often did utilise Biblical arguments to support their case. However, the Bible also served the abolitionist cause as well. Arguments rooted in so-called 'scientific racism' could be countered only by *formal* scientific analyses, the sorts of things with which the average person would not be concerned.

107. Alfred Rosenberg, *Dietrich Eckart: Ein Vermächtnis* (München, 1928), in George

L. Mosse, *Nazi Culture*, p. 77.

108. Taken from a letter sent to all *Gauleiters* — for purposes of propaganda — dated 30 September 1941, Bundesarchiv, Sammlung-Schumacher, Gruppe XIII, 382. Of course, as is well-known, the viewing of Jews as representing some sort of disease had ample precedents, particularly in the writings of Paul de Lagarde.

109. For a most perceptive and disquieting discussion of this see Saul Freidländer, *Reflections of Nazism: An Essay on Kitsch and Death*, translated from the French by Thomas Weyr (New York, Harper and Row, 1984), pp. 41–6.

4 THE NATIONAL SOCIALIST RELIGION IN POWER: THE SANCTIFICATION OF NATIONAL LIFE

In the previous chapter we were primarily concerned with the ideational content of the National Socialist religion. While occasional references were made to the consequences attendant upon the translation of the several principles under consideration into power, this was an area that was left largely untreated. We must now concern ourselves with several crucial aspects of the National Socialist rule in Germany, the sum of which can be described as constituting the 'sanctification of national life'. In this regard, we will be looking at five general areas: (1) the relationship of the National Socialist religion to the state; (2) the National Socialist approach to knowledge; (3) the National Socialist approach to aesthetics; (4) the *necessity* for the National Socialist religion to perpetuate a state of bourgeois stasis, and (5) how this religion faced up to the awesome challenges posed by war. *The* major campaign of National Socialism, i.e., that mounted against the Jews, will largely be left to the following chapter, although obviously we will be considering it to a limited extent in this one.

It is a commonplace to view modern history as in large measure representing the triumph of the state over the several forms of organised religion which have been considered as providing the spiritual foundations of civilisation in the West. The increasingly secularised character of this civilisation has been commented upon *ad infinitum*, and for very good reason. Most assuredly, traditional religious forms have withered in the face of the increasing application of science and technology to life. Often, the emergence of the so-called 'totalitarian state,' in the guise of Soviet Russia (at least during the Stalinist period), Hitlerite Germany, or — more rarely — Mussolini's Italy, has been viewed as somehow crowning a pattern of development which has seen the modern state accrue more and more power unto itself while, at the same time, increasingly infringing upon those spiritual realms which, according to liberal precepts, ought to be left to the individual or at least to religious rather than secular agencies. The writer will not be making any observations with regard to the Soviet Union or to Fascist Italy. In considering National Socialist Germany, however, it is his contention that Hitler was concerned with reversing a trend that had prevailed in Germany in particular and in the West in general, *viz.*, the continuous growth of state power at the expense of religious principles and that, in fact, there was no totalitarian state in National Socialist Germany. Rather, that, in large measure, the state was supposed to be merely an instrument — and at times a not very significant one — by virtue of which the religion of National Socialism was applied to national life.

In his work *Totalitarianism* Professor Schapiro made the extremely important point that Hitler's ideology never really 'exalted the state', instead choosing to view it as an instrument of a party headed by himself, i.e., the state derived what significance it had as an expression of his own will.[1] With the triumph of Hitler in 1933 'The victory over the state was complete'.[2] In fact, Schapiro went so far as to declare that to use the term 'totalitarian state' was to use 'a contradiction in terms'.[3] Furthermore, that most perspicacious commentator upon Nazism in particular and totalitarianism in general, Professor Hans Buchheim, has pointed out that, in National Socialist eyes

> . . . the bearer of political power is not the state, as an impersonal unit, but this is given to the Führer as the executor of common *völkisch* will.[4]

Indeed, Buchheim maintained, political theoreticians in the Third Reich were concerned with 'destateifying public life' and replacing state authority with the *Führerprinzip*.[5] The so-called *'Gestapo'* (*'Secret State Police'*) was not really a state police at all, according to Buchheim, while the SS 'in a constitutional organisational sense . . . never had anything to do with the *Wehrmacht*. The *Wehrmacht* was an organ of state power, the *Waffen-SS* an organ of the Führer's power.'[6]

As for the Nazis themselves, it is important to point out that they generally did not accept the notion of the total, or 'totalitarian' state. According to one National Socialist theorist, what had appeared with Hitler's coming to power was a totality of *leadership, not a totality of state in any form.*[7] Indeed, fully recognising that creative politicians shaped the state and not the other way around, one had to observe that, with the coming to power of National Socialism, the state was no longer in the centre of public life but was now on the edge of 'political-historical events'.[8] How much the Nazis succeeded either in taking over the state *completely*, or relegating it to being an institution of little significance in all areas of political activity is open to debate. What cannot be questioned are two facts: (1) that, as far as the Nazis themselves were concerned, the state was an institution that had only instrumental purposes, and (2) that the activity which was central to National Socialist goals, i.e., the implementation of racial politics, had to be carried on outside the formal state structure. Certainly, for Hitler, the state always had been an institution which, contrary to the teachings of generations of German philosophers and political theorists, had a purely instrumental function. In *Mein Kampf*, we find the following:

> *the state represents no end, but a means. It is, to be sure, the premise for the formation of a higher human culture, but not its cause, which lies exclusively in the existence of a race capable of culture.*[9]

In so far as the National Socialist movement itself was concerned, particularly to the degree that Hitler viewed it as 'revolutionary', the state could not be allowed, through 'jurists and law-makers', to inhibit it.[10] In a secret speech to Nazi officials on 23 November 1937, Hitler was quite specific in declaring that 'Today, a new basis for [the] state has been established, [one] whose characteristic is that it does not see its foundation in Christendom or in state thought but primarily in the unified *Volksgemeinschaft*.'[11] This speech was highly significant because it revealed that Hitler was decisively breaking with traditional concepts of the state. Most instructive, for our purposes, was his break with the traditional Christian *justifications* for the state. That this was done not to strengthen the state *vis-à-vis* religion but rather to assure the triumph of *völkisch* life principles was clearly revealed in a statement made by Hitler in 1938.

> I would like to be certain that the struggle against the internal enemies of the nation will never be damaged in a moral bureaucracy or by its inadequacies but [that] there, where the formal bureaucracy of the state should prove itself to be unsuitable to solve a problem, the German nation will set in action its living organizations in order to assist in the breakthrough of its life's necessities. What the state, according to its essence, is not in the position of solving will be solved through the movement. For even the state is only [one] of the organizational forms of *völksich* life, conducted and dominated . . . by the immediate expression of *völkisch* life will — the party, the National Socialist movement.[12]

Hitler believed, as we can see, that the state had a particular character or 'essence' which might have prohibited it from actively combatting 'internal enemies of the nation.' Rather, what was needed to provide for the 'breakthrough of its [the German nation's] life necessities was the action of the National Socialist movement, that 'living' element of the people's political expression. The struggle against internal enemies, a struggle that might well necessitate measures of the most extreme kind, concerned life itself. Only that movement itself rooted in the laws of life was spiritually equipped to carry out such actions as might be deemed necessary to preserve the integrity of the German people. These actions subsisted at the very heart of the National Socialist revolution — in fact, some have maintained that they *were* the revolution — and the traditional impedimenta of a 'moral' state (as reflected in a 'moral' bureaucracy) made it singularly ill-suited for the tasks at hand.[13] It might very well be true that 'totalitarianism' in any form was inherently antithetical to the state, inasmuch as the latter, through various constitutional arrangements, does not lend itself to the singularly extra-legal activities of the totalitarian leader or leadership clique. National Socialism, however, a movement which, in its own eyes, apotheosised the unfolding of natural developments, could and did press a wellnigh religious claim against the state.

The 'National Socialist *Weltanschauung*,' defined as 'the all-embracing attitude of the German race' was perceived as being grounded in a fusion of scientific confirmation and religious affirmation.[24] State forms might change, but the nation and its *Weltanschauung*, both rooted in nature and finding their natural expressions in the *Führerprinzip*, remained.[15] Thus, the formal, quite conscious assault of the National Socialist movement upon state power was undertaken not only to assure the personal and idiosyncratic power-needs of the Führer. The religion-grounded *Weltanschauung* — an important expression of which was the annihilation of perceived natural enemies of the Nordic peoples — absolutely necessitated the abolition of that 'state-worship' so often identified with German political history. Indeed, when viewed against the background of National Socialist religiosity, such worship could well have been viewed as blasphemous. Religiously-grounded undertakings, for example, the annihilation of the Jews, thus had to take place outside any formal control and, of course, in secret. The most that could be asked of the 'state' was that it help to facilitate such operations, something that it was willing to do so long as they were shrouded in conscience-salving euphemism. Most certainly, if such were done the 'state' would hardly be so untoward as to inquire as to the fate of those whose extermination was deemed necessary in keeping with the laws of life.[16]

Obviously, a German state remained and, to the degree that ministerial posts and bureaucratic positions were staffed by National Socialists, we can speak of the 'National Socialist state.' At the same time, as many have noted, party and state could and did run afoul of each other from time to time. Certainly, it was Hitler's purpose that, to the greatest degree possible, the state apparatus be dominated by members of his movement. One cannot gainsay the fact, however, that hypothetically and, as it turned out, in practice, those programs consonant with the broader ideological interests of the Nazi movement were formulated and, to some extent, took place largely outside the state. The obedience and willingness to follow orders unquestioningly which one associates with a sort of stereotyped Prussian civil servant had their roles to play, of course. Further, there can be little doubt that many conservative, bourgeois Germans voted for National Socialism and thereafter lent it strong support because they associated 'traditional German values' of order and respect for state authority with the movement. For the Nazis themselves, though, these were merely means to the grandiose end of translating into power beliefs central to their naturalistic religion. Hitler had in fact, at least in part, succeeded in reversing a well-established trend and, with his triumph and that of the National Socialist movement, religious idealism was to supplant that traditional statism so often identified with Western Civilisation in general and, in more exaggerated form, with Germany in particular.

Yet, as we have seen, this was not a religion in the traditional Judaeo-Christian meaning of the word (although, as we have seen, Hitler and at least some of his colleagues often utilised the language and some of the ritualistic forms of Christianity). In its fusion of a wellnigh positivistic view of science with general mystical and pantheistic concerns usually and correctly associated with Germany's romantic past, National Socialism proffered a religion of nature necessarily secular in many ways. This allowed for a singular variety of pragmatism to inform the attitudes and actions of the National Socialists. As we shall see, this pragmatism — something that did not have to appear artificial or forced, since it was a reasonable corollary of the religion of nature — proved to be a most convenient implement in rallying intellectual and 'scientific' support for National Socialism.

The fact that the state was observed as receiving a mandate of sorts from the National Socialist *Weltanschauung* suggested to many that National Socialist education had to be strengthened. A new type of individual had to be the ultimate goal of the National Socialist revolution, 'a *Volk*-bound German man'.[17] The restructuring of the German state in particular and German political life in general necessitated that areas of scientific endeavour be brought under the guiding principle of the National Socialist ideology. Since the National Socialist ideology was rooted in life-sustaining religious principles, it quite naturally followed that distinctions between the political expression of this ideology and hallowed 'spiritual' and 'scientific' realms had to be abolished. It was in this context that the very real pragmatism inherent in National Socialism came to the fore.

When the term 'pragmatism' is used, it is not done so with reference to philosophical pragmatism *à la* Charles Peirce, William James or John Dewey. Nor can one claim that National Socialist pragmatism was precisely analogous to that of Fascism in general. Fascists often grounded their usually disingenuous use of the term in simplistic notions of 'action for action's sake.' There were certainly resemblances between the National Socialist use of pragmatism and that of Fascists in general. For National Socialists, however, pragmatism was sewn into the very fabric of their secular religion. It was not something that had to be imposed upon it in any extrinsic manner, especially not in realms hypothetically the preserve of the intellectual community.

In assuming that there was a fundamental difference between the realms of spirit and of politics, one had to posit a fundamental distinction between some sort of metaphysically-grounded 'mind' and a mundane world of practical activity. As is well known, such a distinction had been assumed by generations of German philosophical and political speculators. Furthermore, it has to be recognised that the preservation of precisely such a distinction had allowed numberless German *Kulturmenschen* to sit back in abstract diffidence while the National Socialist movement struggled for and eventually attained power. With the National Socialists *in* power, however, it became incumbent upon the party faithful to make certain that, to the greatest degree possible, the intellectual life of the community was subject to basic life-grounded principles, recognition of which had served to restrict the role of the state. After all, the National Socialist movement, grounded in life itself, had to represent an essential reconciliation between the two apparently dissimilar but in reality identical forms of life-expression, practical and spiritual. In a word, there could be no distinction between the world of mind, as this embodied the ideational contents of the laws of life and the world of the deed, as this was represented in the National Socialist movement. For men who lived in conformity with nature, i.e., Nordic men, the two worlds were one and the same. Thus, there could never be a contradiction between science and the goals of National Socialism 'because these [the goals] have been built up from practical knowledge of the laws of nature and history'.[18] The National Socialist takeover of political power hardly constituted the end of the struggle. Rather, it was '*but the foundation for the restructuring of all areas of life according to the living principles of the National Socialist Weltanschauung*'.[19] The

National Socialist movement recognised that man was part of a natural and historical order; that he did not live 'on an island of sacred contemplation . . . but in the midst of happening [*Geschehen*] itself'.[20]

This being the case, thoughts of some sort of timeless objectivity on the part of science had to be abandoned as being disingenuous. The National Socialist *Weltanschauung* emerged from life. Any true science was possible only on 'the basis of a living *Weltanschauung*'. It was *Weltanschauung* that bound science to life.[21] Thus, for National Socialists, it was commonsensical(!) that adherence to scientific principles had to be congruent with faith in the National Socialist ideology. This being the 'case', it was no wonder that intellectuals and scientists who failed to adhere to National Socialist precepts could be viewed, as the Führer himself put it, as 'degenerate' representatives of a 'degenerate science', as 'estranged from life'.[22] Such intellectuals and scientists represented a phoney academic 'impotent neutrality' since they bore 'no relation to political reality and to the fateful struggle of the nation'.[23] According to Heinz Wolff, Nazi student leader, the very notion of 'objectivity', rooted as it was in scientific liberalism, encouraged people to forget that science was made by 'living men,' by 'men of flesh and blood'.[24]

It is important to point out that, in declaring scientific objectivity to be impossible, National Socialist ideologues were paralleling a variety of thinking which some have seen as having first emerged with the 1935 work of the Polish Jewish physician Ludwick Fleck. In this work, *Genesis and Development of a Scientific Fact*, which was concerned with correlating concepts of syphilis and those epistemological conclusions drawn from them with the theory underlying the Wassermann reaction, Fleck made the point that all knowledge, even the most 'scientific', was really social knowledge. In a word, preconceived concepts have to shape even the most 'objective' scientific hypothesising and experimentation. 'Any kind of learning', he said, 'is connected with some tradition and society, and words and customs already suffice to form a collective bond'.[25] Thus, there could be no talk of a 'value-free' or 'objective science'. Fleck's work was little known at the time, and even if it had been, the Jewish pedigree of the author would probably have prevented National Socialists from taking it very seriously, even if they had understood it. None the less, it is obvious that the sort of 'relativism' involved here — an approach to what has come to be called the 'sociology of knowledge' that more recently has been crowned by the work of Thomas Kuhn — can be subject to radical misuse. This is particularly true, of course, if relativistic interpretations of knowledge are placed at the disposal of people who, in the end, are guided by absolutes of which only they have complete knowledge. Fleck himself was in both the Auschwitz and Buchenwald camps, and both of his sisters and their families were exterminated. Spared because of his medical knowledge, Fleck survived the war. Whether he ever reflected upon National Socialist application of hypotheses analogous to his own is uncertain.

In any case, Nazi ideologues attacked scientific and intellecutal objectivity not only because they saw it as an impossibility. For them, it was essentially irrelevant to the grandiose life-struggles being undertaken by the German nation in particular and by Nordic man in general. This was particularly the case since the tendentiousness of National Socialism was justified through the claim that it bore those life-principles which constituted the very foundation of scientific investigation in the first place. For a teacher, it would now be necessary to demonstrate that he or she had earned the right to enjoy freedom of teaching by showing strength of character.[26] Naturally, what was meant by 'strength of character' was the individual's willingness to adhere to that which stemmed from the life-source of all knowledge, the National Socialist *Weltanschauung*. The 'age of liberal dissolution and sham-freedom' was past, Ernst Krieck declared, and a new age of active participation of institutions of higher learning in the life of the nation was dawning.[27] 'Academic freedom' in the old sense, something that had reflected lack of concern and character, was to be eliminated. For Martin Heidegger, 'academic freedom' had meant 'unconcern'. It had been a 'capricious exercise of intentions and inclinations [and] was noncommitment'.[28] For knowledge to have any meaning to it at all, these National Socialist critics were saying, it had to be relevant to the needs of the time, needs which necessarily were determined by that movement rooted in the laws of life which, after all, constituted the source for all knowledge. It is here that we can observe that wedding of pragmatism to idealism that we have mentioned earlier. Since the National Socialist movement embodied life-principles it alone could determine what aspects of knowledge served these principles, indeed, in reality, what aspects in fact constituted knowledge at all. Just as the state apart from the National Socialist *Weltanschauung*, was a lifeless mechanism, devoid of meaning, so was knowledge also devoid of life, i.e., in reality, not knowledge at all, unless it served the purposes of the National Socialist movement. Thus, the National Socialist regime, which has often been described as having its spiritual roots sunk deep into *Biedermeirisch* soil, could actively encourage modern scientific developments, since these would serve the vital task of defending the National Socialist *Weltanschauung*. Further, because of the material necessities involved in translating this into reality, ideological pressures in various areas of education had to be soft-pedalled. At the same time, adherence to the 'laws of life' would dictate that in areas such a philosophy, the social sciences, and so on, the Nazi leadership could determine which approaches were life-sustaining and which were not. In all of this the term 'relevance', something that has become a most fashionable one in the United States in recent years, was of singular importance. What was irrelevant to the Nazis was that variety of knowledge that indicated lack of commitment and 'liberal' indifference to the interests of the whole. The natural religion of National Socialism achieved practical expression in the sanctification of the nation. With the turning of the German nation into a sanctified *Volksgemeinschaft*, knowledge that did not serve the interests of this community was not merely extraneous, it was heretical.

Despite, however, the obviously strong hypothetical basis for it there never was a truly systematic National Socialist policy on higher education. To be sure, there was no lack of sympathy for National Socialism in academic circles, and the actual purging of Jewish faculty was often greeted with enthusiasm. There was, among some, even the joyful anticipation that patterns of thought deemed specifically Jewish, e.g. relativity theory and psychoanalysis, would also be purged, and to some extent this was done.[29] Yet particularly in technical areas 'experts' were needed, and this was especially the case if National Socialist ideals were to be implemented through military adventures. This, plus almost continuous quarreling between those concerned with the establishment of educational policy — Alfred Rosenberg, Rudolf Hess, Minister of Education Bernhard Rust and the educator-turned-ideologue Ernst Krieck — allowed for a certain degree of 'scientific freedom' to prevail in the universities.[30] Again, we can observe that pragmatism which we have noted as a crucial element in the National Socialist religion. Since this faith had to be introduced to the German people as a whole 'in small doses' why disturb matters unduly? Particularly in technical areas, experts were needed, and, so long as educators and scientists were willing to go along with the general policies of the regime or, as was usually the case, paid little attention to them, why 'rock the boat'?

In areas, however, which can be described as having been not of immediate importance, certain measures could be undertaken. In 1935, for example, the ageing editor of the *Historische Zeitschrift*, Friedrich Meinecke, was replaced by a true National Socialist historian, Alexander von Müller. To some extent, Meinecke had attempted to accommodate both himself and his historical thinking to National Socialist historical fantasies; but, it had not been enough and besides, an alarming number of his students had been Jewish.[31] In the area of psychology, as indicated above, psychoanalysis, a decidedly Jewish enterprise, was purged, along, of course, with no small number of its practitioners. This must bring up the obvious question: if the National Socialist regime had survived for a longer period of time, would it have made serious efforts to bring all knowledge into conformity with an educational policy supposedly reflective of 'laws of life'? This is a question which cannot be answered with certainty. Yet there can be no doubt that the Nazis believed that they had discovered and were acting in terms of such 'laws.' As difficult as it is to imagine a 'German physics', or a 'German biology', it is equally difficult to imagine a successful, long-term National Socialist regime refraining from far-ranging attempts to bring reality further into congruence with assumed beliefs.

As mentioned earlier, National Socialist attacks upon 'scientific objectivity', as vulgar as they were, revealed a questioning of the very basis of scientific judgement that was and still is generic, if not necessarily to scientific establishments as a whole, then at least to many engaged in that enterprise which might be called 'philosophy of science'. Further, as Nancy Stepan has recently pointed out, the history of at least the biological sciences reveals that there is a measure of truth in this. Not only hypothesising, but even experimentation and the evaluation of results thus obtained were greatly influenced by the overriding belief in assumed natural differences between the races.[32] Stepan has focused mainly upon British biology, and most of her emphasis has been on application of hypotheses stemming from evolutionary and genetic speculation. Yet, based on the evidence, she thought it apposite to make the following assertion about the overriding influence of racial thinking upon the sciences in general. 'Its long life testifies to the deep psychological need Western Europeans, scientists among them, seem to have felt to divide and rank human groups, and measure them negatively against an idealised, romanticised picture of themselves.'[33] To no small degree, it would seem, the processes of generalisation central to scientific endeavours have been influenced on a broad scale by commonly held beliefs, and the assertions made by Dr. Fleck in the 1930s would seem to have been overly modest. Under the circumstances, what would have occurred in a situation of total control — something that never prevailed in the Third Reich — dominated by a religious movement which not only accepted but glorified scientific subjectivism in the name of sacred *racial absolutes* can only be imagined. As we will see later, less scientifically-gifted sorts would find it very easy to restructure an environment of extermination along those lines conveniently provided by racial assumptions.

An area in which National Socialist life-principles could be, and were, applied with rigour was the field of aesthetics. Here, we are not going to be concerned with Nazi art policy *per se;* this is a subject that has been covered rather thoroughly elsewhere.[34] Rather, we will be addressing a question of particular importance with regard to the National Socialist religion, viz., that of how this policy represented a logical extension of certain fundamental principles into an area usually observed as being characterised by at least a modicum of independence.

A common — and certainly justifiable — approach to studying the art policies of so-called 'totalitarian' regimes is to emphasise the areas of propaganda and social control. Certainly, these concerns were of importance in National Socialist art policy. We must understand, however, that the National Socialists, representing as they saw it natural, life-affirming forces, were able to bring to bear that argument which we have observed in other realms of life: anything that is estranged from the community is estranged from life. Thus, artists who appeared to be self-consciously alienated from the warm-hearted collectivity of the *Volksgemeinschaft* were not really creating art at all, since art had to represent and affirm life.

Artists who articulated individuality through their works had to be perceived as being isolated souls, uprooted from the folk-community which had supplied art's life blood in the first place. If one considers certain aspects of National Socialist 'art criticism,' one can be struck by a certain 'democratic' aspect to it. Art should be for the 'people', and the 'people' had to be the final judge. Kurt Karl Eberlein pushed this to logical conclusions, when he declared that any art that did not throb with the values of land and community smacked of 'culture', and, as such, was 'alien to the people'.[35] This, he thought, was the fate of all art 'cut off from blood and soil'.[36] While Eberlein's views were, even by National Socialist standards, rather hyperbolic, his emphasis upon the folk-bound nature of artistic creativity was consonant with that of all National Socialists. Crucial here is the notion of art as 'affirmation'; in the end, a people's affirmation of itself. Here, Adolf Dresler's remarks are apposite. 'Art', he said, 'is the life-expression of a people. Hence, the people must demand that art be a reflection and authentic representation [*Richtsbild*] of its soul'.[37] Furthermore, 'each phenomenon in the life of a people' had to be represented in a manner that best approximated its 'world-view [rooted] longings'.[38] In a somewhat earlier work, Paul Schultze-Naumberg also spoke of such 'longings' and, according to him, the most crucial of them, the 'point of departure' for all German art, had to be 'the heroic man', for Germans, one necessarily Nordic.[39] Now, after a degenerate liberal age, one characterised by that toleration of the inferior and the ugly dictated by a 'misunderstood *Caritas*', so extraordinary a being would indeed become 'the point of departure' for all art, the most crucial aspect of which, according to Schulze-Naumberg (following the lead provided *gratis* by Hitler) was architecture.[40] In any case, it was 'youth and the spirit in which it grows up' that would provide the best assurance that an art grounded in 'blood and soil' (the *only* true art, after all), 'will find its true face'.[41]

In such a situation, there was little room for any variety of artistic 'formalism', or, except of course for those judgements to be made at such celebrations of philistinism as the 'Exhibition of Degenerate Art' in July 1937, formal art criticism. Art criticism, particularly if it was brought to bear against the proliferation of vacuous Nordic nudes and their muscle-bound defenders which increasingly were emerging as aesthetic representatives of the new, 'Aryan man', was cynical and degenerative. As Paul Josef Goebbels put it, in an edict of 27 November 1936 which banned art criticism altogether, it was representative 'of the time of the Jewish domination of art'.[42] Criticism simply confused the people who ought, Goebbels declared, to be allowed to form their own opinions on what constituted true art. In this regard, Alfred Rosenberg who, from time to time, disagreed with Goebbels over what constituted 'Nordic' or 'Aryan' art, certainly agreed with him. The standard of opinion to be brought to bear in judging the worth of a piece of art could be that of '*any* healthy SA man'.[43] In all matters aesthetic, the voice of the people — a voice of which the National Socialist movement was the highest possible amplification — had to prevail. As Hitler declared, the artist could not *be* an artist if he created only for himself. He created not only for some narrow, artificial clique, but as everyone did, for the people.[44]

In any case, if the *Volk* is perceived as life-bearing, all true art *has* to be *Volkskunst*. For Goebbels, in a speech of 15 November 1933, the artist attained creative life 'in the life of the Volk'. What the Minister of Propaganda and Public Enlightenment stated was that the artist — while dependent upon certain 'eternal laws' for his talent — actualised his potential in the body of the *Volk*, that entity which had provided him with the spiritual contents of his art in the first place.[45] From this, it was only natural that Goebbels drew the following conclusion (expressed in a speech of 17 June 1939, upon the occasion of the second annual Reich Theatre Festival Week): 'It is not true that the artist is unpolitical, for political means nothing else but to serve the public with understanding'.[46] In this extraordinary statement one can see with clarity how National Socialism, in its own mind, was able to bring together the practical realm of politics and that of creativity. In reality, the two were not 'merely' inextricably intertwined, but were in fact the same. To create was a political act because creativity, to *be* creative, involved serving 'the public with understanding'. By the same token, politics partook of the aesthetic. In fact, the National Socialist movement was adamant in viewing politics, i.e., serving the people, as a work of art. Thus, when Goebbels stated that the artist was not interested in bloodless figures of the intellect, but with *Life*, he was not talking about a van Gogh-like grasping for infinity within appearances, but about art as politics.[47] Naturally, by politics, Goebbels was not referring to the give-and-take of interest-clashing, but to the policies which were expressions of the National Socialist life principle.

Parenthetically, the objection can be made that one ought not to take the speeches and writing of Goebbels seriously. After all, he was 'Minister of Propaganda and Public Enlightenment'. Yet if one considers the tone and *content* of his diaries one has to accept the fact that, for him, even as a disseminator of propaganda, there was a marked identification with the salient principles of National Socialism. Goebbels' admitted cynicism was always counterbalanced by what he at least saw as a fundamental idealism and by his occasional anger at the German people in general and the party in particular for being unable to live up to it.

Consideration of the National Socialist approach to aesthetics points out an interesting phenomenon; 'politics' were viewed as being rooted in mystery, as almost aesthetic in nature. On the other hand, as we have seen, aesthetics could not be a mysterious, individual matter. In a 19 July 1937 speech delivered at the opening of the 'Exhibition of Degenerate Art' at the House of German Art in Munich, Hitler underscored this attitude towards aesthetics. During the course of his usual tirade against modern art and its supporters — 'Bolshevist art collectors or their literary children' — Hitler strongly condemned such notions as 'inner experience'. 'Whether someone has a strong will or an inner experience he proves through his work and not through garrulous words'.[48] In a word, art obtained its justification as art by externalising itself in mundane forms, forms amenable to the understanding of every member of the *Volksgemeinschaft*.

With the opening of this exhibition . . . [there is] the beginning of the end of German art insanity and accordingly the cultural annihilation of our people. From now on, we will conduct an inexorable work of purification against the last elements of our cultural degeneration.[49]

With these words, Hitler began a thorough-going attack upon modern art which, as is well-known, resulted in the virtual banishment of all of its forms from the Third Reich. It is instructive to note, however, that Hitler was not only referring to modern art when he spoke of 'German art insanity'. In a much broader sense, he was condemning what he saw as necessarily resulting from the artistic 'inner experience', i.e., from something which, extraneous to the life of the *Volk*, or perhaps representing something that was downright hostile to it, was not, indeed *could* not have been, art. Most assuredly, if such pernicious forms were allowed to thrive, the 'cultural annihilation' of the German people was assured. In a world of *Mythus*-grounded politics, art had to be mundane.

If an artist refused to adhere to the aesthetic principles laid down by National Socialism, then indeed there had to be something wrong with him. As Hitler put it,

I have inexorably adhered to the following principle: If some self-styled artist submits trash for the Munich exhibition, then he is either a swindler, in which case he should be put in prison; or he is a madman, in which case he should be put in an asylum; or he is a degenerate, in which case he must be sent to a concentration camp to be 're-educated' and taught the dignity of honest labour. In this way I have ensured that the Munich exhibition is avoided like the plague by the inefficient.[50]

It is important to point out that, while what became the official National Socialist agency concerned with art-policy, the *Reichskulturkammer*, was quite adamant in declaring what did *not* constitute folk-art (and hence. in reality, what was not art), and while the head of the section on 'Fine Arts' Adolf Ziegler, offered certain examples of what healthy 'Aryan' art ought to be, there was no 'official style' *per se*. Yet one was not necessary, at least not after the massive assault undertaken against that perceived of as degenerate. From around 1936 onwards there was a veritable and, for the most part, spontaneous outpouring of paintings and sculpture which conformed rather neatly to National Socialist canons, often not clearly articulated, of what true 'folk art' ought to be. A fine summary of the paintings has been provided by Sybil Milton.

romantic landscape paintings; peasants with large families; suckling infants in their mothers' arms; formal portraits of leading Nazi personalities, especially Hitler; stylized Nordic racial prototypes in heroic military or athletic poses; pseudo-erotic classical allegories of nude female 'muses'; still lifes; genre paintings; and flatout plagiarisms of the Old Masters.[51]

Certainly, if, as Adolf Dresler believed, degenerate art had reflected a decline in traditional family values, the new 'National Socialist Art' would reflect that wholesomeness that was being restored in Germany.[52] It may have been true that, as the *New York Times* reported, there were three times as many patrons of the 'Degenerate Art' exhibition as of the 'German-Aryan Art' one which appeared at the same time.[53] There can be no question, however, but that the 'call' for an art form representative of those 'folk-values' constitutive of the new 'Aryan man' brought forth a strong answer. As Expressionist, Post-Expressionist, and Dada 'degenerates' either fled into exile or, like Emil Nolde, originally a strong supporter of National Socialism, went 'underground', a new, 'wholesome' art, from which all varieties of egotistical aesthetic individualism had been expunged, took their place.[54] We can never know for certain the degree to which, in the eyes of those relatively small number of folk interested in art, Arno Brecker's monumental sculptures, or the paintings of Paul Keck or Elk Eber took the place vacated by those identified with a more degenerate age. We can say that, to all intents and purposes, an 'Aryan art' rendered immune from criticism, became, without significant protest, the chosen art in which the general sanctification of national life was presumably reflected. As suggested above, there could be no place for any sort of artistic individualism, something which, in its very essence, suggested estrangement from national health, and thus was 'anti-natural' as well.

With so obvious (and necessary) an emphasis upon true art as 'natural,' it is hardly surprising that in the offical guide-book for the exhibition of Degenerate Art, non-representational examples were deemed as 'consummated insanity' ('*vollendeter Wahnsinn*').[55] The exhibition had been divided into nine parts concerned with a variety of representations of artistic decadence. Here, paintings were classified according to sloppy workmanship (group number one), moral degeneration (group number five), and 'Deadening of the last Remnant of any Race Consciousness' (group number six), the influence of Jews upon art (group number eight), and so on. Yet, despite these engaging themes, it was the non-representational art brought together in the final 'grouping', number nine, that was supposed to 'crown' the exhibition. Here the editor of the guide,

Fritz Kaiser, pulled out all the stops. Such completely sick 'works', he cried, were hardly works of art at all. One could not be content with just laughing at them but had to combat this 'art' and the spirit responsible for these works '*with rage*'.[56] For the bearers of those values which both came out of and advanced a national community sanctified by nature, what represented the epitome of self-serving subjectivism had to be viewed as unnatural. Or, if there was some place for them in the natural world, they were at the lowest possible level. It was the art of psychotics or savages.

'There is no place for cultural Neanderthalers in the twentieth century', Hitler proclaimed in a speech of 10 July 1938, 'at least not in national socialist Germany'.[57] True genius did not necessarily mean insanity, or anything approaching it: quite simply, it was measured in better-than-average works.[58] Furiously, Hitler lashed out against Dada, Cubist, and various other 'modern painters.' In contrast to them, the Greeks and Romans produced art that, after 2000 years, still brings forth feelings of awe. It is with this art that one could find 'a standard for the tasks and accomplishments of our own time'.[59] As is well known, Hitler's own artistic tastes, (at least those displayed publicly) and apparently with the possible exception of Goebbels, those of most of the important members of the National Socialist party, were *Biedermeirisch* in the extreme. They preferred paintings that one could expect to find hanging in youth hostels or dentists' offices. Quite naturally, the National Socialist rulers, being in a position to do so, could impose their own, extremely conservative tastes, upon the nation. Furthermore, as has been pointed out accurately and often, rulers striving to attain 'totalitarian' rule cannot suffer alienated, spiritually unassimilable souls to express themselves in print, music, stone or canvas. In this context, parallels have been drawn — some of them quite misleading, others not — between National Socialist art policy and that of the Soviet Union.[60]

It must be seen, however, that that sanctification of the German nation which was a logical corollary of the National Socialist natural religion, at the very least provided a convenient rationalisation for the imposition of conservative canons of art criticism. A 'modern artist', one who, for example paints blue horses or abstract forms, would not be serving the interests of the nation. As Goebbels had put it, by not performing a political act, he or she would not be performing an aesthetic act. That which could be viewed as 'unnatural' by the vast mass of German citizenry — and the average German, like the average individual all over the world, most certainly did *not* care for 'modern', 'abstract', or 'non-representational' art — obviously was not in keeping with those life-affirming forces, adherence to which was necessary if art was to be art. Thus, it was absolutely *necessary* that the National Socialist 'revolution' reject 'modern' art in any form and, for its aesthetic, utilise a forced, at times virtually hackneyed, realism which expressed itself in lithe Nordic bodies, happy harvest scenes and columns of victorious troops. It is certainly true that such art can be viewed as serving the sole interest of social control. Nevertheless, it was ideologically consistent that the National Socialists place emphasis upon a fundamental bourgeois conservatism as constituting an important aspect of their 'revolution'. That 'revolution of spirit', the object of which was to bring into being a nature-bound *Volksgemeinschaft* (while, of course annihilating all those who represented an affront to such a community), could not be undone by individuals who, though they also might have viewed themselves as revolutionaries in their several fields, drew upon spiritual resources anti-natural in character.

Seen in this context, Hitler was being perfectly consistent when he stated that anyone whose work displeased him was a criminal or a madman. It is certainly true that, a Herbert Read put it, 'Whenever the blood of martyrs stains the ground, there you will find a doric column or perhaps a statue of Minerva'.[61] For the National Socialist movement, however, itself concerned with aesthetics in so many ways, an art policy rooted in nineteenth century, self-satisfied bourgeois philistinism was absolutely essential if the, to it, most important revolution of all were to be advanced — that one which would bring Aryan man into harmony with those life-forces which set him apart from all others.

Of course, the SS-man was supposed to be the prototype of the 'New Man' of National Socialism, if not the very being himself. It is not surprising, therefore, that at least some in this organisation were extremely sensitive to the close relationship between artistic representation of this extraordinary being and the actual SS-man and his activities (at least those activities more publicly acknowledged). In the second-to-last year of the 'Thousand Year Reich' there appeared a work entitled *German Artists and the SS*. It was introduced by *Obergruppenführer* Gottlob Berger, who took time off from what must have been his increasingly frustrating job as head of Waffen SS recruitment, to do so.

It is the goal of the SS to involve the highest *völkisch* life-values of honour and truth in each decision and in every deed. If, however, art is the expression of the will to struggle of our time, so will it be filled with the same life-values which are also striven for as a final fixed aim by the SS. Each picture, each drawing, each sculpture documents the sense of this struggle in which the SS man participates.[62]

What followed in this most curious book were photo-reproductions of paintings that evidently had appeared either at an exhibition sponsored by the SS or at perhaps a variety of exhibitions which had then been culled for styles and themes appropriate to the assumed spiritual and physical tone of the organisation. In any case, the SS organisation had been presented with a variety of works which mirrored or embodied its nature, its struggles, the goals for which it fought, and the petty-bourgeois bathos which was so often the dialectical counterpoint of its almost unmeasurable brutality. Several of these works will now be described.

In Th. C. Protzen's painting '*SS Junkerschule Bad Tölz SS*', the training school for the *Waffen SS* is depicted in its almost poignantly bucolic setting. Set amidst a gentle forest and against the awe-inspiring Bavarian Alps, there is a distinctly religious aspect to this painting. Here, in grandoise buildings which somehow seem to belong in a landscape blessed by Providence, SS warriors are being trained to carry out their sacred tasks. Indeed, there can be little doubt that the artist was striving to bring together nature and that sanctified organisation of which it was the highest representation. In his own contribution to National Socialist 'aesthetic theory', Franz Rodens made the claim that in the at times disquieting landscapes of Caspar David Friedrich (a romantic painter with a somewhat greater claim to artistic permanence than Th. C. Protzen) one could sense a racially-conditioned quality which provided for ' a totally new relationship to nature'.[63] While Friedrich made his own contributions to the rising German nationalism of the Napoleonic era, he might have been somewhat surprised at this evaluation. There can be no doubt, though, that the sanctification of nature through nationalism (and vice-versa) was definitely a goal of Mr Protzen. In Fritz Klimsch's classical sculptured rendition of Nordic beauty, 'Youth' ('*Jugend*'), there was a depiction of young womanhood which 'elevates her to the ideal picture [or 'prototype'; the term '*Idealbild*' could be translated that way as well] of our race'.[64] The almost stultifying sentimentality of 'Our Faith — Our Victory' ('*Unser Glaube — Unser Sieg*') a contribution of Frid Kocks which shows a handsome SS warrior dreaming of a tender, almost childlike young woman, was counterbalanced by a coarsely brutal, almost comic-book like, drawing by Hans Schweitzer-Mjölnir, 'Waffen-SS Champions Against the World Enemy' ('*Waffen SS Vorkämpfer gegen den Weltfeind*'). The unnamed editor of *German Artists and the SS* was most certainly attempting to make the following points: the SS trooper who dreamed of a Gretchen-like unsullied beauty awaiting him at home, would undertake the most brutal of campaigns in her defence. Defeat of the Soviet apeman, over whom the troopers with classical visages are triumphantly advancing, is necessary if the New Aryan Man, a being sanctified by nature, is to emerge. While, as mentioned earlier, there never was an official statement as to what the 'style' of true National Socialist art had to be, the representative works drawn from a collection apparently dear to at least the SS leadership reveal what National Socialists thought 'true' art, i.e., what Adolf Dresler described as 'authentic representation' of the national soul, ought to 'look like'. In this regard, it is of interest to bear in mind that, as a commentator upon National Socialist art and Soviet Socialist Realism has stated, National Socialist art was not concerned with 'reality' as such, i.e., with some sort of 'realism' much less 'naturalism'. Rather, it was concerned with capturing some sort of higher 'truth' (*'Wahrheit'*).[65] Much more than Socialist Realism, at least as it developed through the Stalinist period and for a while thereafter, National Socialist art was concerned with wellnigh 'sacred topics'. In view of its concern with capturing the essence of that providentially-ordained 'New Man,' this is not surprising.

A more 'popular' effort at artistically representing the 'New Aryan Man' and his historical and contemporary world was the *'Standartenkalender'* published primarily for SA and SS faithful, but available for all who wanted it, by the Nazi publishing house, Franz Eher of Munich. Each page of the calendar consisted of three or four days of a month and under each date there was recorded an event crucial in German history, or the history of the National Socialist Party, or a day of birth or death of a figure crucial in a Nazified German history. Under the dates and the recorded occurrences there was a picture, generally of some scene perceived as somehow being representative of the 'New Order' or some important statement, e.g., a longwinded and almost embarrassingly sentimental tribute to mothers for the May 1937 segment ending in Mothers' Day, which we will consider later. When page-consuming utterances such as that for Mothers' Day were not presented, pictures were often accompanied by appropriate quotations. It is not surprising, in view of the National Socialist search for spiritual roots, that quotations from Meister Eckhart and the Eddas (presumably reflecting the spirit of the 'original' Aryans) could be found, along with those from more conventional anti-Semites such as Martin Luther, and from Nazi leaders. Throughout the calendar, depending of course, on 'key' dates and occurrences, scenes of rural peace, industrial vigour, or youthful enthusiasm vied with sterner representations of the armed forces, or with

Himmler himself, in the case under consideration addressing SS leaders in Frankfurt-am-Oder. Himmler, along with a noteworthy quotation from him, was featured because the lead date of the 1937 calendar was 7 October 1900, the birthday of the *Reichsführer-SS*. The quotation can be rendered as follows: 'The truth is a concern of the heart; never of the intellect. The intellect is inclined to stumble; the heart must always beat the same pulse, and if it ceases then a person dies, exactly as a people when it breaks faith'.[66] This quotation, which aptly demonstrates how unabashed romanticism can be put at the disposal of police bureaucrats always striving for greater efficiency, and the perhaps disquieting photograph under which it was placed, can be compared to an offering of two weeks earlier. Here, the most tranquil of scenes imaginable, 'In the Lüneburger Heath', complete with sheep lounging about under trees, had been presented.

As was the case with *German Artists and the SS,* the *Standartenkalender*, albeit in a more 'popular' manner, offered a mixture of nature-bound romanticism, ideological sternness, and outright sentimentality. Somehow, one was to sense a striving, a vision, one whose ultimate meaning was perhaps inaccessible to all but the most-initiated, but whose presence could be seen in all aspects of the daily life of a people elected by Providence to be bearers of eternal truths. A 'revolution of the spirit' was thus complemented by, if not grounded in, that sacred stasis which testified to the sanctification of national life.

The National Socialist commitment to stasis in areas other than art has been commented upon quite often and in many different contexts. What is meant by stasis is not that the Nazis were committed to such policies as 'no growth' or to preserving some sort of countryside/village idyll. Indeed, during the National Socialist reign, small farms continued to disappear, cities continued to grow, and industry developed at a marked pace.[67] However, during the National Socialist years in Germany, there was no meaningful change in the class structure of German society and no substantive alterations in those patterns of development associated with bourgeois, industrialised Germany. Often such lacks have been singled out as pointing to a disingenuousness on the part of Germany's National Socialist rulers. The lack of social change, to say nothing of actual revolution, has been seen as proof that Hitler came to power simply to preserve the bourgeois *status quo*, and thus that, knowingly or not, he was simply a tool of capitalist powers. Ignoring all of those problems of interpretation inherent in vulgar Marxist hypotheses on National Socialism, one must come to the conclusion that, while there certainly was a large degree of disingenuousness in National Socialism's use of the term 'revolution', lack of revolution and adherence to stasis were of crucial importance to the implementation of Nazi policies, most particularly those central to the National Socialist religion.

As the Nazis saw it, theirs was 'a revolution of spirit' the primary purpose of which was to make Aryan man conscious of his place in a natural world filled with enemies. In order that Aryan man celebrated by National Socialist aesthetics assume his proper place in such a world, the eradication of these enemies had to occur; 'biological mysticism', as Rauschning put it, dictating the necessity of such a solution. Under such conditions, questions of radical departures in formal social relationships, patterns of ownership and distribution and so on were both distracting and beside the point. They were beside the point because, with the National Socialist movement in power, a great natural truth had been realised and the German nation placed under the suzerainty of the laws of life. If all actions of the National Socialist regime were in conformity with such laws, then revolution was being continuously carried out under conditions of a radical immanency, i.e., a state in which every event or deed which followed from National Socialist policy was an expression of mystically grounded truth, and thus sanctified through its very occurrence.

Not only the pursuit of knowledge, artistic creativity and other presumably more esoteric realms were thus sanctified. Even presumably 'mundane' events usually associated with the more pedestrian aspects of modern society supposedly pulsed with that excitement attendant upon the actualisation of spiritual potential. Speaking at a construction site, Hitler expressed this notion most clearly: 'Perhaps the greatest miracle of our time is [that] buildings arise, factories are established again, streets are laid out, railway stations constructed, but over all there grows up a new German man:!'[68] The new German man was defined in terms of his activities, activities which, because they were being undertaken by new men acting in conformity with the laws of life, were sanctified. For this new man there were no problems that could not be solved. New cities would be built; inexpensive cars would be made available to the German people. Such activities, which German romantics would have viewed as representing alarming concessions to Western materialistic civilisation, were positive ones, indicative of the fact that, for nature-bound Aryan humanity, nothing was impossible.

As one can imagine, the National Socialist ideology had an extraordinary advantage — it could allow any petty-bourgeois bromide or smug philistine attitude to be sanctified through the divinity of life itself. At an exhibition dedicated to the German woman, Alfred Rosenberg made the observation that the National Socialist movement recognised this woman as constituting the 'life-source' of the German people. It had been the German woman that had protected the 'racial intactness' *(Unversehrtheit)* of 'our *völkisch* life', and the National Socialist *Weltanschauung* grasped this role for the first time.[69] 'You, the German mothers, are the life-source of the German people', Wilhelm Frick proclaimed. 'In your loving and tender hands lie the fate and future of the German nation'.[70] The thanks of German soldiers, presumably being proffered at that time, to their mothers were the most beautiful expressions of gratitude of the German nation.[71]

National Socialist emphasis upon motherhood and the family has been commented upon often. Involved was not merely a propaganda ploy and/or some smooth attempt at social intergration, although these most certainly had roles to play. Of far greater importance was the perceived role that women had in that sanctification of national life that was central to National Socialist concerns. The woman, in Nazi eyes, would continue to fulfill tasks for which nature had prepared her. She would be wife and mother. However, through grasping basic natural principles, the movement could liberate women from a sense of worthlessness by making them *aware* of the life-sustaining character of their roles. Thus, while accepted feminine activities would proceed as before, the carrying out of these activities while *conscious* of their sacred purpose elevated women to the position of being racial comrades and fellow battlers for the National Socialist world order. The syrupy sentimentality of 'Mothers' Day' became as profound an expression of the sacred nature of Aryan life as a work of art.

Yet, while the 'life-bearing', i.e., familial and procreative, functions of womanhood were exalted by the National Socialist regime, the 'new German woman' was supposed to be a race comrade in every sense of the word. While not to the same degree as the 'new German man' — for such would amount to that 'masculinising' of the woman identified with despised feminists — she was to be hardened. The 'new German woman', eschewing the soft fashions, lipstick and rouge identified with her decadent Western counterpart, was to be an athlete. The 'social butterfly' of the old days was to be replaced by a lithe, tanned creature of nature who preferred javelin-throwing to dancing, and whose feminity would not be affronted by occasional excursions in marching boots.[72] The emphasis upon a sort of 'physical liberation' of German women, as well as upon a certain shared comradeship in struggle, added, or seemed to add, a significant dimension to the housewife/mother role central to the National Socialist view of women, and convinced some, largely of middle class origin, that women had a future with National Socialism.[73] Particularly since the position of women had not altered significantly during the Weimar period, even with the presumed assistance of a liberal constitution, a movement which not only exalted women in the time-honoured traditional roles, but seemed to offer the sort of physical liberation described above, had to have proved attractive, despite the obvious misogyny displayed by many, from the Führer on down, with regard to women's role in politics.[74]

Also, it is crucial to recognise that, at least for some Nazis, the most prominent of whom was Heinrich Himmler, the traditional, bourgeois home, at least with regard to women's functions in it, had to be challenged in the name of that assumed 'higher morality' attached to the breeding of a superior race. The *Lebensborn* experiment, whose importance is still open to debate, represented a radical departure from traditional bourgeois home-values, particularly as concerned women. Yet even in his efforts, as some saw it, to encourage illegitimacy in the name of racial advancement, the *Reischsführer SS* could not be completely consistent, and always feared the consequences of disrupting, much less damaging, German family life in general.[75] Even his famous 'Chosen Women' (*Hohen Frauen*) were to be intellectually and physically groomed to serve, in the end, traditional functions of supporting 'their men' and pro-creation.[76]

In the end, and to an extent which would hinder the utilisation of German women in the war effort, the 'traditional' view of women, i.e., as homemakers and mothers — and, *Lebensborn* to the contrary, usually within the accustomed hearth-bound family — emerged as predominant.[77] Athleticism and various activities which could be described as being vaguely 'paramilitary' might have been encouraged, and women did play a role in anti-aircraft defence and as air raid wardens once the war became serious. Yet, athletic prowess and various quasi-military roles really came to be viewed either as preparation and conditioning for the bringing of healthy children into the world, or as extensions of a sort of 'nurturing' role.[78] To a surprising degree, it would seem, the petty-bourgeois conceptions of women which often found articulation in the most banal of pronouncements imaginable reflected deeply held beliefs on the part of the National Socialist leadership. Women who had believed that National Socialism, despite its known misogyny, could somehow serve as a road for advancement had to have been disappointed as the realities of their situation became clear. As in the case of Jews and various others deemed inferior 'biology was indeed destiny' and 'although women joined the vast array of women's organisations and heard themselves praised by hours of propaganda, they remained only privates in a civilian army commanded by Nazi men'.[79] On the other hand, there can be little doubt that German women as a whole, much like their menfolk, found the exaltation, by National Socialists, of traditional female activities, and of home life in general, to be of comfort. As Gerda Lerner has pointed out, 'ideology and prescription internalised by both women and men' has played what has to be seen as a 'causative' role in determining gender relations throughout the world. How much more had this to be the case when the most moralistic petty-bourgeois 'ideology and prescription' was part and parcel of a supposedly religious revolution of values.[80] For most National Socialists, at least petty-bourgeois in attitude, if not, strictly speaking, in background, moralistic jeremiads in defence of the 'traditional' roles of women came naturally and were, of course, of immense agitational value. National life most assuredly must appear to be 'sanctified' when commonly-held usages and attendant beliefs are turned into articles of faith. As regards women, it was precisely just such an 'article' that, in the end, her primary task was one aptly portrayed by H. A. Bühler in his painting 'Homecoming' (*Heimkehr*) which shows an exhausted soldier burying his head in the lap of his wife or girlfriend; the succouring of menfolk fighting for a movement in which she had to remain a 'private'. A traditional 'Womanly Role' had been sanctified.

In this regard, it is perhaps fitting that we conclude our consideration of the National Socialist religion and German women with lines taken from the *Standartenkalender*, for 6-9 May 1937. Sunday, 9 May, was 'Mother's day' and a poem by the eminently forgettable Otto Paust was provided for the occasion. The poem was entitled 'Mother Means Homeland' (*'Mutter heisst Heimat'*), and the author has provided what he thinks to be key lines of this piece, confident that, in this case, absolutely nothing whatsoever has been lost in translation.[81]

> Mother!   From your sheltering womb
>   sprang our life — we grew tall.
>   Mother! In your helping hand
>   we found in wonderland
>   homeland . . .

After a few lines in which the poet expresses his conviction that homeland means family and happiness and mother means thankfulness for all things great and beautiful, upon which all must fasten their gaze and expectations, the piece continues:

Mother means yet more: [it] means Fatherland.
Mother means love and flaming bond
for brother and sister of every class.
To serve the homeland, deeply, bravely and true,
means: loving you, Mother, in sacred awe.
You gave us life — we became Nation.
From you grew the future in daughter and son.
Mother! From your sheltering womb
grew Germany's life — Germany grows tall.
Mother! In your helping hand
the *Volk* finds, in wonderland
Homeland.

Although there are no doubt others of this genre to be found in other
languages, it is doubtful if any poet, no matter how awash in bathos he
might have been, has ever succeeded in producing a piece in which procreative and conventionally-nurturing functions have been, quite literally, sanctified to the degree that they have been in this one offering.
Probably, though, the most crucial line must be 'Mother means yet more:
[it] means Fatherland'. In a word, the most important value of
Motherhood was nurturing the *Father*land; that tradition-bound *Volk*,
in the end aggressively masculine in character, which was sanctified by
those same timeless truths embodied in motherhood. The poem began
with emphasis upon mother and children. It ends with these children part
of a timeless *Volk* finding, 'in wonderland' its timeless homeland. Again,
we can see — particularly bearing in mind the presumed readers of the
poem — how sanctified tradition, gilded over with thick layers of sentimentality, could be put into the service of a movement which, in the
days ahead, would slaughter large numbers of women and children for
the most 'idealistic' of motives.

It was the sanctification of traditional social institutions and petty-
bourgeois morality which found expression in the National Socialist
movement that allowed its adherents to declare (and probably believe)
that charges that the Nazis were modern-day heathens were totally false.
Goebbels, in a 4 December 1935 speech in Saarbrücken, attacked people who made such accusations.

> Is it heathen that one restores the ethos of the family? And restores
> a sense and purpose to life to the worker? Is it heathen to once more
> build up a state on moral principles, to drive out Godlessness and
> to cleanse theatre and film from the contamination and plague of
> Jewish-liberal Marxism — is this *heathen*?[82]

As a matter of fact, the propaganda minister maintained, through such activities and through the Nazi *Winterhilfe* charities, the National Socialist movement was actually practising Christianity.[83] Indeed, some clergymen, impressed by the moralistic idealism of the Nazis, drew parallels between the Christian religion and the National Socialist *Weltanschauung*. Like Christianity, as one eminent Protestant theologian Cajus Fabricius put it, National Socialism had not gained its view of the world from any system of philosophy 'but from the stern realities of life. One fact in this struggle for existence has become an overpowering reality to them — the Führer.'[84] As one might expect, Cajus Fabricius drew a distinction between *Weltanschauung* and religion, maintaining that National Socialism definitely had no religious pretensions.[85] He no doubt would have been distressed to learn of what Hilter — who, according to Goebbels in a 8 April 1941 entry in his diaries, once declared that it 'had crippled all that is noble in humanity'[86] — really thought of Christianity. It is important to note, however, that, in its presumed grasping of life in its totality, National Socialism's exaltation of pious, *Volk*-bound morality allowed it to gain a great deal of support from individuals and groups which did not accept or could not have accepted the major underlying principles of the movement's own very real religious tenets. Once again, we can reflect upon the pragmatic character of this presumably most idealistic of political movements. One of the advantages that a 'revolution of the spirit' must always have over that formal class revolution espoused by the Marxist left is that, under most circumstances, the individual race-comrade can decide just how far this revolution is to be carried, at least from the point of view of his own participation in it.

The sanctification of national life that resulted from application of National Socialist principles to Germany allowed the movement to define pragmatic political actions in thoroughly idealistic terms. In a word, Nazi attitudes and policies towards the state, towards the pursuit of knowledge, and towards art, as well as the movement's general adherence to a petty-bourgeois morality, were justified simply by virtue of their existence. In the natural religion of National Socialism, the dichotomy between 'is' and 'ought' had been bridged, but in a fashion rather unanticipated by the great Hegel, who, as is known, spent a considerable portion of his intellectual life engaged in the same enterprise. The fact that a petty-bourgeois morality, to some extent rooted in the Judaeo-Christian tradition, could successfully be placed at the service of a cause engaged in uprooting this tradition, root and branch, testifies to the congruence of National Socialist ideals with certain perceived needs of modern life.

In order that the National Socialist religion of life be successfully translated into reality, it was necessary that the greatest war of history be fought. In reality, there was one unified war, of which the general race-war against 'international Judaism' and more mundane forms of combat were constituent parts. Nevertheless, while acknowledging that campaigns such as the 1940 Battle of France, the Battle of Britain of the same year, and the later campaigns in Russia were, or came to be, viewed by Nazi ideologues as being part and parcel of a general war of annihilation against Jewry, it is obvious that different sets of demands were posed by different varieties of combat. The war of annihilation against a largely unarmed Jewish population required a different approach, and different patterns of rationalisation, than did warfare in the conventional sense. While these two aspects of Nazi warfare cannot be entirely separated, we will consider the 'campaign' against the Jews at length in the following chapter. For now, we must focus upon how National Socialist principles were applied to so-called 'conventional' warfare, i.e., that involving the usual, mundane impedimenta of modern war — planes, tanks, artillery pieces and so on — and, of great importance, how these principles bore up *under stress*. Consequently, we will be focusing on the response of the National Socialist leadership to those situations which the German people had to confront when the war became 'serious,' i.e., from the beginning of the Russian campaign in June 1941, until the end of the war. Quite naturally, it is of immense interest to observe how a so-called 'life-affirming' *Weltanschauung*, presumably rooted in the laws of life as they are expressed in nature, confronted serious and unpleasant situations posed by real events.

How committed National Socialists would respond to the increasingly severe demands posed by war was in large measure revealed in an article in the *Völkischer Beobachter* of 25 February 1941. To put this in some perspective, we must recall that, by this date, the German *Luftwaffe* had sustained its first major defeat in the Battle of Britain. The campaign against the Soviet Union, Operation Barbarossa, was in the final planning stages and campaigns in North Africa were about to begin (an at that time unanticipated operation in the Balkans against Yugoslavia and Greece would be undertaken beginning on 6 April 1941). The article was concerned with the original Twenty Five Point Program of the National Socialist German Workers' Party which had appeared on 25 February 1920. This program, it was declared, was not like others, it was not just ink on paper. On the contrary, 'it lives and flows in the blood of the German race'.[87] Indeed, the party program was one of the weapons with which Germany 'was beating England'.[88]

There are several pertinent remarks that can be made about this article. First of all, by 1941 it was obvious that a substantial number of the twenty-five points had never been translated into action, nor was it likely that they ever would be. This was particularly true with regard to the so-called 'socialist' aspects of the program. Yet, according to the article, the program 'lives and flows in the blood of the German race'. In part, so baldly melodramatic a statement can be viewed as being informed by certain mundane propagandistic concerns. There is another angle, however, from which it can be considered. Since the National Socialist program was rooted in the very life-concerns of the German people, precise implementation of every one of the twenty-five points was unnecessary. All that really mattered was the Aryan life-spirit which informed the program as a whole. Since the program was created by a party which in essence *was* the German people, it was — as an entity which *in toto* was greater than the sum of its parts — always being actualised, most particularly in the extraordinarily successful policies of the Führer. Once again, we can see how National Socialist idealism could so easily express itself in the pragmatic idiom, a process which followed logically and almost effortlessly from the fundamental character of the religion of nature. In essence, what was being said was that any sort of National Socialist action was the party program incarnate.

The military successes enjoyed by the Nazi war machine — with the rather major exception of the defeat over Great Britain — allowed for the facile identification of National Socialist ideology with day-to-day political and military events. Under certain conditions, National Socialist propaganda — a term which perhaps ought not to be used in too glib a fashion, since, more often than not, the National Socialist leadership itself tended to believe what it was conveying to the German people — was able to declare that military events were demonstrating the emergence of a Nazi 'new man', awesome in depth of character and absolutely fearless in batttle. Two examples of this, described very well by Jay Baird, will suffice. On 9 April 1940, Germany conquered Denmark and undertook a campaign to conquer Norway, In Norway, heavy fighting centred upon the vital port of Narvik, which served Germany as a shipping point for much-needed Swedish iron ore. A small contingent of German troops, reinforced only by the surviving crew members of German destroyers sunk during naval engagements with the Royal Navy, succeeded in holding off a far larger Allied force. Against great odds, the commander of this force, General Major Eduard Dietl utterly frustrated Allied efforts in the Narvik area (not to deprive General Major Dietl of his due, but this would appear to have been a very easy thing to do in 1940).[89] For Goebbels, Dietl symbolised the Nazi 'new man', fearless in combat and capable of fighting successfully against unimaginable odds.[90]

1940 was a good year for the emergence of 'new, National Socialist men'. On 10 May 1940, while more conventional German army units were crashing over the borders of the Netherlands, Belgium and Luxembourg, glider detachments landed near Fort Eban Emael and several bridges, keys to the Albert Canal portion of the Belgian defence system. The fort was to have delayed the German advance for almost a week. It fell in 36 hours to 85 men who, armed with grenades, flame-throwers and hollow-charge explosives, were able to subdue a garrison which, depending on the source, numbered anywhere from 800 to 1200 men, until reinforcements could arrive to seal the victory. The rest of the glider detachments were able to secure most of the Albert Canal bridges intact.[91] Total losses for the plucky little band which neutralised Eben Emael were six dead, 19 wounded while the units which secured the bridges lost only 38 dead. The overall commander of the operation, Captain Walter Koch, was depicted by Goebbels as representing the same type of new, National Socialist man as had General Major Dietl. Koch knew no fear of any man, was possessed of depth of character and was absolutely honourable.[92]

What was significant about these men, from the point of view of the National Socialist ideology was the 'fact' that they were living manifestations of those principles that constituted the substructure of this ideology. They were the 'new man' in the making, a man whose very existence testified to the effectiveness of a *Weltanschauung* grounded in natural laws of life. Truly, as National Socialists saw it, such people as Dietl and Koch were living the National Socialist ideology, and no amount of reflection upon the truth or falsehood of this ideology could detract from this. The party program, or most assuredly the spirit that was embodied in it, lived in the astonishingly successful exploits of German soldiery. Point by point fulfillment of the program, with the notable exception of those aspects of it concerned with racial policy, was unimportant so long as its spirit was realised in combat (later, as we shall see, Hitler himself would have a few comments to make upon the matter).

As mentioned earlier, with the invasion of the Soviet Union on 22 June 1941, National Socialist religious principles were to be subjected to a strain hitherto unknown. First of all, this was a clash between life-bound principles and those which subsisted at the base of an ideology devoid of life. This was a campaign, as a *Völkischer Beobachter* article of 19 July 1941 put it, against the new Soviet man, something that had emerged out of a 'political retort'.[93] The unified German people was confronting a variety of peoples held together only by autocracy and orthodoxy. Bolshevism had thoroughly atomised these peoples who were either incredibly stupid or 'fanatical slaves in a completely soulless system'.[94] In this article, there is the obvious belief that the Russian campaign represented a clash between a 'soulless system' and a *Weltanschauung* which expressed itself in idealistic terms. None the less, even the most optimistic Nazis were fully cognisant of the fact that they had embarked upon a course of action which was risky in the extreme. This would quite literally be a campaign to the death.

To the awesome challenges posed by the Russian campaign, one had to offer increasing amounts of idealism, something which demanded '*more than* the fulfillment of duty'.[95] Everyone, SA man (Victor Lutze, author of this article, headed the now virtually powerless SA) and factory worker, had to go beyond the call of duty. Furthermore, as many high Nazi officials pointed out, with the Russian campaign it was no longer a question of mere *German* idealism. All of Aryan Europe was united in a campaign against Jewish/Bolshevik barbarism. As Gunter d'Alquen, *Hauptsturmführer* of the Waffen SS put it, those Norwegians, Danes and Flemings and Dutch who served and fell with honour in the Waffen SS knew that they were 'soldiers of Adolf Hitler in the struggle for the victory of National Socialism — the clear expression of the great Germanic idea'.[96]

The emphasis upon a clash of ideas, or ideals, particularly important once Germany found herself at war with, at first, the Soviet Union and then the United States, was evident in Wolfgang Willrich's edited work, *Of the Reich's Soldiers (Des Reiches Soldaten)*. In this work, portraits of earlier military heroes, such as Dietl and the *Luftwaffe* ace, Werner Mölders, were presented, along with one of the greatest hero of all, of course, Adolf Hitler. In the introduction to this book, Willrich offered the following comparison of the respective ideals animating the opposing armies:

There, the power of gold with the claim to world domination, pushes for a struggle of annihilation; here, the idea of the *Reich* calls for a just world order. There, the Jew, hating out of his ugliness, rules over the commercial greed and blind lust for domination of the Anglo-Saxon world powers and their vassals, and over the fanatical and incited wretched masses of Red Russia; here, a new Europe, borne by racial pride and dedicated to [its] traditional culture should gather itself around the *Reich*, battling for its independence from World Jewry in all areas and securing its own creative race character from decay.[97]

Truly, Willrich implied, idealism *had* to triumph over materialism; good over evil. Here, the role of family ethics, particularly strong in rural settings, with the strong emphasis upon the elevated position of the 'woman and her ethically decisive influence in the family' was crucial, and it was no accident that many who bore the Knight's Cross came from such backgrounds.[98] All of the values embodied in National Socialism were now being put to the sternest of tests. The emphasis upon the severity of the tests imposed upon Germany, particularly since the beginning of the Russian campaign, was emphasised by Walther Tröge, in his edited book of wartime art. In this regard, he pointed out that 'all works which originated in Russia or under the influence of the eastern front experience are . . . harder, more biting and perhaps more gruesome'. This had to be so if wartime art was to remain true in depicting the exigencies imposed by a harsher struggle.[99] In Tröge, perhaps more than in Willrich, one can sense an emphasis upon grim determination, something that was reflected in a painting by R. Lipsus which depicted German Troops advancing across a muddy steppe, under a leaden sky. The Russian campaign, a war which truly had become a 'world' one — these would be the ultimate tests for the German people as bearers of National Socialist ideals.

With the beginning of the Russian campaign, one can observe an increasing emphasis upon will, always of importance in Hitler's *Weltanschauung*, more particularly upon the will to conquer, to overcome fate. The pragmatic element so prominent in National Socialism was still there, i.e., decisions made and policies undertaken by the National Socialist regime were correct simply by virtue of their occurence. Nevertheless, even though Barbarossa had been occasioned by unprecedented military victories that had been responsible for enormous Soviet casualties and had brought in approximately 2,500,000 Soviet prisoners by October 1941, everyone seemed to realise that unprecedented amounts of labour and sacrifice would be necessary if the operation were to be successful in the end. Most certainly, calls for sacrifice in the name of the National Socialist *Volksgemeinschaft* had been issued ever since the movement came to power in 1933. With the Russian campaign, however, there was the sense that a great deal more than ever before would have to be sacrificed; this, despite the fact that, as we now know, total war mobilisation in Germany really did not begin until 1943. Some of this sense was reflected in Hitler's official thanking of the army and home front, which appeared in the *Völkischer Beobachter* on 5 October

1941. The Führer praised the sacrifices of the army, but spent a good deal of time on those of the home front. 'Behind the front of sacrifice', he declared, stood millions of German farmers, workers, and women doing their jobs. *'We can truly say: for the first time in history, a whole people is now in combat, a portion on the front, the rest at home'.*[100] After the war, necessarily a successful one of course, the National Socialist movement would *'go back to the old party program, whose fulfillment now appears to me* [to be] *more important perhaps than on the first day'.*[101] The 'Lord God', Hitler went on to say, never helps lazy people or cowards, people who refuse to help themselves. If the German people strove assiduously on its own behalf *'then even the Lord God will not refuse you his help'*![102]

Hitler's message of 5 October 1941 was a significant one in so far as National Socialist ideology was concerned. As we mentioned before, demands for sacrifice and hard work always had been made by the National Socialist leadership. However, both in profound — at least as they saw them — ideological/religious works and in more baldly propagandistic pieces, leading National Socialists had come down strongly upon two points: (1) that there was an absolute congruence of the National Socialist ideology with 'laws of life' (hence, as we have seen, pragmatism seemed to have been sewn into the very fabric of this ideology), and (2) that the Nazi party program, even if specific points of it had not as yet been implemented, was living in the very life of the German people. Now, in the 5 October message, Hitler quite bluntly stated that the realisation of the party program was up to the German people. If this people was successful in the greatest war in history, then it could look forward to the program being implemented *after the war*. For Hitler, even as his armies were driving upon Moscow, this program was *not* alive in the life-blood of his people. This people had to stand on guard against laziness and cowardice for, after all, the 'Lord-God' — and here, Hitler might well have been indirectly referring to himself as this God's messenger — helps those who help themselves. In other words, there was the possibility that the National Socialist program, one rooted in the laws of life, would not be translated into action. The fate of Germany had been thrust into the hands of the German people. So had that of the party program. To be sure, dedicated National Socialists continued to adhere to the belief that their *Weltanschauung*, their 'religion of nature,' was rooted in life and that the movement, to the degree that it faithfully acted in conformity with 'life,' was justified in whatever it did. In this regard, idealism continued to express itself in the pragmatic idiom.

Under massive pressures, however, such as those generated by the Russian campaign, it became psychologicallly unbearable for the National Socialist leadership to be able always to see the movement and the German nation as being coextensive. After all, what would happen if the German nation in particular and Aryan man in general should somehow fail to accomplish those tasks presented to them by the laws of life? As we shall see, while the nation as an axiological principle and racial entity remained sanctified, its members were more and more called upon to adhere to principles, ideas, and patterns of action that, as Hitler often suspected, were not really inherent in the German people as a whole, but had to be brought out from this people by the movement. In a word, as the war became, at first, increasingly serious for Germany, and later downright disastrous, that sense of immanency that had played so strong a role in the National Socialist religion, while never disappearing altogether, began to decrease in prominence. Those Germans who did their duty, as the National Socialist perceived this duty, 'lived' the ideology; those Germans who did not — and, as we shall see, an increasing number of them were perceived as not doing so — could not have been seen as doing so.

Although more 'radical' National Socialists like Hitler and Goebbels had always retained a certain degree of suspicion towards the army, this suspicion became extremely pronounced after the successful Russian counterattack before Moscow, which began on 6 December 1941. After about a month, the counterattack was contained, but only after the German army had lost well over 100,000 casualties and only after the Führer, seemingly providentially, was able to prevent a rout through his 'stand fast' order (something that would, of course, have somewhat more negative effects during the Stalingrad battle.) In any case, as Wellington might have put it, the Moscow affair had been 'the nearest run thing' and the handling of the situation by the professional military came under sharp criticism. An entry in Goebbels' diary for 24 January 1942 points this out clearly. The army, he said, had treated its wounded soldiers very badly. They had been left in unheated freight cars, often without blankets and badly fed. The party, Goebbels stated, really ought to take over the care and transport of wounded soldiers.[103] In a similar vein, Goebbels, in an entry of 28 March 1942, spoke of the marked superiority of the *Waffen-SS* compared to the army in looking after their men. However, since most army generals were reactionary, such was to be expected.[104] At the same time, Goebbels adhered to the notion that those who stuck to their duty with grim determination *were* the ideology in action. 'There are ideologists in our midst', he said in a diary entry of 27 February

1942 (during the course of one of his routine attacks on Alfred Rosenberg), 'who believe a man from a submarine crew, on emerging from the engine room dirty and oil-bespattered would like nothing better than to read *The Mythus of the Twentieth Century*'. This was nonsense. Such a man needed light materials to read. After all, 'He is living our way of life and doesn't have to be taught it'.[105] Elaborating further, Goebbels declared that, 'After the war we can talk again about ideological education. At present, we are living our ideology and don't have to be taught it'.[106] Here, we can observe the old pragmatic approach again. Those of us — propagandist, soldier, or U-boat sailor — who are doing our jobs in the service of the National Socialist regime are representing the National Socialist ideology, or, rather, *are* the ideology. In such a situation, formal ideological education, to say nothing, one would suppose, of the Twenty-Five Point Program of 1920, were things that were rather beside the point.

As in Hitler's October 1941 message, Goebbels placed immense demands on the German people. This can be seen very clearly in a speech of 15 March 1942, in which he declared that the war was not to be won simply by shouting 'Heil Hitler'. Rather, one must work, most especially in as much as morale and spirit rested in labour.[107] Then Goebbels went on to make a statement that was immensely significant with regards to how the 'natural religion' of National Socialism responded to stress. He referred to the seemingly mundane call to the German people to work hard and support the war effort. 'Naturally', he said, 'this is not the National Socialism that is preached in the grandiose hymns of our party. This is National Socialism for home consumption. There must be this also. Even Catholics don't go to Easter High Mass three times a day'.[108] While these lines were received with a certain degree of merriment ('*Heiterkeit*', as it appears in the transcript), what Goebbels said was of extraordinary importance. The National Socialism 'preached in the grandiose hymns' of the Nazi party was the National Socialism of High Mass. It was *the* National Socialism rooted in life, the bearer of religious principles externalised in racial policies of which the German people knew a great deal but about which they could not know all. Naturally, 'National Socialism for home consumption' was also rooted in the 'laws of life'.

As has been mentioned before, there was often congruence between so-called propagandistic efforts and the genuine beliefs of the Nazi leadership. For example, the dignity and spirit of labour were elements that had been emphasised both privately and publicly before and after 1933. In his 15 March 1942 speech, however, Goebbels was drawing a line between the National Socialism of the High Mass and that which had to be proffered to a public in which war enthusiasm had to be aroused and maintained. Through labour and dedication this public was to be imbued with National Socialist principles. As in Hitler's October 1941 statements, Goebbels had maintained that the success or failure of National Socialism was, in reality, dependent upon whether or not the German people was willing to expend those efforts commensurate with the demands of a war in which life itself was engaged in mortal combat with all those estranged-from-life forces that threatened to extinguish it. The German people, on the front lines and at home, had to strive to live National Socialism so that it did not have to be taught.[109] In a word, for Goebbels, 'ideological instruction' was almost tantamount to a confession of defeat, both for the German people and for that movement which, through its presumed adherence to natural laws of life, *was* the German people in its most highly developed form.

With the beginning of the invasion of Russia, one can observe an increasing tendency to separate the National Socialist movement from the German people in general and the army in particular. Naturally, this phenomenon was not totally unprecedented. Elitism had always played a role in the Nazi attitude towards mass politics and, most particularly, in Hitler's concept of leadership. However, in the motto '*Deutschland ist Hitler, Hitler ist Deutschland*', expressed, by Rudolf Hess at the 1934 Nuremberg party rally, among other places, a fundamental National Socialist principle had been stated. Namely, that there was, through the movement's adherence to natural life principles, a wellnigh ontological identification of the National Socialist leadership with the German people even if this leadership had to be viewed as representing an elite group within this people. This notion was not put on ice for the duration of the war. Nevertheless, there can be little question but that the Nazi leadership, both publicly and privately, responded to the increasing stresses of an increasingly unsuccessful war by, at times, abandoning the pragmatic idealism emphasised above in favour of a new, more mundane variety of pragmatism that was informed by an increasingly dualistic view of movement and people.

The movement could provide the German people with principles and set an example of selflessness in defence of the sanctified 'nation'. If the people who comprised this nation did not respond positively, however, then it would go under, even as the sacred principles of National Socialism remained true. Through defeat, the German people in particular and Aryan man in general would demonstrate that, at best, they did not grasp these principles and at worst, were not worthy of them, something which Hitler in more pessimistic passages in *Mein Kampf,* thought probable.

Naturally, this did not mean that hallowed themes were dropped from Nazi propagandistic efforts. Racist concerns remained as central as ever. As an example of this, we can consider the response of the SS journal *Das Schwarze Korps* to the stubborn Russian defence of Stalingrad. In the 29 October 1942 issue, the almost peevish complaint was raised that if English or American soldiers had been there, they would have had the decency to surrender, and not have continued the fanatical, suicidal resistance with which the German 6th Army was being confronted. 'Thus', in the journal's view, 'Stalingrad represented the quintessence of the Soviet contempt for the human race'.[110] Furthermore, Nazi propaganda after the surrender of the 6th Army continued to emphasise, some say more than ever before, anti-Jewish themes.[111] Here, we can consider one of the most important National Socialist speeches ever given. On 18 February 1943, sixteen days after the surviving remnant of the 6th Army capitulated, Goebbels gave his famous 'total war' speech. In this we can see Goebbels bringing to bear the salient element of National Socialist ideology: the Jewish threat — in this case externalised in the form of Bolshevism — not only to Germany, but indeed to Western civilisation as a whole. Throughout the address, we can observe that which Goebbels had once professed to despise — ideological instruction (parenthetically, in his calling attention to Jewish liquidation commandos and Jewish terror in general, we can also see a good deal of projection).

The very existence of Western man was at stake, Goebbels declared. 'Behind the storming Soviet divisions *we see already the Jewish liquidation commandos*; behind these, however, arises *terror*, the spectre of starving millions and complete European anarchy'.[112] 'Eastern Bolshevism', he continued, 'is not only terroristic *teaching*, but also terroristic *praxis*'.[114] It pursued its goals recklessly and consistently, with absolutely no consideration or thought of human happiness. All this was part-and-parcel of a unified, trans-European Jewish threat. 'In any case', Goebbels said, to an increasingly enthusiastic crowd, 'Germany has no intention of bowing down before this Jewish threat, but rather, *in due course* meeting it, if necessary under [conditions] of the *most complete* and *most radical* elimination of Jewry'![114] The Soviet allies of international Jewry cared nothing about human life. Their throwing in of masses of men and tanks against the German lines had proved that beyond a shadow of a doubt.[115] '*What is sitting before me*,' Goebbels continued, '*is a cross-section of the whole German people at the front and in the homeland* — is that not so?'[116] Stormy applause and cries of '*Ja*' greeted this rhetorical question. 'To be sure *Jews* are not represented here!' More applause and cries greeted the pronouncement. Finally, Goebbels made his most strident demand: do you want total war; total and *radical* war? To this, the cries of '*Ja*' were deafening.[117] From 18 February 1943, well after Great Britain, the Soviet Union and the United States had declared total social and economic commitment to a world war, Germany was officially doing the same.

It is true that after he delivered his 'total war' speech, Goebbels is supposed to have said, 'This hour of idiocy! If I had said to the people, "Jump out of the third story of Columbus house", they would have done it too.'[118] This would suggest a most cynical attitude on Goebbels' part, with regard to that 'cross-section of the whole German people' he had just finished exhorting to give their all to the war effort. Yet, we must not forget two things: (1) that Goebbels, in his warning of Jewish 'liquidation commandos' and a general Jewish/Bolshevik peril, was expressing something which he himself believed, and (2) that he thought it necessary to rally the German people not by focusing upon the requirements posed by conventional war, but rather by emphasising the point that the war was in fact one of racial annihilation. All else had failed. Thus, *one had to fall back upon the central core of the Nazi ideology*, one grounded in religious truths. If one were determined to provide the educative experience necessary to arouse the German people to the point of superhuman sacrifice, then the message proffered had to be an expression of the National Socialist *Weltanschauung*. There is a most interesting assumption here. Goebbels, who despised ideological instruction, thought it necessary to emphasise *the most radical aspects* of the National Socialist ideology in his effort to rally the German people. In the final analysis, National Socialist propaganda and National Socialist principles proved to be one and the same. There can be little question but that Goebbels was very cynical with regards to the commitment of the German people to the war effort. They would respond to any message, stridently presented, with enthusiasm. Yet the message presented by Goebbels was *the* message of National Socialism, *viz.*, we are engaged in a racial war with international Jewry; either Aryan man or the international Jew must perish. At the same time, Goebbels thought it highly unlikely that his audience and, for that matter, the German people in general, was imbued with — to utilize a Rankean phrase — that particular 'spiritual energy' that would drive it on its own, to grasp those life principles embodied in the National Socialist movement. From now on, it was up to this movement, clinging assiduously to that in which it most strongly believed, to educate the German people to the point where it would willingly sacrifice itself for an ideology congruent with life itself.

Throughout the immediate post-Stalingrad period until the end of World War II, Goebbels, as did other Nazi leaders, continued to differentiate sharply between the National Socialist movement and those individuals and institutions who, through their deficiencies, demonstrated that they were not properly imbued with the National Socialist spirit. Naturally, events on the Eastern Front drew a fair amount of commentary. There, of all the units, German or Allied, i.e., Romanian, Italian, and Hungarian, the SS ones performed the best. This was so because of National Socialist indoctrination. 'Had we brought up the entire German *Wehrmacht* exactly as we did the SS formations, the struggle in the East would undoubtedly have taken a different course'.[119] The poor Duce, Goebbels opined, was in a terrible position overall. He had no units like the SS, only a monarchical army 'which of course is not equal to such a brutal war of ideologies'.[120] It is of interest to note that, even with the declaration of 'total war', the Führer adhered to certain fundamental views concerning, among other things, the natural role of women in the struggles to come. 'But even during total war', he remarked, 'one must not fight the women. Never yet has such a battle been won by any government. For women constitute a tremendous power and as soon as you dare to touch their beauty parlours they are all up in arms against you'.[121] Just how much this was indeed a 'war of ideologies', at least in Nazi eyes, was amply revealed in this remark.

At the same time, the National Socialist leadership sought to deprecate the idealism of so-called 'liberated' women, i.e., those ensconced in the Allied camp. American women in particular seemed unwilling to make those sacrifices which, hopefully their German counterparts were willing to make in the face of total war. In a *Völkischer Beobachter* article of 13 April 1944, a story that appeared in the *Philadelphia Inquirer* was reproduced at some length, accompanied, of course, by the expected ideologically-tinted exhortations to do better. American women appeared to manifest unpatriotic attitudes. They cheated on their ration cards and seemed to be completely unwilling to volunteer for nursing tasks and for war industries.[122] Feminine dishonesty and lack of idealism in America had been accompanied, as was to be expected, by a breakdown of family morality and a rise in juvenile delinquency.[123] With that total lack of humour often associated with Teutonic modes of idealism in any form, the *Völkischer Beobachter* went on to implicate the pathological influence of Frank Sinatra upon American women. Under such circumstances, it was no wonder that such women seemed to be unwilling to make necessary sacrifices.

It does not require a profound knowledge of psychology to determine that, in this article, the editors of the *Völkischer Boebachter* were projecting their own concerns regarding the dedication of German women onto their American counterparts. As several authors have pointed out, National Socialist attempts to rally women to the war effort — attempts which were to no small degree hobbled by persistent ideological qualms — met with what can be described as limited success.[124] At the same time, one can observe a none-too-subtle effort to wean German women away from those materialistic urges that Hitler himself saw as characteristic of women in general. Such use of awful example and implicit or explicit exhortation can be viewed as characteristic of any regime under stress. In the case of National Socialism, however, it represented an important development within the framework of the ideology. *Again*, recognising that calls for sacrifice and labour had always been an important part of the National Socialist message, we must once more point out that, under the stress of serious military reverses, it had become imperative that the National Socialist regime at times set itself apart from those whose very spirit it claimed to embody. It was its task to point out such things as lack of idealism showed by so-called 'liberated' American women, in the profound hope that a spiritual awakening would somehow be called forth in the ranks of the German people.

As we have seen with the uncomplimentary references to American women, German propaganda, which had always emphasised the barbarous character of Soviet Russia, with its 'Jewish liquidation commandos', tended, as Americans came to play an increasingly important part in the war, more and more to focus on what it perceived as negative aspects of the American character. Particularly after the Normandy landings on 6 June 1944, articles decrying the barbarous nature of the Americans became common. In the 14 July 1944 *Völkischer Beobachter*, for example, there was an essay in which 'character types' of American prisoners were described. 'There are outspokenly gangster types among them' the essay proclaimed.[125] A search of the pockets of American prisoners revealed switch-blade knives ('*Flammendolche*') and brass knuckles. These were the murderers who were fighting to 'free Europe'.[126] A similar article on much the same subject appeared two days later, and the issue of American barbarism, something which stemmed from the same Jewish source, of course, as Soviet barbarism, became a topic which enjoyed much popularity, at least in the columns of the *Völkischer Beobachter*. One of the most interesting, in this regard, was an article appearing in the 3 November 1944 issue of this newspaper entitled 'The Black Flood' ('Die schwarz Flut'). Here, it was maintained, one could see palpable evidence that Jews were using Negroes to destroy the white race. For some reason, CIO leader Sidney Hillman was singled out as being particularly nefarious in this respect. The American '*Mischkultur*' was in large measure the product of such '*Swing-Juden*' (!) as George Gerschwin and Irving Berlin.[127] Hypnotised by Negroid rhythms, the American public, through the strong Jewish influence, was exhibiting signs that 'negroid mass eroticism' was now socially acceptable.[128] Implicit in this article was the rhetorical point: Do you want Europe to be ruled by racial degeneracy? Once again, we can perceive that as the war situation grew ever worse, the Nazi leadership strove to educate the German people through emphasising not peripheral issues, but those elements which subsisted at the racial core of the ruling ideology. Throughout all of this, one gets the notion that the National Socialist leadership at times perceived itself as being in the position of the kindly schoolteacher who had been charged with the divine task of explicating certain fundamental principles to an increasingly restless class of schoolchildren.

As has been stated previously, the educative efforts described above in large measure resulted from the National Socialist movement's occasionally 'pulling away' from the German people, this being necessitated by certain radical turns in military fortunes. As we have noted, a *Weltanschauung* ultimately rooted in mystery and in a radical identification of spirit and nature — a corollary of which had to have been a pragmatic view of events as self-justifying — must have found itself in trouble as mundane life seemed no longer to conform to the 'laws of life'. In this context, it is most interesting to note that, as the 'real world' became ever more painful for Nazism, that aspect of the 'Hitler Cult' which always had emphasised the Führer's singularity became strengthened to the point that he was now often portrayed as being rather apart from the world, approximating that transcendental God of the Jews so despised by Nazi ideology.

As an example of this, we can consider the 20 April 1944 issue of *Das Schwarze Korps*. In a front-page birthday tribute entitled 'He is Victory!' ('Er ist der Sieg!'), it was acknowledged that 'the Führer seldom speaks to us. Too seldom.'[129] The article went on to state that, while it was often difficult to describe 'an immediate personal effect of his power over our hearts', he was still there, always working and thinking. Thus, any sacrifice demanded by Hitler was necessary even though he could not always experience what was going on in the lives of 'Grenadier Schulze or woman-worker Müller'.[130] Shades of the old-fashioned Judaeo-Christian father-figure God whose ways, while just, were 'often strange'! Significantly, the article declared that history would not ask whether *Feldherr* Adolf Hitler fought on the Volga or in the Carpathians, but whether he secured the 'victory of life' for his people, 'greatness and freedom' to the Reich, and a 'happy future' for Germany's children.[131] Here, we can see a major problem involved in bolstering Hitler's historical position. German forces might well have been driven from the Volga to the Carpathian Mountains. Hitler, as commander-in-chief of the German armed forces, was presumably responsible for their fortunes. Mundane military affairs, however, did not matter any more; what counted was whether or not *Feldherr* Adolf Hitler had secured the 'victory of life' for the German people.

What we can see here is a rejection of immanency altogether. 'Laws of life', the bearers of which represented the highest elements of the sanctified German nation, were now the preserve of a movement which, in transcendental fashion, went beyond this world. In a cruel war in which *material* success was being obtained on all fronts by the Allies, spirit and matter, so triumphantly brought together by numerous Nazi ideologists, were once again separated. For the German people, all that was left was a desperate belief in an increasingly remote *Führer*, the only vestige of National Socialism possessed of any reality.[132]

Naturally, most ideologues were not consistent in their rejection of that monism central to the National Socialist religion of nature. As we will see, Hitler himself made at least one statement in which he showed a rather strong degree of consistency in adhering to certain basic tenets of the National Socialist religion. Thus, though defeat loomed, high Nazis often attempted to reaffirm their loyalty to that identification of matter and spirit essential to the National Socialist *Weltanschauung*. As we have pointed out earlier, the strengthening of the 'Führer Cult' was a logical result of the bending of the National Socialist ideology under stress. On the same day as the SS honoured Hitler in their journal, 20 April 1944, an article by Alfred Rosenberg appeared in which he demonstrated that, as presumably chief ideologist of the National Socialist Party, he would continue to adhere to that old version of the Hitler Cult which emphasised the unity of Führer and people. In the titanic struggle now raging in Europe, Rosenberg maintained, the National Socialist *Weltanschauung* was being strengthened and steeled. This *Weltanschauung* was bound up with one personality, and 'act and idea, struggle and construction were continuously tied to the phenomenon of the Führer'.[133] In fact, that will to victory of 'front and homeland' was symbolised in Hitler.[134] Goebbels, in his 1944 Christmas speech to the German people, went even further. After praising the German people for bearing up so well under Allied air attacks and for being unified in their beliefs in the face of so many tests, he declared that 'The Führer is our pride and our hope'. He was 'our one and everything' and, 'he belongs to us as we belong to him, totally and completely, with body and soul'.[135] It might be of some importance to note that, at the time Goebbels was making this address, German troops were enjoying some material success, at least against the Americans in the West, where the Ardennes counterattack, which had begun on 16 December 1944, had not yet been fully contained.

With the eventual failure of the Ardennes counterattack, and the resumption of enemy advances on all fronts, the Führer disappeared to the myth-shrouded gloom of his bunker. Now, he truly became a transcendental spirit, removed from the continuous string of military disasters that were visited upon Germany from January 1945 until the end of the war. The man who, after the assassination attempt of 20 July 1944, had declared that he saw his survival as indicative of Providence's concern that he remain in power and complete his divinely-sanctioned tasks, was silent now, and, in Goebbels' last diary entries we can see the anguish of one who could no longer adhere to the heroic religious immanency embodied in the National Socialist *Weltanschauung*. From this point on, brave stances assumed by National Socialist propagandists, while reflecting, in many ways, beliefs central to the movement, had little to do with nagging personal doubts and bitter recriminations.

The army, Goebbels said, had failed because it had not become National Socialist. German generals, unlike their Soviet counterparts, had not become committed to an ideology. The army had to become National Socialist 'in outlook and bearing' if there were to be any possibility at all of sustained, much less successful, struggle.[136] The trouble with the army, Goebbels maintained, in considering the collapse of defences around Trier, was that it was not revolutionary enough. Röhm had been right in 1934, but he could not have been listened to, much less followed, because if his schemes had been acted upon, such actions would have been the doings of 'a homosexual and an anarchist'.[137] If Röhm had been a 'solid personality', 100 generals rather than 100 SA members would have been shot on 30 June 1934.[138] Here, we can clearly see that element which had become most prominent in body public and private National Socialist pronouncements ever since the beginning of the Russian campaign, *viz.*, the tendency to differentiate rather sharply between the National Socialist movement as the bearer of certain life-rooted ideals and other groups, most important of which was the army, which simply could not live up to these ideals. National Socialist education had been lacking — Goebbels himself had often deprecated it so long as soldiers and sailors were 'living' the ideology — and now the chickens had come home to roost. Now, the troops have 'infected the home front with their bad morale because they have not been brought up as National Socialist'.[139].

Goebbels, however, did not limit his criticism to the army, and to party failure to educate it. 'A fateful development seems to me to be that now neither the Führer in person nor the National Socialist concept nor the National Socialist movement is immune from criticism.'[140] A major source of the problem, according to Goebbels, was the 'bourgeois' character of so many in the movement. Here, in attacking Speer, Göring, and others, Goebbels seemed to be harking back to his pre-1925 'left-wing revolutionary National Socialist' period.[141] For Goebbels, the Führer himself, who 'correctly perceives what has happened . . . [but] seldom draws the right conclusions', had failed to provide that leadership commensurate with National Socialist goals.[142] The great leader of the German people who was supposed to be, none the less, a man of the people, had stopped speaking to those who were supposed to be dying for his regime. In desperation, Goebbels stated, he was continuously attempting to get the Führer to reverse his policy on this, citing the examples of Churchill and Stalin.[143] All efforts had been in vain. In a most revealing diary entry of 8 March 1945, Goebbels summed up what the National Socialist regime had to do — and had *failed* to do — in order to retain the confidence of the German people. ' . . . If National Socialism could once more present itself to the people as a pure ideology, freed from all manifestations of corruption and time-serving, it could still today turn out to be the great victorious ideology of our century'.[144]

Previously, Goebbels had been confident in the National Socialist movement as the bearer of an ideology rooted in life-forces. At the same time, as he once stated it, there had to be an ideology for 'home consumption.' Now, Goebbels' cynicism regarding the German people was being augmented if not replaced by a fundamental despair regarding the National Socialist movement itself. In a word, this movement was threatened with extinction because it was *not National Socialist enough.* Ideological purity had not been maintained and the harassed minister of propaganda did not exempt his Führer from this charge. The petty demands and overpowering temptations posed by mundane life had proved too much for a natural religion which supposedly both bore life and received its axiological charge from it. The National Socialist *Weltanschauung* was still valid, but the men who bore it had proved to be frail reeds. Similarly, that sanctified concept of 'the nation' remained pure, but the people who comprised it were too weak and too uneducated to grasp the religious ideals in terms of which the nation obtained its divinity.

Goebbels, as cynical as he often proved to be, hesitated, even in private, to declare that, in failing to live up to the rigorous standards posed by an ideology rooted in life, the German people deserved whatever fate attended it. He had hinted at such an attitude on several occasions — and perhaps he believed it — but, Goebbels had never baldly stated what had to have been the logical conclusion if he was to have adhered to the identification of matter and spirit central to the National Socialist *Weltanschauung*. According to Albert Speer, at least one person was willing to do so.

Around the middle of March 1945, Speer and Hitler talked about the economic future of a defeated and devastated Germany. Hitler's views on the matter were recapitulated in a letter sent by a troubled Speer some days later.

> From the statements you made that evening the following was une-quivocally apparent — if I did not misunderstand you: If the war is lost, the people will be lost also. It is not necessary to worry about what the German people will need for elemental survival. On the con-trary, it is best for us to destroy even these things. For the nation has proved to be the weaker, and the future belongs solely to the stronger eastern nation. In any case only those who are inferior will remain after this struggle, for the good have already been killed.

> These words shook me to the core. And a day later when I read the demolition order and, shortly afterward, the stringent evacuation order, I saw these as the first steps toward carrying out these inten-tions.[145]

For many Germans, the National Socialist movement and its ideology *were* Hitler. Now, with the nation going under, their leader revealed that, in at least one lucid moment, he grasped how a true believer in the identity of nature and spirit had to respond when the 'laws of life' dictated that people presumably ordained to manifest them in their highest form failed in its sacred task. Many people, Speer included, thought that Hitler's indifference to the fate of his people and his willingness to lay waste that portion of Germany not already blasted by Allied bombs and artillery, were signs of madness. In a psychogenetic sense, they might have been correct. From the viewpoint of a dedicated Nazi ideologist, however, Hitler was being perfectly consistent. Events had demonstrated that the National Socialist religion had *not* attained incarnation in the

German people. If it had, then this people would have been victorious on every front. The religion had proved to be too honestly stringent in the demands it had placed upon frail humanity. Despite desperate, last-minute efforts by Goebbels and Rosenberg, for once united in a common effort, to call attention to the absolute *necessity* of the German people's recognising that the fact that the Führer lived in them — a recognition which had to assure victory — this people had failed to do so. Thus, it had to die.

The National Socialist religion of nature, in its positing of an absolute identification of nature and spirit, had allowed for a radical subordination of all state institutions, knowledge, and high culture to it while, at the same time demanding that a petty-bourgeois social stasis, presumably commensurate with the 'state of nature' itself, be maintained. During periods of political and military success, the pragmatism inherent in this doctrine proved to be a most valuable ideational and propagandistic weapon — the 'natural' correctness of the National Socialist idea was demonstrated through the successes of those who bore it into battle. When the adherents to 'laws of life' began to be *overwhelmed* by life, however, the Nazi ideology, this extraordinarily powerful natural religion, had to devour itself and, in the end, there could only be nihilistic destruction. While there can be little doubt that Hitler's personal pathology had much to do with his orders that defeat-threatened Germany be razed, it is also true that in a situation in which life was devouring life, the nihilistic ravings of March 1945 could, at the very least, have received substantive ideological rationalisation. For a movement rooted in nature, there could be no appeal to any sort of higher authority for justification, and those individuals, who, with unbounded arrogance, had deprecated humanity in order that a mystery-grounded naturally-determined racial elite rule on earth for one thousand years, found themselves condemned by their own naturalism. For, in the final analysis, in a cruel world of nature, stripped of any sort of extrinsic teleology, simple material might must always prevail, and truth must necessarily be measured in casualties suffered and inflicted, indices of war-time production, and general fortunes of war.

This serves to explain a phenomenon described in some detail by Hannah Arendt. While talking about totalitarian movements as a whole — but necessarily focusing upon the Nazis in particular — she pointed out that, unlike religious fanatics, members of such movements do not hold to the faith in defeat. With the destruction of the mundane world of National Socialist 'realities' there could be no martyrs, at least in the traditional sense of the term.[146] In my opinion, Arendt too easily dismissed the religious elements of National Socialism. In this particular regard, however, her argument that the National Socialist permutation of totalitarianism was a '*pseudo*-religion', in the strongest sense of the term, would appear to be verifiable.

While the National Socialist *Weltanschauung*, by virtue of its devotion to principles of nature, had to have cut out the grounds for its own existence as defeat loomed for Germany, it did serve to provide the ideational substructure for Hitler's most successful campaign — the extermination of the Jews. Here, self-proclaimed authentic and natural men waged a victorious war against what they declared were unnatural enemies of life. It is to this war that we must now turn.

Notes

1. Leonard Schapiro, *Totalitarianism* (New York and London, Praeger, 1972), p. 26.
2. Ibid., p. 68.
3. Ibid., p. 71.
4. Hans Buchheim, *et al.*, *Anatomie des SS-Staate*, Band I, *Die SS-Das Herrschaftsinstrument Befehl Und Gehorsam* (München, Deutscher Taschenbuch Verlag, 1967), p. 16.
5. Ibid.
6. For Buchheim's discussion of the role of the Gestapo, see, Hans Buchheim, *Totalitarian Rule: Its Nature and Characteristics*, translated from the German by Ruth Heim (Middleton, Connecticut, Wesleyan University Press, 1968), p. 96. For his discussion on the role of the SS, see *Anatomie des SS-Staates*, Band I, *Die SS-Das Herrschaftsinstrument Befehl und Gehorsam*, p. 182.
7. Ernst Krieck, *Völkisch-Politische Anthropologie*, Band II, *Das Handeln und die Ordnungen* (Leipzig, 1937), pp. 64–5.
8. Ibid., pp. 72–3.
9. Adolf Hitler, *Mein Kampf* translated from the German by Ralph Manheim (Boston, Houghton Miflin, 1962), p. 391, emphasis is Hitler's.
10. Hermann Rauschning, *Hitler Speaks: A Series of Political Conversations with Adolf Hitler on his Real Aims* (London, Heinemann, 1939), p. 200.
11. Max Domarus, *Hitler: Reden und Proklamationen 1932–1945*, Band I, Zeiter Halbband 1934–1938 (München, Suddeutsche Verlag, 1965), p. 761. The 'polycentric' nature of the 'National Socialist State' is discussed in John Hidon and John Farquharson, *Explaining Hitler's Germany* (Totowa, New Jersey, Barnes and Noble, 1983), p. 69 and pp. 75–9.
12. Ibid., p. 525.
13. The description of Nazism as being an 'anti-Jewish revolution' is to be found in George L. Mosse, *The Crisis of German Ideology, Intellectual Origins of the Third Reich* (New York, Grosset and Dunlop, 1964).
14. Institut für Zeitgeschichte, *Schulungsbrief Nr. 5, NS Welstanschauung*, 15.12.44, reel no. MA 332, frame 9380476.
15. Ibid.
16. Buchheim, in volume one of *Anatomie des SS-Staates*, has a most interesting discussion of this. See in particular that on pp. 277–82.
17. Ernest Krieck, 'Charakter und Weltanschauung', Rede zum 30 January 1938, *Heidelberger Universitätsreden, Neue Folge*, Nr. 4 (Heidelberg, Carl Winter Verlag, 1938), p. 5.

18. Bernhard Rust, 'Das nationalsozialismus und Wissenchaft', *Das national sozialistische Deutschland und die Wissenschaft*, Heidelberger Reden von Reichsminister Rust and Prof. Ernst Krieck (Hamburg, Carl Winter Verlag, 1936), p. 22.

19. Ibid., p. 10-11. Emphasis is Rust's.

20. Ibid., p. 15-16.

21. Ibid., p. 19.

22. Institut für Zeitgeschichte, *Blick in Aufgabe und Arbeit des 'Amtes Rosenberg.'* *Weltanschauung und Wissenschaft*, reel no. MA 608, frame 55672.

23. Ibid., frame 55673

24. Heinz Wolff, 'Politik und Wissenschaft,' in *Völkischer Beobachter*, Münchener Ausgabe, Nr.25. 54.Jahrgang, 25 January 1941, S, 1.

25. Ludwick Fleck, *Genesis and Development of a Scientific Fact*, foreword by Thomas S. Kuhn, translated by Fred Bradley and Thadeus J. Trenn (Chicago, University of Chicago Press, 1979), p. 42.

26. Ernst Krieck, 'Die Erneuerung der Universität', *Frankfurter Akademische Reden*, Johann Wolfgang Goethe-Universitat (Frankfurt, n.p., 1933), p. 10.

27. Ibid.

28. Martin Heidegger, 'Die Selbstbehauptung der deutschen Universität'. *Rede gehalten bei der feierlichen Übernahme der Rektorats der Universität Freiburg am 27 May 1933*, Breslau, 1933, in Joachim Remak (ed.), *The Nazi Years: A Documentary History* (Englewood Cliffs, New Jersey, Prentice-Hall, 1969), pp. 58-9. For an interesting discussion of how Heidegger's variety of 'existentialism' could have led him to give initial support to National Socialism, see Hazel E. Barnes, *An Existentialist Ethics* (New York, Alfred Knopf, 1967), pp. 418-23.

29. Matthias Heinrich Göring, first cousin of Hermann Goering, was able to preserve a limited degree of freedom for psychological research and practice in his Göring Institute. Yet, there can be little doubt that Freudian psychoanalysis suffered greatly when compared to other forms of psychotherapy. See Geoffry Cocks, *The Göring Institut* (New York, Oxford University Press, 1984).

30. See Reece C. Kelly, 'Die gescheiterte nationalsozialistische Personalpolitik und die misslungene Entwicklung der nationalsozialistischen Hochschulen', in Manfred Heinemann (Hrsg.), *Erziehung und Schulung in Dritten Reich* Teil 2. *Hochschule, Erwachsenbildung* (Stuttgart, Klett-Cotta, 1980).

31. Robert A. Pois, *Friedrich Meinecke and German Politics in the Twentieth Century* (Berkeley and Los Angeles, University of California Press, 1972), pp. 121-3.

32. Nancy Stepan, *The Idea of Race in Science: Great Britain 1800-1960* (Hamden, Connecticut, Archon Press, 1982), pp. xx-xxi, 4, 144, 182.

33. Ibid. p. 189.

34. Probably the best treatment of Nazi art policy *per se* is still Hildegard Brenner *Die Kunstpolitik des Nationalsozialismus* (Hamburg, Rowohlt, 1963). On how this policy influenced works of art see Berthold Hinz, *Art in the Third Reich*, translated from the German by Robert and Rita Kimber (New York, Pantheon, 1979).

35. Kurt Karl Eberlein, 'Was ist deutsch in der deutschen Kunst?', in George L. Mossse (ed.) *Nazi Culture: Intellectual and Social Life in the Third Reich* (New York, Grosset and Dunlap, 1966), p. 165.

36. Ibid.

37. Adolf Dresler, *Deutsche Kunst und entartete 'Kunst': Kunstwerk und Zerrbild als Spiegel der Weltanschauung* (München, Deutschen Volksverlag, 1938), p. 6.

38. Ibid., pp 6-7.

39. Paul Schulze-Naumburg, *Kunst aus Blut und Boden* (Leipzig, Verlag E. A. Seeman, 1934), p. 37.

40. Ibid., pp. 34, 42.

41. Ibid., p. 47.

42. Paul Josef Goebbels, Unititled Article, in Mosse, *Nazi Culture*, p. 162.

43. Alfred Rosenberg, *Selected Writings*, Robert Pois, (ed.) (Jonathan Cape, London, 1970), p. 161. Emphasis is Rosenberg's.

44. Dresler, *Deutsche Kunst*, pp. 29-30.

45. Paul Josef Goebbels, *Goebbels-Reden* Band I: 1932-1939, herausgegeben von Helmut Heiber (Düsseldorf, Droste Verlag, 1971), p. 134.

46. Ibid., p. 219.

47. Ibid., p. 222. For an interesting analysis of how aesthetics became involved in a major 'political' concern, that of production and working conditions, see Anson G. Rabinbach, 'The Aesthetics of Production in the Third Reich' in *Journal of Contemporary History*, 1976, *17*, no. 4.

48. Domarus, *Hitler*, p. 709.

49. Ibid.

50. Hitler, *Secret Conversations*, 1941-1944, with an introductory essay on the *Mind of Adolf Hitler* by H. R. Trevor-Roper, translated from the German by Norman Cameron and R. H. Sterns (New York, Farrar, Straus and Young, 1953), Conversation of 29 July 1942, p. 489.

51. Sybil Milton, 'Artists in the Third Reich' in Henry Friedlander and Sybil Milton (eds.), *The Holocaust: Ideology, Bureaucracy and Genocide* (Millwood, New York, Kraus–International Publications, 1980), p. 116. Those close to Hitler knew of his fascination with the morbidly sensual works of Franz von Stuck. Understandably, psycohistorians have made much of this. See Robert G. Waite, *The Psychopathic God, Adolf Hitler* (New York, Basic Books, 1977).

52. Dresler, *Deutsche Kunst*, pp. 8-9.

53. Milton, 'Artists in the Third Reich', in Friedlander and Milton, *The Holocaust*, p. 118.

54. Nolde's involvement with National Socialism and the psychological sources for it are considered at length in Robert Pois. *Emil Nolde* (Lanham, Maryland University Press of America, 1982).

55. Fritz Kaiser (Hrsg.) *Entartete 'Kunst', Führer durch die Ausstellung* (Berlin, Kaiser, 1937), p. 22.

56. Ibid. Emphasis is Kaiser's.

57. Domarus, *Hitler*, p. 877.

58. Ibid.

59. Ibid. p. 878.

60. Herbert Read, *The Philosophy of Modern Art* (New York, Meridian Books, 1959), p. 113.

61. See, for example, Hellmut Lehmann-Haupt, *Art Under a Dictatorship* (New York, Octagon Books, 1973). Also Martin Damus, *Sozialistischer Realismus und Kunst im Nationalsozialismus* (Frankfurt/M, Suddeutsche Verlag, 1981).

62. *Deutsche Kunstler und die SS* (Berlin, n.p., 1941), no page.

63. Franz Rodens, *Vom Wesen Deutschen Kunst* (Berlin, Franz Eher Verlag, 1941), p. 54.

64. *Deutsche Kunstler*, Nr. 17.

65. Martin Damus, *Sozialistischer Realismus*, p. 9.

66. *NSDAP Standartenkalender*, 1937 (München, Franz Eher Verlag, 1937), p. 81.

67. The best descriptions of this are still to be found in David Schoenbaum, *Hitler's Social Revolution: Class and Status in Nazi Germany, 1933-1939* (New York, Anchor Books, 1967).

68. Domarus, *Hitler*, p. 642.

69. Alfred Rosenberg, 'Frau und Mutter — Lebensquell des Volkes', in *Völkischer Beobachter*, Norddeutsche Ausgabe, Nr.224, 52.Jahrgang, 12 August 1939, S. 5.

70. Wilhelm Frick, 'Unser erster Gruss gilt den Müttern', in *Völkischer Beobachter*, Norddeutsche Ausgabe, Nr.139, 54.Jahrgang, 19 Mai 1941, S. 2.

71. Ibid.

72. Leila J. Rupp, *Mobilizing Women for War. German and American Propaganda. 1934-1945* (Princeton, New Jersey, Princeton University Press, 1978), pp. 45-6.

73. The drawing power exercised by the National Socialist ideology upon middle class women in particular is one of the major themes of Jill Stephenson, *The Nazi Organization of Women* (London, Croom Helm; New York, Barnes and Noble, 1981).

74. On the failure of the Weimar Republic to provide for truly meaningful change for women see Renate Bridenthal and Claudia Koonz 'Beyond *Kinder, Küche, Kirche*: Weimar Women in Politics and Work,' in Berenice A. Carroll, (ed.) *Liberating Women's History: Theoretical and Critical Essays* (Urbana, Illinois, University of Illinois Press, 1976).

75. An excellent description of the clash between Himmler's 'Utopian' views of racial improvement and his basically bourgeois approach to morality is provided by Larry V. Thompson, '*Lebensborn* and the Eugenics policy of the *Reichsführer SS*' in *Central European History*, 1971, IV, no. 1 (March).

76. Felix Kersten, *The Kersten Memoirs 1940-1945*, introduction by H. R. Trevor Roper, translated from the German by Constantine Fitzgibbon and James Oliver (New York, Macmillan, 1957), pp. 75-6.

77. Thompson, 'Lebensborn', p. 76-7.

78. Jill Stephenson, *Women in Nazi Society* (New York, Barnes and Noble, 1975), pp. 186-7.

79. Claudia Koonz, 'Mothers in the Fatherland: Women in Nazi Germany', in Renate Bridenthal and Claudia Koonz (eds.), *Becoming Visible: Women in European History* (Boston, Houghton Miflin, 1977), p. 471.

80. Gerda Lerner, 'Placing Women in History: A 1975 Perspective', in Carroll, *Liberating Women's History*, pp. 363-4.

81. *NSDAP Standartenskalender*, 1937, p. 37.

82. Goebbels, *Reden*, p. 273. Emphasis is Goebbels'.

83. Ibid. p. 274.

84. Cajus Fabricius, *Positive Christianity in the Third Reich* (Dresden, H. Püschel, 1937), p. 70.

85. Ibid., p. 8.

86. Paul Josef Goebbels, *The Goebbels Diaries 1939-1941*, foreword by John Keegan, translated and edited by Fred Taylor (New York, Penguin Books, 1984), p. 304.

87. 'Das Parteiprogramme', in *Völkischer Beobachter*, Suddeutsche Aufgabe, Nr.56, 54.Jahrgang, 25 February 1941, S.2.

88. Ibid.

89. An excellent description of Dietl's inspired defence of Narvik is to be found in Telford Taylor, *The March of Conquest, The German Victories in Western Europe, 1940* (New York, Simon and Schuster, 1958), pp. 128-9, 138-48.

90. Jay Baird, *The Mythical World of Nazi War Propaganda, 1939-1945* (Minneapolis, University of Minnesota Press, 1974), pp. 81-2.

91. For a good discussion of these actions see Taylor, *The March of Conquest*, pp. 210-14. The fall of Fort Eben Emael was responsible for the rapid retirement of the Belgian army from its first line of defence. While this army was able to rally and to put up a reasonably decent fight, it never fully recovered from the near rout occasioned by the fall of its most modern fortress.

92. Baird, *The Mythical World*, p. 95-6.

93. Theodor Seibert, 'Der Sowjetmensch', in *Völkischer Beobachter*, Norddeutsche Ausgabe, Nr.200, 54.Jahrgang, 19 Juli 1941, S.1.

94. Ibid., S.2.

95. Viktor Lutze, 'Idealismus,' in *Völkischer Beobachter*, Norddeutsche Ausgabe, Nr.222, 54.Jahrgang, 10 August 1941, S.1. Emphasis is Lutze's.

96. Gunter d'Alquen, 'Die germanischen Kameraden', in *Völkischer Beobachter*, Norddeutsche Ausgabe, Nr.246, 54.Jahrgang, 3 September 1941, S.6.

97. Wolfgang Willrich, *Des Reiches Soldaten* (Berlin, Verlag Grenze und Ausland,

1943), p. 9.
  98. Ibid, p. 18.
  99. Walther Tröge, *Feuer und Farbe: 155 Bilder vom Kriege* (Wien, Wilhelm Frick Verlag, 1943), no page number.
  100. Adolf Hitler, 'Der Dank des Führer an Front und Heimat,' in *Völkischer Beobachter*, Norddeutsche Ausgabe, Nr.278, 54 Jahrgang, 5 Oktober 1941, S.4 Emphasis is Hitler's.
  101. Ibid. Emphasis is Hitler's.
  102. Ibid. Emphasis is Hitler's.
  103. Paul Josef Goebbels, *The Goebbels Diaries, 1942–1943*, edited and translated by Louis P. Lochner (New York, London, Hamish Hamilton, 1948), pp. 10–11.
  104. Ibid., p. 105.
  105. Ibid., p. 64.
  106. Ibid., p. 65.
  107. Goebbels-*Reden*, Band II., 1940–1945, p. 107.
  108. Ibid., p. 108.
  109. Ibid.
  110. Baird, *The Mythical World*, p. 177.
  111. Ibid., p. 195–6.
  112. Goebbels-*Reden*, p. 178. Emphasis is Goebbels'.
  113. Ibid., p. 180. Emphasis is Goebbels'.
  114. Ibid., p. 183. Emphasis is Goebbels'.
  115. Ibid., p. 184.
  116. Ibid., p. 203. Emphasis is Goebbels'.
  117. Ibid., p. 205.
  118. Ibid., p. 208, fn. 99.
  119. Goebbels, *Diaries*, entry for 8 May 1943, pp. 278–9.
  120. Ibid., p. 279.
  121. Ibid., entry for 10 May 1943, p. 288.
  122. 'Mrs. Babbitt Versagt . . . Amerikas Frauen und Roosevelts Krieg', in *Völkischer Beobachter*, Norddeutsche Ausgabe, Nr.104, 57.Jahrgang, 13 April 1944, S.3.
  123. Ibid.
  124. Rupp, *Mobilizing Women*, p. 188 ff, 136, Appendix; Stephenson, *Women in Nazi Society*, pp. 186–8.
  125. Untitled essay in *Völkischer Beobachter*, Norddeutsche Ausgabe, Nr.196, 57.Jahrgang, 14 Juli 1944, S.6.
  126. Ibid.
  127. Dr. Dietrich Ahrens, 'Die schwarze Flut', in *Völkischer Beobachter*, Norddeutsche Ausgabe, Nr.301, 57.Jahrgang, 3 November 1944, S.4.
  128. Ibid.
  129. 'Er ist der Sieg!', in *Das Schwarze Korp*, 16. Folge, 10. Jahrgang, 20 April 1944, S.1., in Helmut Heiber Hildegard von Kotze, *Facsimile Querschnitt durch Das Schwarze Korps*, (München, Scherz, 1968), p. 196.
  130. Ibid., pp. 196–7.
  131. Ibid., p. 197.
  132. This theme is discussed throughout Ian Kershaw, *Der Hitler-Mythos: Volksmeinung und Propaganda im Dritten Reich* (Stuttgart, Deutsche Verlagsanstalt, 1980). According to the author, the most crucial element in the '*Mythos*,' was the identification of Hitler with national rebirth (p. 63). The 'Hitler Mythos' was generally impervious to challenge until late 1942–early 1943, roughly just before, during and after the Stalingrad disaster, (p. 150).
  133. Alfred Rosenberg, 'In tiefer Verehrung', in *Völkischer Beobachter*, Norddeutsche Ausgabe, Nr.111, 57.Jahrgang, 20 April 1944, S.1.
  134. Ibid., S.2.

135. Paul Josef Goebbels, 'Weihnachten-Fest der starken Herzen', in *Völkischer Beobachter*, Norddeutsche Ausgabe, Nr. 346/347, 57.Jahrgang, 26/27 Dezember, 1944, S.2.

136. Paul Josef Goebbels, *Final Entries 1945*, edited, introduced, and annotated by Professor Hugh Trevor-Roper; translated from the German by Richard Barry (New York, Putnam, 1978), entry for 15 March 1945, p. 146.

137. Ibid., entry for 27 March 1945, p. 248.

138. Ibid.

139. Ibid., p. 247.

140. Ibid.

141. Ibid., pp. 250–1.

142. Ibid., p. 247.

143. Ibid., p. 253.

144. Ibid., p. 79.

145. Albert Speer, *Inside the Third Reich: Memoirs*, translated from the German by Richard and Clara Winston (New York, Macmillan, 1970), p. 440.

146. Hannah Arendt, *The Origins of Totalitarianism*, (New York, Harcourt, Brace, Jovanovich, 1973), pp. 363–4.

5 THE NATURAL, AUTHENTIC MAN AND THE ROAD TO AUSCHWITZ

For Hitler, the National Socialist movement drew its strength 'from a complete and comprehensive recognition of the essential nature of life'.[1] What was of ultimate, indeed chiliastic, significance was the emergence of a new man, one totally in keeping with the laws of nature. 'The new man is among us', Hitler proclaimed in 1934. 'He is here! I will tell you a secret. I have seen the vision of the new man — fearless and formidable. I shrank from him.'[2]

As one might imagine, occultist panderers to the perplexed have made a great deal of these lines. Accepting the fact that the career of the man makes actual contact with the devil a moot point, we must recognise that Hitler was sincerely convinced that he was offering people, or at least Aryan people, a radically new approach to life, something which must be described as a new religion. As we have seen, it was grounded in a fundamental rebellion against the hoary Judaeo-Christian dichotomy between man/God and nature. As could be expected, the Hitlerian emphasis upon the 'natural man' found wide resonance among the party faithful. Of prominence here, as we have seen, was the notion that the National Socialist movement was itself rooted in a basic understanding of certain natural laws. In this regard, it is of interest to note that, in a 1936 address, the once liberal, now convinced Nazi philosopher and educator Ernst Krieck, could declare that contradiction between the sciences and the goals of the National Socialist state was precluded because these 'have been built up from practical knowledge of the . . . laws of nature and history'.[3]

The Nazi claim to have grasped the concept of life 'in its total width and depth' allowed National Socialists to declare openly that their movement was rooted in and, through grasping its essence, was the highest moment of, a unified *life*, in which nothing could be perceived as dead, or even inorganic. 'There is no inorganic nature, there is no dead, mechanical earth', Ernst Krieck enthused. 'The great mother has been won back to life.'[4] In grasping life in its totality, the National Socialists naturally had grasped the 'whole man' as well. Traditional Judaeo-Christian conceptions of man, which had fragmented him between body and spirit, were to be overthrown and some National Socialist ideologues even spoke of a new National Socialist medicine — quite homeopathic

117

in nature, it would appear — which would treat the 'whole man'.[5] At the same time of course, the 'whole man' could become such only within the 'life-whole' of the *Volksgemeinschaft*, where falsely assumed gaps between nature and spirit could be bridged.[6]

The goal of the National Socialist movement was the creation of a new human type, the natural man before whom Hitler said he shrank. This was a being who was totally in harmony with a natural world of which he, through understanding its totality, was the highest expression. It is hardly overstating the case to point out that, whether or not, in his heart of hearts, he really thought that he was such a man/god, and, as we have seen, he claimed that he did not, Hitler was viewed as providing at least a model or prototype for the sort of 'natural man' being conscientiously and seriously cultivated in Himmler's SS.

In this extraordinary being, several of the most crucial elements of the National Socialist religion came together. This creature was immortal; not, of course, in the traditional, Judaeo-Christian sense, but because of his or her (usually *his*, one gets the feeling) participation in the life of a race which not only lived in perfect harmony with eternal natural laws, but *embodied* these laws. As we have seen, Himmler had faith in a sort of 'race-karma', and his beliefs in reincarnation obviously were of a piece with these. Certainly, he was somewhat singular in his adherence to mystical forms. Yet his own version of immortality was merely a somewhat more exotic permutation of the, literally, 'death-defying' credo of the National Socialist religion, a credo of which the 'fearless new man' was to be the ultimate expression. Of course, as indicated earlier, this existed in sharp counterpoint to the very real morbidity of the leading figures in the movement; something which bordered on necrophilia, and which found expression in the actual symbol of the SS itself. The other element central to National Socialist religiosity, anti-transcendence, was also central to the vision of the 'new man.' Obviously, if this being not only lived in accordance with natural laws, i.e., the 'laws of life', but was their embodiment as well, he or she not only lived in a sort of sublime stasis, but had to make certain that the rest of life was brought into conformity with its underlying, unchanging laws. After all, to live in accordance with these laws, to be, in effect, their embodiment, essentially meant living outside history.

This 'new man' or totally 'natural man', needed no extensive justification. He justified himself by virtue of his very existence. Out of this there emerged the notion of National Socialist 'authenticity' (this was a concept which could be found among Fascists in general, but we will be focusing exclusively on National Socialism). It is here where what

J. P. Stern called the politics of '*Erlebnis*' came into play. Hitler was able

> to translate the notions of genuineness and sincerity and living experience (designated in German by the word 'Erlebnis' and its various compounds) from the private and poetic sphere into the sphere of public affairs and to validate this move by the claim that he, the exceptional individual with his intimate personal experience of 'the little man's weal and woe', is the Nation's representative by virtue of the genuineness of that experience.[7]

Throughout one chapter, Stern continually emphasised the role of authenticity in Hitler's appeal to the nation, at times suggesting that it served the function of actually substituting for a 'consistent ideology' while it served a 'pseudo-religious' purpose.[8] In a very real sense, the author implied, there was a variety of existentialism at work here, in which 'authenticity, commitment and what, for want of a better word, we may call personal truth' had usurped traditional political values that previously could be analysed in public, more-or-less 'objective' terms.[9]

It is perhaps parenthetical to our discussion, but, with regards to Nazi emphasis upon authenticity, the issue arises of the obvious link between Adolf Hitler (or any of his chosen minions) as the 'authentic man' and Nazi ritualism. In her above-cited work, Mary Douglas posed the ritualism of established religious and social systems against that 'exaltation of the inner experience' which emerges whenever such systems are challenged.[10] Here she made a most instructive point, something with which Stern could only agree, that, for those in rebellion against established socio-religious forms (and, of course, attendant ritualistic patterns), what matters is 'a man's inner convictions'.[11] Clever or smooth use of language is to be distrusted and, indeed, 'incoherence is taken for a sign of authenticity'.[12] Of course, the author points out, those who rebel against established ritual, whether they know it or not, will establish ritualistic patterns of their own, 'ritualisms of enthusiasm' as she referred to them.[13] With regard to National Socialism, it is obvious that its 'natural' (that is to say, *secular*) religion allowed for authenticity to find immediate and *self-conscious* expression in a carefully contrived pattern of ritualism. What Stern described in his own work was a truly extraordinary utilisation of the notion of authenticity in which ritualism defined itself *in terms of* the inner experience. At the same time, the latter avoided solipsism through expression in forms pregnant with existential content. Perhaps, one could maintain that, in providing a doctrine in which transcendental concerns were irrelevant or superfluous, the Nazis, through their self-justifying 'authentic' religion of nature, in fact *alleviated* ritualism through infusing ritual and symbol with that authenticity which was *ipso facto* inner experience.

In any case, Professor Stern has touched upon an issue that is of crucial importance in understanding the nature of National Socialism. While there might well be very good reasons for bringing in the question of existentialism's role in the emergence of National Socialism's concepts of authenticity — particularly inasmuch as Martin Heidegger had found it initially quite easy to reconcile his variety of existentialism with Nazi goals — it is the feeling of this author that the emphasis upon authenticity came directly out of the Nazi natural religion. Through the Nazi merging of nature and spirit — the aforementioned '*Alles ist Leben*' concept is of central importance here — there could be no question but that all acts undertaken by Hitler in particular and the National Socialist leadership is general *had* to be *essentially* authentic. It would be a violation of natural laws even to suggest that they could be false. All National Socialist actions, from the invasion of Poland to the extermination of the Jews, and finally, to Hitler's orders to Speer that all of Germany be razed so that nothing of value could survive her collapse (presumably according to the National Socialist ideology, nothing of value would have been left anyway, since Germany had been defeated), were endowed with authenticity through virtue of their having occurred in the first place. To *deny* their authenticity would have been tantamount ot denying the validity of the laws of thermodynamics. The person who lives in harmony with, or better, *embodies* the laws of nature (and, in the end, these have to be one and the same), is authentic and, necessarily, all of his actions must be as well.

It was in large measure the National Socialist claim to authenticity that seemed to fascinate C. G. Jung. In his famous 'Wotan' essay of 1936, one in which he stated that a natural demiurge in the symbolic form of Wotan was confronting a rather superficial Christianity in Germany, he made the following engaging statement:

> We thus pay our silent tribute to the Germanic time of storm and stress, but, we never mention it, which makes us feel superior. Yet it is the German who has the best chance to learn, in fact he has an opportunity which is perhaps unique in history. He is expressing the perils of the soul from which Christianity tried to rescue mankind, and he can learn to realize the nature of these perils in his own innermost heart.[14]

Here Jung was not suggesting that he was about to lend unqualified support to the National Socialist movement. Rather, he was stating that, because of the awesome issues involved in the confrontation between National Socialism — 'Wotan', if you wish — and Christianity, the Germans who were enduring this confrontation were somehow more authentic, more attuned to certain perils in their 'innermost heart[s]'. It is difficult to tell, at this point, just what Jung means by 'perils', i.e., whether one was to view them positively or negatively. As is so often the case, unfortunately, his tortured mysticism is opaque enough to virtually obscure what he had in mind. One thing is certain however: Jung viewed the National Socialist phenomenon as representing an outburst of psychic authenticity, one that somehow elevated the Germanic people above their more jaded neighbours. National Socialism might well have been persecuting Jews, and Christians, for that matter. In his 'Wotan' essay, Jung was quite straightforward in acknowledging that.[15] He made no judgment on this however, and the reader cannot help but feel that, at least in 1936, such issues were not very important for him. In any case, what really seemed to matter for Jung was the authentic spirituality that National Socialism seemed to have aroused in the German people, a spirituality that, in the end, might dictate that 'Wotan' overthrow Christ, albeit perhaps temporarily.

Authenticity could be observed as being expressed in the mysticism of the deed, something that had to have been a logical corollary of the National Socialist natural religion. It is here, perhaps, that one can consider the point raised by J. P. Stern, *viz.*, that National Socialism represented a crude variety of existentialism. In a situation in which spirit and matter are viewed as one, *without* the guiding force of an Hegelian-variety teleology, those presumably rooted in 'laws of life' had to be judged according to their actions, i.e., the degree to which their actions conformed to those principles discovered by the National Socialist leadership. Presumably, the latter, as pointed out above, were *always* authentic by virtue of being what they were. This enabled the leadership to proffer a new variety of 'socialism,' presumably to demonstrate that the term 'National Socialism' had not been partially drained of meaning through primary emphasis upon racial policies. Thus, in a speech of 19 November 1938, Goebbels declared that the 'socialism' of National Socialist Germany was not one of theory and programs, but 'clear, realistic socialist *action*'.[16] Accomplishments, not theories, defined the character of this socialism. The same theme is discernable in Goebbels' 10 October 1939 speech concerned with the National Socialistic *Winterhilfe* campaign. *Winterhilfe* achievements 'were demonstrative signs of the social solidarity of our German people', he proclaimed. This was true socialism, socialism of the deed.[17]

Informing this approach to socialism, one which obviously had strong pragmatic overtones, was the National Socialist claim upon authenticity. What was authentic was National Socialist action; unauthentic was anything that ran counter to it. In a speech of 3 October 1944, to the leaders of *Gaue* Köln-Aachen, Goebbels, obviously under somewhat of a strain, came down especially hard upon the notion that National Socialism lived through deeds, through action.[18] Here, he made the interesting observation that the Soviets did not collapse before Moscow in December 1941 because they *thought* that they could hold out; on the other hand, because the Germans did not think that they could fight there in such cold, they fled.[19] Parenthetically, one is tempted to ask if Goebbels was suggesting that the Soviets be made honorary National Socialists. As was to be expected, wartime stresses had compelled him to emphasise the relationship between the National Socialist ideology, authentic to the core, and those actions which, if successful, were the ideology in action. Failure, such as that before Moscow in 1941, could only be testimony to an unauthenticity that ran counter to National Socialism. In any case, one must note that the *Gaue* representatives addressed on 3 October 1944, must have been unauthentic in the end because Aachen fell to the American First Army on 21 October 1944. Thus, those aspects of the Nazi religion of nature which emphasised authenticity ran into the same problems as those aspects which emphasised the identification of nature and spirit.

This speech was, however, written in 1944, at a time in which a *Weltanschauung* which emphasised the authenticity of all actions rooted in this radical identification of spirit and nature — a corollary of which, as we have seen, had to have been a crudely pragmatic view of events as self-justifying — must have found itself in trouble. During the salad years of National Socialism's coming to power and the triumphs which followed this, the *political* and *social* power of such a *Weltanschauung* was extraordinary. More important, though, is the fact that the Nazi concern with unleashing or creating the 'natural, authentic man' was rooted in certain fundamental and thoroughly understandable (if not always rational) human desires. The wish to live in close harmony with nature (to live authentically) and revulsion against the admittedly often alienating life-patterns of urban existence — these are phenomena extant throughout a Western world increasingly uncomfortable with the problems attendant upon first mechanised, and now automated, societies. Taken but slightly out of context, many of the statements of Nazis quoted in this work would be applauded by the average, somewhat unreflective, environmentalist. Before too many parallels can be drawn between Nazi and more contemporary concerns with the natural man, a substantive, and perhaps decisive, difference must be pointed out, *viz.*, that the National Socialists chose to view at least one group of people, the Jews, as at best existing at a level of nature so low as to be comparable with disease-bearing germs, or even as being essentially *outside* of nature.

Here we do have occasional variations in the Nazi *Weltanschauung*. Two hundred years of cultural and social conditioning and more recent economic developments had in large measure determined who the enemy of 'natural man' would be. There was little argument about that. Most Nazis, however, chose to include the Jew within the realm of nature, albeit at the very low level described above, while others sought to banish the Jew altogether from the natural world. As an example of the first approach, we can consider a 22 April 1936 article published by Himmler in *SS Leitheft*, 'Why will there be Training about the Jewish problem?' ('Warum wird über das Judenproblem geschult?') 'The Jew', Himmler declared, 'is a parasite which, like the parasites of the animals and plant world, lives from the strengths and productive labour of host peoples. The Jew is the blood-sucker of the world.'[20] The same viewpoint was expressed by Goebbels in a 15 November 1938 article in the *Völkischer Beobachter*, where he attempted to explain to Reuters correspondents the rationale for post-*Kristalnacht* anti-Jewish measures. Germans, he said, were mainly interested in getting the Jews out of the country. A population of 80 million was rebelling against the provocations of 600,000 Jews. This was not civil war[!], Goebbels declared, 'but a people's reckoning with its parasites'.[21] Walter Darré, Reich Peasant Leader and, until 1942, minister of agriculture, provided an ingenuous rural application of this concept in his explaining why the unwholesome Jewish race had been able to flourish on good German soil. Even the best soil, he pointed out, can support weeds (*Unkraut*), and the conscientious farmer had to weed his fields in order to take care of this problem. Thus, 'in the peasant sense', the Jewish laws served this purpose in that they 'free us from the weeds of Jewish blood'.[22] The agricultural expert might well have been engaging in word-play here, because *Unkraut* can also mean parasites when the word is applied to humans.

A very common image of the Jew was that of being a disease. Uses of this image were legion; a few examples will suffice. The 22 December 1941 issue of the *Völkischer Beobachter* contained a speech given by Alfred Rosenberg on the occasion of the 50th anniversary of the death of the nineteenth century Geman racist Paul de Lagarde. He praised Lagarde for combatting Jewish emancipation and for recognising that Jews had only a negative role to play in Germany. With approval, he quoted his famous statement: 'One does not negotiate with trichina and bacillus . . . They will be annihilated as quickly and as thoroughly as possible.'[23] This opinion would no doubt have met with the approval of Supreme Party Judge Walther Buch, who made the following observation:

> The Jew is not a human being. He is an appearance of putrescence. Just as the fission-fungus cannot permeate wood until it is rotting, so the Jew was able to creep into the German people, to bring on disaster, only after the German nation, weakened by the loss of blood in the Thirty Years' War, had begun to rot from within.[24]

Hitler himself while, as we shall see, at times tending to exclude the Jews from the world of nature altogether, also utilised the disease concept.

> The discovery of the Jewish virus is one of the greatests revolutions that have taken place in the world. The battle in which we are engaged today is of the same sort as the battle waged during the last century by Pasteur and Koch. How many diseases have their origin in the Jewish virus![25]

On at least two occasions, Hitler excoriated those German bourgeois who expressed dismay at the expelling of Jews and the sending of them to the east. Jews, he said, had 'accomplices all over the world' and could adapt to any place, any climate. 'Jews can prosper anywhere, even in Lapland and Siberia.'[26] The bourgeoisie did not realise that the 'Jew is a parasite and as such is the only human being capable of adapting himself to any climate and of earning a living just as well in Lapland as in the tropics'.[27] In Hitler's comments in particular, one can notice what Lucy Davidowicz has called two contradictory images of the Jew. He was at once vermin and a 'mythic omnipotent super-adversary' against whom war was necessary.[28] The images are not contradictory if we bear in mind that the Jews were being placed within the context of a natural world of which Aryan man, as apotheosised in the National Socialist movement, was the highest possible expression.

The Jewish enemy here had been included in the world of nature, but at so low a level as to preclude his positive participation in the sanctified activities of those men able to live in conscious harmony with the laws of life. Indeed, as we have seen, this enemy of natural man was perceived as being part of the natural only as a disease or parasite might be, i.e., as some sort of negative regulating mechanism. Such a being could also serve to pervert normal, healthy instincts. Darré, as did so many other Nazi ideologues, looked longingly to the German past. In this case, he discovered that the ancient, pre-Christian Germans were unashamed of nakedness. This was all to the good, Darré maintained. People should be uninhibited and proud of their naked bodies. However, Christianity brought in a sense of shame, while the materialistic Jews made life sexual and shameful. Nakedness, used in an exploitative manner, became part of the work of Jewish decomposition. 'Jewish desecration of German women corresponded to the witch-persecutions of the Church; both have a common spiritual father — Jahwe!'[29] Here the Jew, functioning at the very lowest level of life, had been linked to a God divorced from nature and devoid of life. Thus, in the *Alles ist Leben* world view of the Nazis, there were two realms: (1) a higher, nobler one, in which men lived in honest harmony with nature and themselves, and (2) a lower (or just low) realm, inhabited by parasites, human and otherwise.

In their pantheistic *Lebensphilosophie*, described in the first portion of this study, the Nazis had sought to infuse a, to them, secularised and disenchanted world (to use Dr. Richard Rubenstein's expressions) with a new sense of mystery and enchantment. The elevation of nature to the position of divinity, and the setting apart of a portion of humanity as being, at least partially more natural than others, allowed genuine nature mystics to pursue the most ruthless of policies in dealing with beings of a low order. Hence, sensitive souls like Himmler, for whom every aspect of the natural world throbbed with sacred mystery, could pursue a policy very much in keeping with the coldest and yet 'fairest' of natural laws: that the weak or degenerate must perish. As Rubenstein has pointed out, 'In nature men have the same rights as flies, mosquitoes or beasts of prey.'[30] As opposed to 'an urban civilisation developed from Jewish liberalism', the Nazis posited a remystified world whose eternal tensions and rhythms pulsed in the veins of the chosen.[31] Nature herself, acting through the agencies of those living in harmony with her, would defend this world by purging it of the unclean.

As indicated above, there were some who chose to place the Jew outside the natural realm altogether. Probably the most straightforward, to say nothing of being the most important, of these individuals was Hitler himself. In *Mein Kampf*, he made the following comment regarding Jews: 'Their whole existence is an embodied protest against the aesthetics of the Lord's image.'[32] Here, of course, Hitler was stating that the Jews, so hideous in appearance as to preclude their being made in God's image, were not really human, a point which had been underscored in the posing of 'Aryan art' against 'Degenerate Art' in 1937. Implicit in this was the idea that what was not 'human' could not be natural. In an extraordinary 1934 conversation with Herman Rauschning, Hitler carried this further. The Jew, he declared, was part of the world of Satan. 'The Jew', he said 'is the anti-man, the creature of another god. He must have come from another root of the human race.' The Jew and the Aryan were thus set one against the other. Since the Aryan was called 'human being', the Jew had to be given some sort of name. 'The two are as widely separated as man and beast. Not that I would call the Jew a beast. He is much further from the beasts than we Aryans. He is a creature outside nature and alien to nature.'[33] In a very real sense, Hitler was being rather more consistent than many of his followers. We have seen the 'natural man' as this being was conceived of by major Nazi ideologues, Hitler included. The opponents of so noble a creature worshipped an alien god, one divorced from life. Jahwe was the god of the wasteland, ideally suited for people who were utterly divorced from the natural world; for people who, during the course of history, had become increasingly identified with the lifeless, soulless, city. For reasons known only to divine nature, these people had been given approximately human form. Since they were divorced from life-giving nature, however, and hence from the laws of life itself, it was only this *form*, this external husk that allowed one to call them 'human'.

There can be little doubt that, while most Nazis usually 'allowed' the Jew to participate in nature at the lowest possible level, the image of the Jew as utterly *alien* to nature also entered into the picture from time to time. This could help to explain why someone like Himmler, who loved defenceless animals, could engage in policies of mass extermination. As Josef Ackerman has said, the qualities of love for animals and contempt for human life often go together.[34] The Jew as an unnatural, *anti*-natural being who willfully inflicts pain upon creatures of nature, can be seen in a review of 'The Eternal Jew', which appeared in the *Völkischer Beobachter* on 9 December 1938. The review ended with a condemnation of Jewish ritual slaughter of animals. Emphasised here was the 'brutality' of the Jews, who did not allow the animals to be stunned before they were slaughtered. Such practices were unthinkable in National Socialist Germany.[35] In this context, the Jew is made to appear utterly life-alien, unnatural, below the level of existence attained by those creatures so cruelly slaughtered by him. Within the context of a confrontation between 'natural man' and unnatural humanoid, the at first seemingly curious combination of love of animals and contempt for certain humans becomes, on reflection, not so curious.

From what we have seen above, it would be almost logical that authentic, natural men were driven to wage war upon beings, or anti-beings, who existed at the lowest level of natural life or, as Hitler once suggested, were outside the realm of nature altogether. Indeed, in his speech of 30 January 1939 Hitler prophesied that if there were to be any European war — one no doubt instigated by the Jews — then it would see 'the annihilation of the Jewish race in Europe'. According to Lucy Davidowicz, this was Hitler's 'declaration of war against the Jews'.[36] In this regard, Eberhard Jäckel has offered a most interesting observation. Hitler, when he referred to his statement regarding the annihilation of the Jews, recalled that he had made it on 1 September 1939 — in other words, when Poland was invaded. This error offers conclusive proof, Jäckel has maintained, that Hitler identified the war itself with the Jews.[37] There is little doubt that such was the case. The very tenor of the National Socialist religion called for such a conflict. Eventually, nature-bound, authentic men had to confront and annihilate a deracinated pestilence whose very existence represented a threat to life itself.

To be sure, in recent years, a controversy has developed between those who maintain that policies of extermination emerged quite logically from the Nazi ideology as a whole, or at least Hitler in particular, and others who suggest that what policies there were emerged in an almost *ad hoc* manner, as harassed and confused SS leaders, caught between ideological demands and demographic and military necessities, took actions into their own hands; actions which, over time, tended to coalesce into a general policy. Hitler, it has been argued, might well have approved of this policy once it did emerge; but neither he nor the National Socialist leadership in general was responsible for its being implemented in the first place. Tim Mason has dubbed those who believe in a direct link between Hitlerian ideology and the policies of extermination 'intentionalists', and those who view such policies as emerging in a sort of *ad hoc* manner, 'functionalists', and these labels have now come into general use. In my opinion, Gerald Fleming, in his work, *Hitler and the Final Solution*, has succeeded in establishing the fact that, even if there was no written order for the extermination which can be traced to Hitler, the *role* of the Führer in establishing such policies was central, and that it remained so up to the end of the war.[38] In any case, it should be obvious that the author thinks that the National Socialist religion of nature described in this work not only implicitly provided for extermination policies as a 'final solution', but, in fact made them logically and, above all, *ethically* necessary. Especially as Germany found itself in a situation of total war, those 'enemies of life' perversely held responsible for the situation could and had to suffer the fate promised them by Hitler, even if tactical considerations and moral cowardice dictated that he could not allow himself to be linked with such action in the public eye.

On 12 November 1941, an article entitled 'The Jewish Enemy' ('Die jüdische Feind') appeared in the *Völkischer Beobachter*. The author of this article, Seibert (probably Theodor Seibert, the first name was not provided) stated that when the German armies were fighting the English and the French, one could sense something human in these opponents. Now, however, with the struggle against Bolshevism and 'Rooseveltism', two phenomena of international Jewry, what was involved was the simple act of self-preservation against a foe who was an 'enemy of life'.[39]

'The war against the Jewish International', Seibert proclaimed, 'is a life and death struggle which must be and will be ruthlessly pursued unto the end'.[40] Less than a month later, Dr. Goebbels himself confronted the issue of the war against the Jews. The Jewish question, he declared, was one 'which cannot be confronted with sentimentality, but in clear recognition of the historical guilt which Jewry has heaped upon itself'.[41] Goebbels recalled the 30 January 1939 speech of Hitler, in which annihilation of the Jews was predicted if Europe were to be engulfed in war. Now, with war raging, one could no longer shrink from the consequences.[42]

Einsatzgruppen actions, i.e., the mass executions of Jews and others condemned by the 'laws of life', had been under way since the invasion of the Soviet Union. With the conclusion of the Wannsee Conference in January 1942, these actions were rationalised and became the basis for yet more systematic policies. In some of Goebbels' diary entries of February and March 1942, we can observe the emotional writhings of one who was attempting to face the consequences of this without 'sentimentality'. On 14 February 1942, Goebbels recorded his views on the catastrophe world Jewry would suffer along with the Bolsheviks. Hitler had expressed his desire on this score. 'There must be no squeamish sentimentalism about it. The Jews have deserved the catastrophe that has now overtaken them.'[43] On 18 February 1942, after seeing the film *The Dybuk*, Goebbels made the following entry:

> Looking at this film I realised once again that the Jewish race is the most dangerous on the face of the earth, and that we must show them no mercy and no indulgence. This riffraff must be eliminated and destroyed. Otherwise, it won't be possible to bring peace to the world.[44]

By 7 March 1942, Goebbels had convinced himself of the absolute necessity of what was occurring around him.

> The situation is now ripe for a final settlement of the Jewish question. Later generations will no longer have either the willpower or the instinctive alertness. That is why we are doing good work in proceeding radically and consistently. The task we are assuming today will be an advantage and a boon to our descendants.[45]

Events in Poland proceeded apace:

> Beginning with Lublin, the Jews under the General Govenment are now being evacuated eastward. The procedure is pretty barbaric and is not to be described here more definitely. Not much will remain of the Jews. About 60 per cent of them will have to be liquidated; only about 40 per cent can be used for forced labour.[46]

All of this was justified because what was involved was 'a life-and-death struggle between Aryan race and the Jewish bacillus'.[47]

In these entries, one can observe a most interesting progression with regard to attitudes towards the Jews. One starts out with a 'dangerous' race, and ends up with a 'bacillus'. Naturally, in public statements, Goebbels had had to keep pace with the strident statements and demands of Hitler and the SS. Of course, there had always been an aspect of Goebbel's psyche that was fully committed to radical measures against the Jews. With the *reality* of extermination, however, it became necessary for him to gird himself fully in the National Socialist belief that Jews were not 'merely' subhuman 'parasites', but in fact an abstract sort of plague, one which, none the less, had assumed embarrassingly human form.

A person who had to face the question of annihilating the enemies of life more directly was Heinrich Himmler. It is in this incredibly strange man, a combination of mystical, nature-worshipping *Schwärmerei* and intense, bureaucratic coldness, that one can observe the apotheosis of that pernicious yet genuinely-sensed idealism which was summoned forth by the National Socialist religion in its 'finest' hour. Because of the extraordinary significance of Himmler's well known 6 October 1943 address to SS leaders on the Jewish question, this will be quoted at length.

> The sentence, 'The Jews must be exterminated', with its few words, gentlemen, is easily expressed. For those who must carry out what it demands it is the hardest and most difficult there is. You see, naturally, that they are Jews; it is quite clear, they are only Jews. If you consider however, how many — even party comrades — have sent

either to me or to some other such post, their notorious petition in which it says that all Jews naturally are swine; that, however, so-and-so is a really decent Jew to whom one need not do anything . . . In Germany, we thus have so many millions of people who have their famous decent Jews, that this number is already greater than the number of Jews.[48]

Obviously, with regards to the Jewish exterminations, there could be no exceptions. But, one could ask — and probably a great many SS men did — how about women and children? Himmler was unequivocal.

I have decided to find a complete clear solution even here. I do not consider myself justified to exterminate the men — that is, to slay or to have [them] slain — and to allow avengers in the form of children to wax large for our sons and grandsons. The heavy decision to have these people disappear from the earth must be grasped. For the organisation that must attend to this, this task was the heaviest that we have had thus far. It has been carried out without — as I believe I am able to say — our men and leader having suffered damage to spirit and soul. This danger is quite close. The path between both possibilities that here exist — either to become too brutal, to become heartless and no longer respect human life, or to become soft and muddled to the point of nervous breakdown — the path between this Scylla and Charybdis is frightfully narrow.[49]

Naturally, the SS was not to profit from the exterminations. Nothing was to be stolen from the Jews. Such, generally, had not been done, at least according to Himmler, and he went on to praise the SS for assuming the responsibility for the exterminations, 'and then taking the secret with us to our graves'.[50]

In these inelegant lines, the spectacled, weak-chinned *Reichsführer* — everybody's perfect bureaucrat — made his own indelible contribution to twentieth century Western culture. In destroying the Jews — who, at one point, he did refer to as 'people' — one must not 'become heartless and no longer respect human life'. What was obviously at stake here was the destruction of things, unnatural beings utterly remote from the proverbial fallen sparrow or the lilies of the field, for that matter. For Himmler, the worshipper of nature, man was nothing special. The SS, on the other hand, was, and it was a tribute to their humanity that killing things which somehow had succeeded in attaining human form did not come easily. Such killings ought not to be done enthusiastically, much less with sadistic relish. In the case of an SS-*Untersturmführer* who, on his own initiative and with his own hands — and with great hideousness — killed hundreds of Jews, severe punishment was called for since, in being driven by a 'true hatred of the Jews', he had damaged the order and discipline of his men.[51] After all, 'It is not in the German manner to employ Bolshevik methods in the necessary annihilation of the worst enemy of our people.'[52]

For Himmler, probably in many ways more of a 'biological mystic' than even his Führer, the National Socialist *Weltanschauung* was not sullied by painful but necessary actions against an unnatural enemy.

> As far as anti-Semitism is concerned, it is exactly the same as with delousing. No question of *Weltanschauung* is involved in removing lice. It is a matter of cleanliness. Exactly has anti-Semitism been for us no question of *Weltanschauung*, but of cleanliness . . . Soon we will be deloused.[53]

To this one must offer the caveat that 'delousing' was, at the very least, *called for* by the guiding principles of the *Weltanschauung*. None the less, Himmler had no doubt convinced himself that for 'natural men', operating not even according to, but *as the embodiment* of, new religious principles, cruelty even to lice should be avoided. Actions such as those involved in the 'Final Solution' required the idealistic young SS warriors to negate a substantial portion of their emotional heritage. As Hans Buchheim has pointed out, however, for idealists of the SS stamp, ethics dictated 'that the value of the moral act lies primarily in the amount of self-abnegation involved'.[54] The other side of this abnegation was a '*moral subjectivism*' which, in a perversely Kantian manner, 'finds its satisfaction in the purity of its intentions but does not consider the effects of its activities as a question of conscience'.[55] One has undertaken hideous actions for pure, good motives, and that is all that matters. For the SS man thoroughly imbued with the National Socialist *Weltanschauung*, could any motive be more noble than preserving a sacred natural order from pestilence?

We have noted how the pragmatism inherent in the National Socialist religion of nature was undone by military reverses and, eventually, by crushing defeat. In one area, though, events appeared to confirm the necessity for the 'Final Solution'. Jewish behaviour, in Nazi eyes, came more and more to conform to the archetype of the unnatural being. Rudolf Höss, commandant of Auschwitz, expressed horror at the behaviour of the *Sonderkommando*, the so-called 'special detachments', composed almost entirely of Jews, whose job it was to take the bodies from the gas chambers, pull out the gold teeth and cut off hair, and then to take the corpses to the crematoria.

> They carried out all these tasks with a callous indifference as though it were all part of an ordinary day's work. While they dragged the corpses about, they ate or they smoked. They did not stop eating even when engaged on the grisly job of burning corpses which had been lying for some time in mass graves.

> It happened repeatedly that Jews of the Special Detachment would come upon the bodies of close relatives among the corpses, and even among the living as they entered the gas chambers. They were obviously affected by this, but it never led to any incident.[56]

This behaviour shocked Höss, who concluded thus: 'The Jews' way of living and of dying was a true riddle which I never managed to solve.'[57] As would any decent SS man, Höss recovered from harrowing scenes by turning to nature. 'I would mount my horse and ride, until I had chased the terrible picture away. Often, at night, I would walk through the stables and seek relief among my beloved animals.'[58]

In a truly marvellous way, something which, even in his most repentant moments, seems to have been overlooked by Höss, the National Socialists had succeeded in creating that which they knew existed all along. Through degradation, humiliation, torture, and total dehumanisation, they had created the nonhuman, in fact, non-natural Jewish enemy, seemingly incapable of feeling those normal, human emotions that were characteristics of those decent folk engaged in annihilating them. The prosaic realities of military action — numerical superiority, the superior performance of the Spitfire or P-51 Mustang fighter or the T-34 tank — could undo the success-dependent pragmatism of National Socialism in battle. With an utterly helpless, captive mass, one rendered incapable of significant resistance by the conditioning of recent history, it was extraordinarily easy to provide those circumstances in which hypothesis and reality became intertwined in obscene *praxis*.

Reflection will reveal the fact that, with the possible exception of the Führer himself — and even he did not dare to put down in writing the order for the final solution — National Socialist leaders evidenced uncertainty and, at times, spiritual confusion, when confronted with the monumental task of annihilating an entire people, condemned on the basis of a new religion which, like older ones, required that a leap of faith be made. As we have seen, even Himmler could backslide and, in the midst of a racist diatribe, refer to the enemy as 'people.'

One cannot gainsay the singular fact however that Nazism, part and parcel of a deepseated and genuine rebellion against an increasingly demythologised world, provides us with a disturbing example of how the coldest of modern technological devices and services could be utilised by political mystics, individuals who sincerely believed that they were providing those conditions necessary for the emergence of that natural man in whom the highest of life's forces would be actualised.

In his introduction to Gerald Fleming's *Hitler and the Final Solution*, Saul Friedländer talks of 'the historian's paralysis' in dealing with the Holocaust. This

> comes from the simultaneity and the interaction of entirely heterogeneous phenomena: messianic fanaticism and bureaucratic structures, pathological impulses and adminstrative decrees, archaic attitudes and advanced industrial society.[59]

'Paralysis' is perhaps laudable when one is forced to confront, perhaps even attempt to explain, the unspeakable. Yet, this 'paralysis' can be 'cured' — and how terrible that word sounds — when one bears in mind that the 'messianic fanaticism' that drove dedicated National Socialists to shoot, bludgeon and gas millions of human beings, most of them poignantly unheroic souls who wished only to live, was the expression of a religion of nature emerging from and consonant with the needs of a modern age perceived of as being unhappily devoid of life-sustaining myths. In such circumstances, 'pathological impulses' and 'archaic attitudes' had to find articulation in 'bureaucratic structures' and 'administrative decrees'. After all, these were the idiom of any 'advanced industrial society'. In a way, it is commendable that historians choose not to believe that ideas can shape reality; and, in all those ways amenable to 'scientific' analysis, they do not and never have. Yet, however ill-conceived (in every sense of the word) ideas can be, the victories achieved by National Socialism in its most successful war testify to the hideous possibilities open to those who act as if they not only can, but must, do so.

However weak and inconsistent the natural-religion-grounded *Weltanschauung* appears when it is subject to reason-informed scrutiny, the Nazis were convinced that they had succeeded in fusing the realms of nature and spirit, that the product of this fusion was or would be natural, Aryan man, and that the process of reinforming a decadent, bourgeois world with a new nature-*Mythus* necessitated extermination of those whose very existence was an insult to the laws of life. It was no accident that the most successful purveyors of political mysticism to date provided that the last sight which greeted those who were to be exterminated, before they confronted the expression which crowned the gate to Auschwitz, 'Arbeit macht frei', was that of a large tree, striking in its luxuriance.

Notes

1. Hermann Rauschning, *Hitler Speaks: A Series of Political Conversations with Adolph Hitler on His Real Aims* (London, Heinemann, 1939), p. 243.

2. Ibid.

3. *Das Nationalsozialistische Deutschland und die Wissenschaft: Heidelberger Reden von Reichsminister Rust und Prof. Ernst Krieck*, (Hamburg, Carl Winter Verlag, 1936), p. 22.

4. Ernst Krieck, p. 23. The 'great mother' referred to here is, of course, the Great Earth Mother, a divinity who currently is being exhumed by cultists the world over.

5. As an example of this see Ernst Krieck, *Wissenschaft, Weltanschauung, Hochschulreform* (Leipzig, Armanen Verlag, 1934), pp. 30–4.

6. Ibid., p. 35.

7. J. P. Stern, *Hitler: The Führer and the People* (Berkeley and Los Angeles, University of California Press, 1975), p. 24.

8. Ibid., p. 26.

9. Ibid., p. 44.

10. Mary Douglas, *Natural Symbols: Explorations in Cosmology* (New York, Pantheon, 1970), p. 19.

11. Ibid., p. 51.

12. Ibid., p. 52.

13. Ibid., p. 154.

14. C. G. Jung, 'Wotan,' first published in *Neue Schweizer Rundschau* (Neue Folge, iii Jahrgang, Heft ll) March 1936, in C. G. Jung, *Essays on Contemporary Events*, translated from the German by Elizabeth Welch, Barbara Hannah and Mary Brines (London, K. Paul, 1947), p. 9.

15. Ibid., p. 1.

16. Paul Josef Goebbels, *Goebbels-Reden*, Band I: 1932-1939, herausgegeben von Helmut Heiber (Düsseldorf, Droste Verlag, 1971), p. 324. Emphasis is Goebbels'.

17. Ibid., Band II, 1972: 1939-1945, p. 1.

18. Ibid., p. 411.

19. Ibid., p. 416.

20. Josef Ackerman, *Himmler als Ideologe* (Göttingen, Musterschmidt, 1970), p. 159.

21. Joseph Goebbels, 'Reinliche Scheidung zwischen Deutschen und Juden', in *Völkischer Beobachter*, Berliner Ausgabe, Nr. 319, 51.Jahrgang, 15 November 1938, p. 7.

22. R. Walter Darré, *Neuordnung unseres Denkens* (Goslar, Goslarer Volksbucherei, 1940), p. 16. The weed image was an important one for Darré. An early example of this can be found in a 1930 work, translated as *A New Aristocracy Based on Blood and Soil*. An excerpt from this is available in Barbara Miller Lane and Leila J. Rupp (eds.), *Nazi Ideology before 1933: A Documentation* (Austin and London, University of Texas Press, 1978). See p. 115 in particular. Darré was replaced as Minister of Agriculture in 1942 by Herbert Backe. While his approach to the 'Jewish problem' was certainly representative of the movement as a whole, Darré came to be viewed as 'impractical' with regard to agricultural problems. In this context, his application of 'Blood and Soil' principles

caused him to be criticised as too theoretical. See J.E. Farquharson, *The Plough and the Swastika, the NSDAP and Agriculture in Germany 1928, 1945* (London and Beverly Hills, Sage, 1976), pp. 246–8.

23. Alfred Rosenberg, 'Rosenberg sprach über Lagarde', in *Völkischer Beobachter*, Norddeutsche Ausgabe, Nr. 356, 54.Jahrgang, 22 December 1941, S.3.

24. Walter Buch on the ideas of German honour, in *Deutsche Justiz*, 21 October 1938, in George L. Mosse (ed.), *Nazi Culture* (New York, Grosset and Dunlap, 1966), pp. 336–7.

25. Adolf Hitler, *Secret Conversations 1941-1944*. With an introductory essay on 'The Mind of Adolf Hitler', by H. R. Trevor-Roper, translated by Norman Cameron and R. H. Stevens (New York, Farrar, Strauss and Young, 1953), conversation of 22 February 1942, p. 269.

26. Ibid., conversation of 4 April 1942, p. 322.

27. Ibid., conversation of 15th May 1942, p. 393.

28. Lucy S. Davidowicz, *The War Against the Jews, 1933–1945* (New York, Holt, Rinehart and Winston, 1975), p. 165.

29. Darré, *Neuordnung*, p. 54.

30. Richard L. Rubenstein, *The Cunning of History: Mass Death and the American Future* (New York, Harper and Row, 1975), p. 90.

31. Darré, *Neuordnung* p. 56.

32. Adolf Hitler, *Mein Kampf*, translated from the German by Ralph Manheim (Boston, Houghton Miflin, 1943), p. 178.

33. Rauschning, *Hitler Speaks*, p. 238.

34. Ackerman, *Himmler als Ideologe*, p. 165.

35. 'Jüdisches Schachten in Film', in *Völkischer Beobachter*, Suddeutsche Ausgabe, Nr. 343, 51.Jahrgang, 9 Dezember 1938, S.9.

36. Davidowicz, *The War Against the Jews*, p. 106.

37. Eberhard Jäckel, *Hitlers Weltanschauung* (Tübingen, R. Wunderlich, 1969), p. 83.

38. Gerald Fleming, *Hitler and the Final Solution*, with an introduction by Saul Friedländer (Berkeley and Los Angeles, University of California Press, 1984). In his introduction Friedländer provides both a summary and an analysis of the 'intentionalist/functionalist' debate.

39. Seibert, 'Die jüdische Feind', in *Völkischer Beobachter*, Norddeutsche Ausgabe, Nr. 316, 54.Jahrgang, 12 November 1941. S.2.

40. Ibid.

41. Paul Josef Goebbels, 'Wir können siegen, wir müssen seigen, wir werden siegen!', in *Völkischer Beobachter*, Norddeutsche Ausgabe, Nr. 337, 54.Jahrgang, 3 Dezember 1941, S.2.

42. Ibid.

43. Paul Joseph Goebbels, *The Goebbels Diaries, 1942-1943*, edited and translated from the German by Louis P. Lochner (New York, Hamish Hamilton, 1948), p. 48.

44. Ibid., p. 54.

45. Ibid., p. 75.

46. Ibid., pp. 102–3.

47. Ibid., p. 103.

48. Henrich Himmler, *Himmler Geheimreden: 1933 bis 1945*, Einführung, Joachim C. Fest; herausgegeben von Bradley F. Smith und Agnes F. Peterson (Frankfurt/M and Berlin, Propyläen Verlag, 1974), p. 169.

49. Ibid., pp. 169–70.

50. Ibid., p. 171.

51. Hans Buchheim, *et al.*, *Anatomie des SS-Staates*, Band I., Hans Buchheim, *Die SS-Herrschaftinstrument, Befehl und Gehorsam* (München, Deutscher Taschenbüch Verlag, 1967), p. 267. For the SS's horrified reaction to spontaneous Romanian massacres of the Jews see Hannah Arendt, *Eichmann in Jerusalem: A Report on the Banality of Evil* (New York, Viking Press, 1963), pp. 173–4. Naturally, at the lower levels, free rein was often given to the most extreme forms of sadism imaginable.

52. Ibid.

53. Himmler, *Geheimreden*, pp. 200–1.

54. Hans Buchheim, *Totalitarian Rule: Its Nature and Characteristics*, translated from the German by Ruth Heim (Middletown, Connecticut, Wesleyan University Press, 1968), p. 83.

55. Ibid., p. 84. Emphasis is Buchheim's.

56. Rudolph Höss, *Commandant of Auschwitz*, with an introduction by Lord Russell of Liverpool; translated from the German by Constantine FitzGibbon (New York, Popular Library, 1959), p. 142.

57. Ibid., p. 143. For an interesting discussion of how totalitarianism inherently produces what it thinks to be objectively true, see Hannah Arendt, 'The Concept of History: Ancient and Modern', in Hannah Arendt, *Between Past and Future:Eight Exercises in Political Thought* (New York, Viking Press, 1977). On the necessity for totalitarian propaganda to place emphasis on the movement's infallibility, see Hannah Arendt, *The Origins of Totalitarianism* (New York, Harcourt, Brace, Jovanovich, 1973), pp. 349–50.

58. Höss, p. 146.

59. Saul Friedländer in Fleming, *Hitler and the Final Solution*, p. xxxiii.

6 THE TERROR OF HISTORY AND THE *MYTHUS* OF AN IDEALISED PAST

Throughout this work, we have been concerned mostly with National Socialist religiosity as perceived by the National Socialist leadership. Logical consequences of such, hypothetically and in practice, also have been considered. An important conclusion has been drawn: that, to one degree or another, the leadership and one of its most important instruments of expression, the SS, took at least the guiding principles of this 'religion' very seriously, even if the whole, at times ill-defined body of it, was not so taken. From time to time, we have focused upon the mass of German citizenry. While the writer has assumed that those elements of the religion that attained public expression had a drawing power with regards to the German population at large, the concrete dynamics of this have not been investigated systematically. An important reason for this is that, while it is the writer's opinion that one can establish without *any doubt whatsoever* that the leadership strongly believed in the core of the National Socialist religion — and that claims to the contrary are sophistic, ill-informed and näive — it is probably impossible to determine precisely the degree to which this core found persistent resonance in the German population, although some observations about this will be made in the Appendix. As pointed out earlier, most of this population, if it was religious at all, formally adhered to the 'traditional' religions of Germany. Such people remained Evangelical Lutheran or Catholic and even a justifiably unsympathetic observer of the 1939 German scene such as William Shirer had to comment upon the continued mass purchasing of Christmas trees in pinched wartime conditions. 'No matter how tough or rough or pagan a German may be, he has a childish passion for Christmas trees. People everywhere bravely trying to make this Christmas seem like the old ones in times of peace.'[1] To be sure, the love of a Christmas tree might well have been more informed by residual paganism than significant commitment to Christianity; but the average German did not know this and probably would have been greatly offended if it were called to his attention. Further, for such a person 'Christianity' *was* Christmas, and Christmas *was* the tree, gifts, and often mawkish sentimentality. Of course the 'average' German was, in this regard, no different from the 'average' European or American Christian.

So, in many ways, Germany's religious traditions remained intact, even if its leaders might well have viewed them as vestigial elements of a decadent and degenerative Judaeo-Christian *Weltanschauung*. During the struggle for power, National Socialist campaign strategists pointed out the necessity for declaring, particularly in Catholic areas, that National Socialism was 'not a religious *Weltanschauung*', and, as we have seen, even when in power, the National Socialists found it necessary to shy away from at least persistent confrontation with the traditional forms of German Christianity.[2]

The extraordinarily pragmatic approach of the National Socialist party during the crucial electoral campaigns of the late 1920s and early 1930s — its ability to 'plug in' to what was needed in any given circumstance — and the persistence of various traditional German cultural and religious forms after January 1933, could lead anyone to suspect that, even if the National Socialist leadership took its *Mythus* seriously, the vast mass of the German public did not. The fact that, as we have seen, this leadership thought it necessary to *educate* the public gradually, and in a *very* gradual manner at that, serves to reinforce this suspicion. One scholar has gone so far as to suggest that the Nazis were able to score points against the more rigidly ideological Social Democratic Party by demonstrating to the German public that they were 'unhindered by ideology' and hence more flexible in offering solutions to depression-harassed Germany.[3] Yet, when all is said and done, it is still obvious that the National Socialist movement, besides demonstrating an extraordinary (and oft-discussed) ability to adjust its arguments to given regional and/or class circumstances, was also able to present itself in wellnigh metapolitical terms. Furthermore, there can be no question but that in locales positively sensitised to the mystical appeal of the *Volksgemeinschaft* — rural areas and very small towns in particular — the Nazis were able to present large amounts of the racial *Mythus* with great effectiveness.[4] Such arguments were not used in big cities, Richard Hamilton has suggested, because bourgeois folk, supposedly living in that anomic state traditionally considered conducive to the emergence of National Socialist sympathies, did not take the more strident aspects of the ideology seriously. While virtually all elements of the urban bourgeoisie eventually went National Socialist, the anti-Communist posture of the National Socialists was of decisive importance. While, as stated at the beginning of this chapter, the mass appeal of the National Socialist religion cannot be precisely determined, Hamilton has pointed out something of interest: namely, that the National Socialist ideology, particularly the emphasis upon the mythical *Volksgemeinschaft* and the dialectically related anti-Semitism, was taken very seriously in those areas in which people had not yet *directly* experienced, at least in extreme form, the anomic, alienating conditions associated with urban life. Rather, it would appear, they *feared* these conditions and were hostile to those forces that were in some way associated with them.

At this point it is necessary to devote some time to the somewhat singular nature of German industrialisation. Naturally, the larger cities were of great importance in this process. Berlin, Leipzig, Hamburg, Cologne and Munich — all came to have industrial districts and residential areas or industrial suburbs settled by those who served the factories. The Ruhr industrial region, of course, consisted of a set of medium-large cities, such as Essen, Duisburg, Bochum, and Wuppertal tied together into a roughly defined economic complex. Yet, to a great extent, German industrialisation, unlike that of, say, England, did not take place exclusively, or even largely, within clearly defined urban/industrial areas. Indeed, even though Germany was the most heavily urbanised state in contintental Europe, a substantial portion of the industrialisation process took place in small to medium-sized cities. Hence, that clearly defined line between urban and rural life that often has been perceived as resulting from industrialisation did not exist.[5] In a word, industrialisation in Germany, even in its well-developed stages towards the end of the nineteenth century and later, was rather 'spread-out' and a substantial portion of the so-called industrial proletariat either remained rooted in rural life — i.e., obtained seasonal employment in factories or was employed on a semi-permanent basis — or at the very least, retained strong rural or 'small town' associations.[6] Barrington Moore, in commenting upon what he calls 'the provincial and small-town atmosphere of German pre-war [i.e., pre-World War I] labour politics,' has suggested that much of the German industrial proletariat cannot be seen as having conformed to that archetype central to Marxist hypothesising, or even more loosely defined ideology schemata.[7]

Another, extremely important consequence flowed from the rather singular nature of German industrialisation. Those who were not employed in factories — small-town burghers, professional people and the like, and large numbers of the peasantry as well — while, as suggested above, not experiencing the consequences of industrialisation in a fully articulated urban setting, could perceive various disquieting, *potentially* alienating elements of it in their midst. In summation, substantial numbers of 'small' or 'small to medium-sized' towns, and large portions of the German countryside were on the cutting-edge of social and economic change. Populations in these lived in a sort of 'grey area' in which a variety of contradictions, contrasts and uncertainties added up to ambivalence. It was precisely in these areas where the National Socialist *Mythus* could be most fully articulated and with the greatest effect. According to Moore, the future, for the pre-World War I German worker, was often 'couched in terms of an idealised rural past, or else an idealised version of what they had seen or heard about contemporary life in the countryside'.[8] For those workers in the cities, such associations no doubt exerted an emotional pull of some significance. How much more significant must this 'pull' have been in areas in which appearances — however deceptive — no doubt induced burgher and worker alike to turn towards that 'idealised rural past' which historically had been of immense importance in the sanctified *Volksgemeinschaft*.

Naturally, the terms 'idealised rural past', or 'idealised version' utilised by Barrington Moore suggest that, for him, there *was* no such past, and the version of the rural 'present' was, in large measure, clouded by wishful thinking. Of course, this has been known for a long time, but recent studies have been of particular significance in pointing out just how far off the mark such romantic musings have been. According to romantics — even ones with academic credentials — from Wilhelm Heinrich Riehl on, the large, warm, mutually supportive family was a characteristic of rural life, German or otherwise, and it was this homey complex that was threatened by the insidious forces of modernity. Among others, a recent study of Michael Mitterauer and Reinhard Sieder has established that the 'large pre-industrial family' was a myth.[9] As suggested, this mythical unit was infused with that deliciously suffocating warmth often seen as resulting from a comforting patriarchy in which everyone knew his or her place. Recent studies have suggested that, while economic necessity might have dictated that members of the so-called 'pre-industrial' rural or small-town German family had to have depended upon one another, such an arrangement was not necessarily conducive to the establishing of warm bonds. Indeed, while the death of a child in such a family certainly was of concern, it was of relatively little importance, unless, of course, the child had attained an age at which it was making some sort of contribution to the unit's economic survival.[10] Perhaps even less surprising to students of Central European history is the fact that, for some time in rural Bavaria, wife-beating was apparently more common 'than the ill-treatment of horses'.[11] All in all, the notion of the pre-industrial family, at least in Germany, being a warm-hearted collectivity within which individuals could attain fulfilment is seen to be an absurdity. Indeed, intensive familial interaction, with an emphasis on developing individualism, is far more characteristic of that modern family, supposedly informed by the values of a harsh, alienating, mechanised society.[12] Thus that worshipping of presumed 'vanished solidarities of the past' — a shared tendency, albeit for different respective reasons, of the left as well as the right — must be seen as romanticism, in the worst possible sense.[13]

Yet, when all is said and done, past institutions and social relationships can be seen as being necessarily more tied to nature, as being part and parcel of a mode of being more conducive to the emergence and sustaining of comforting archetypal patterns. There seems to have been something deliciously ahistorical about this and romantics, such as Riehl, can be said to have turned to the past in an effort to escape from history. History is, after all, change, and the emotional demands posed by such change can be taxing. From our point of view, it is on the mark to say that human beings are *historical* beings, and that we are thus, in whatever permutation of freedom we have at any time, always creating or recreating ourselves. As Mircea Eliade has pointed out, however, in *The Myth of the Eternal Return*, in a world in which humans seem to be more powerless than ever before, it is easy and perhaps even justified to view history as disquieting. Indeed, in comparing the situation of primitive human beings grounded in nondynamic, archetypal certainties to that of 'us moderns' he has seen the latter as, at times, being virtually paralysed by the 'terror of history'.[14] This consideration, of course, brings us around to our earlier concerns with such things as 'fear of transcendence', and the need to 'end history'. It is in this context that we must now, once again, focus upon the nature and power of these salient aspects of the National Socialist religion.

In attempting to undercut that traditional interpretation of National Socialism which sees its primary source of support as stemming from a middle class threatened by economic and social extinction, Richard Hamilton has focused upon an important statement by William Sheridan Allen. In describing the state of Northeim's (a town of around 10,000; in the first edition of Allen's work, the pseudonym 'Thalburg' was used) middle class — large elements of which *did* go National Socialist — the latter declared that it had not really been much touched in hard, economic terms, by the depression. Only 'psychologically', Allen stated, had this had any impact on the middle class or Northeim.[15] From our perspective, of course, this explains a great deal. Objectively, of course, large elements of the bourgeoisie were not driven to the brink of poverty by the depression. Certainly, the great industrialists could *not* have been threatened by communism, a movement which, according to all accounts, was in considerable disarray in Germany in the early 1930s.

As we have seen, the areas in which the National Socialist *Mythus* enjoyed its greatest appeal, in rural (particularly Protestant rural) and small town settings, were not those in which some of the drearier aspects of industrialisation and objective alienation had been experienced first-hand. It was precisely in those areas and in those classes, or elements of classes, in which one sensed a narrowing gap between the objective 'is' and a chilling 'might be', that the Nazi religious pull was the strongest. It was here, amongst these people, in large measure, threatened 'only psychologically' that a fetishistic cultural pessimism necessitated the creation of a history-defying, totemistic past. To focus again upon a previously considered example: there was no *objective* reason why elements of the German bourgeoisie *had* to revel in the myth of the large, morally pristine, pre-industrial family. Yet, the effective use of this myth, so central to the overriding notion of *Volksgemeinschaft*, has characterised Fascist ideologies as a whole, and National Socialism in particular.[16] People were driven not only to believe that such things existed, but to *act* as if they did. At the same time, as has been noted, it was of the highest necessity that the Jews in particular be seen as a deracinated element which threatened the whole panoply of archetypes central to a mythological past.

According to Eliade, primitive man, through adhering to the archetypal usages central to fully articulated cosmogonies, is in the position 'to annul his own history through periodic abolition of time and collective regeneration'.[17] As Eliade has seen it, the 'time' of history, i.e., chronological time, is 'profane' time; while the sort of 'timeless time' of primitive cosmogonies, wherein the totems and archetypes which give meaning to the lives of the peoples concerned are rooted, is 'sacred time' (Freud's 'Kairotic time' is perhaps the best 'modern' equivalent of this). No doubt, in part because of the fate of his country, Romania, Eliade has been very sympathetic to those who, in modern times, seek to escape from history. Emphasising its 'timeless' aspects, i.e., transcendence 'of' rather than 'in' history, he has offered acceptance of Christianity as the way by which harassed moderns, deprived of comforting archetypes and repetitions, can escape, or at least minimise the terrors of temporal life.[18] Again, particularly in view of the post-World War II fate of Romania, it is not surprising that Eliade has focused upon Marxism as an approach to salvation which, seeing transcendence as coming out of history and at its end, made no small contribution to its 'terrors'. The National Socialist approach has not been mentioned, at least not in *The Myth of the Eternal Return*. It is obvious, though, that in the National Socialist religious revolution, we can see an effort to escape from the 'terror of history' by essentially *abolishing* it. The very real terror necessitated by such an action was not of crucial significance since it would be directed against those who stood in opposition to the emergence of 'sacred time' within that 'profane time' over which it must inevitably triumph. That singular fusion of idealism and pragmatism, described earlier in this work, provided, at least for dedicated National Socialists, the means by which this process could be actualised within the life of the nation.

With regard to the notion of 'sacred time', and its possible political applications, it is of interest to note that, from the late nineteenth century on, German builders of national monuments, e.g., the monument on the myth-shrouded Kyffhäuser Mountain (1896), had placed emphasis on providing a 'sacred space' in front of such edifices. This originally was to have been reserved for the graves of those fallen for the Fatherland. By the time the Kyffhäuser Monument was dedicated, however, this space was to be occupied by crowds of enthusiastic patriots taking part in nationalistic rites.[19] The monuments themselves were certainly erected to commemorate historical events or persons, e.g., Friedrich Barbarossa (supposedly asleep within Kyffhäuser Mountain), or the victory of Hermann (or Arminius) over the Roman Varus in 9 A.D. It is obvious however that the 'sacred space' was to represent a timeless melding together of past, present and future, a process taking place in the nationalistic ceremonies unfolding upon it. Perhaps, all memorials or monuments are designed to have this effect, but it would appear that the conscious planning of some sort of 'sacred space' was more prominent in the then recently-unified — and thus no doubt less secure — Germany than elsewhere. Whether this obvious effort to instil a sense of eternal *völkisch* truths in those participating in nationalistic rituals could have helped 'prepare the way' for National Socialism's assault upon 'profane historical time' is difficult to determine. There can be no doubt, however, that both phenomena resulted from the same, at times desperate, psychic needs. At any rate, the providing of such a 'space' continued as a function of the National Socialist blending of politics and aesthetics.

As stated above, when considering a nation which remained at least *de jure* Christian, it is difficult to determine precisely — even the most sophisticated efforts to arrive at some sort of quantified answer are, in my opinion, vain — just how many 'average' Germans, engaged in the mundane projects of day-to-day existence, were drawn to the National Socialist cosmogony. None the less, during the interwar period, the 'terror of history' had become very real for the German population, while 'the future as history' seemed to hold in store very sharpened, particular terrors for certain elements of the population.

Dr Leo Schneiderman, in his *The Psychology of Myth, Folklore, and Religion*, has made use of Eliade's 'profane/sacred' dichotomy. For Schneiderman, though, modern man '*is forced to act as if the gods were dead* while knowing in his heart that he is still a man possessed by something other than himself'.[20] The modern human lives in sacred time — or at least is *concerned* with living in it — more than he realises; in a word, 'he is more religious than he consciously knows himself to be'.[21] For many modern Germans, that singularly important aspect of the National Socialist tradition which seemed to provide for the continuous sanctification of modern life through grounding it in accepted elements ('truths') of a timeless *Volksgemeinschaft* had to have exerted a powerful pull. This was certainly accentuated by the accommodation that eternal myth *had* to make, in keeping with the very notion of *Volksgemeinschaft*, for the most banal of petty-bourgeois usages, an accommodation which, in the end, had to render *them* eternal as well.[22] Jean-Pierre Sironneau has had much of value to say about National Socialism as a secular religion. In my opinion, however, he is somewhat wide of the mark in his assertion that the primary reason why National Socialism, indeed, any variety of secular religion, has to be seen as a contradiction in terms, is that it was, or is, grounded in history. Thus, since any true religion had to serve the purpose of liberating people from history, i.e., had to be transcendent, in the anti-historical sense of the term, National Socialism, despite its religious trappings, did not in the end measure up to being one.[23] As I see it, Sironneau's notion of what constitutes a true religion is rather too formalistic. More important, however, in my opinion, is a crucial misinterpretation. Sironneau has declared that National Socialism was anti-transcendent because it was *consciously grounded in history*. Most assuredly, one would have to agree that National Socialism was fundamentally anti-transcendent. Throughout this work, however, we have been considering a 'religion', or 'pseudo-religion', that derived its strength from a pronounced *anti-historical* posture which, *as such*, was anti-transcendent, i.e., seemingly immune from disquieting change.[24] It was *because*, and not in spite, of this posture that National Socialism, whether or not it was in the end a 'real religion', was able to exert a strong pull of religious *nature*. This was most obviously manifest in assumed efforts to create the social *Volksgemeinschaft*.

In such an environment, unpleasant but necessary actions against those who threatened *Gemeinschaft*, something which found solipsistic expression in various soil-bound myths, were themselves actions undertaken 'out of time'. The actual order for the final solution was, it would appear, an oral one. According to Himmler, the deeds of the SS represented a glorious page of history which would never be written. In the '*anus mundi*' of an Auschwitz, Treblinka, Maidjanek or Belzec, time ceased for victim and executioner, and what temporal dimension there was was provided only by those railroad schedules necessary to make certain that sanctified massacre would proceed apace. In a word, those who presided over the actions of *Einsatzgruppen* and the mass gassings, were determined that such experiences would be virtually non-events. Naturally, there was no doubt a very substantial psychological benefit provided by making certain that hideous actions were in effect non-events: one could not be held accountable for deeds which, since they were done 'out of time', had never been perpetrated. Hence, there could be no guilt.

No doubt psychological explanations, ones grounded in theories of denial or cognitive dissonance, are very much to the point. In dealing with the National Socialist phenomenon, however, and, for that matter, others which try to cast 'material' realities in religious terms, it would be dangerously misleading to assume that 'ideas', however abstruse or absurd they might be, cannot develop extraordinary powers of their own. Throughout this work, we have been implicitly concerned with this. The National Socialist religion, born of an amalgam of social, cultural and psychological circumstances, was an articulation of these circumstances. Its leading ideas were grounded in — even if, in due course, they had in part to break from — widely held fantasies. For many, these had played important roles in social relationships and political decision-making. One can condemn the National Socialist religion as an obscenity, informed by false consciousness or bad faith, the sort of bad faith responsible for 'a deliberate decision on the part of mass man to live within the limits of finitude'.[25] Dystopian efforts to render this process 'eternal' testify to the depths of the obscenity. Yet, in Himmler's ability to talk about slaughters 'carried out without . . . our men or order suffering damage to body and spirit', and in Höss's apparent bafflement over the seemingly unnatural behaviour exhibited by those he was in the process of exterminating, we can see how ideas can triumph over physical and moral realities to the point where victims become psychological murderers and executioners, victims. Unconsciously, of course, Himmler, Höss and a multitude of others, were sadists. As they came to see it, however, they, and not gasping, crying children, were the unhappy victims; condemned by pitiless 'laws of life' to preside over a timeless *anus mundi*. Perhaps, in future, all of those Aryan folk who would benefit from those sacred but terrible activities undertaken on their behalf by the most sensitive of human beings could learn about them. For Germany as a whole, it might very well have been true that, as Klaus Vondung put it, National Socialist ritualistic manipulations and thaumaturgical usages were, in the end, inadequate to the task of determining that 'this ideology and its imaginative picture of reality [would] transplant [what was] truly real'.[26] None the less, never before or, up to this point, since, have bearers of a perverse idealism come so close to bringing a world into conformity with religious fantasies born of an unwillingness to accept the vicissitudes of mortality.

In September 1934 William Shirer attended the National Socialist party rally at Nuremberg. He started off his entry of 5 September in the following fashion:

> I'm beginning to comprehend, I think, some of the reasons for Hitler's astounding success. Borrowing a chapter from the Roman church, he is restoring pageantry and colour and mysticism to the drab lives of twentieth-century Germans. This morning's opening meeting in the Luitpold Hall on the outskirts of Nuremberg was more than a gorgeous show; it also had something of the mysticism and religious fervour of an Easter or Christmas Mass in a great Catholic cathedral.[27]

In many respects, Shirer was very much on the mark. Yet, it must be seen that, while the use of certain forms reminiscent of Catholic ceremony was obvious, the purpose of the ritual, i.e., the sanctification of national life, was so radically at odds with the Judaeo-Christian tradition, that reliance upon those analogies implicit in this extremely perceptive observer's remarks can be very misleading. After all, the rituals of Jews and Christians are supposed to bring finite, historical beings into close proximity with a transcendent God-of-history, and hence with the transcendence that dwells within them as well. This was hardly the purpose of those rituals witnessed by Shirer. Rather, they were the sacred rites of that 'new man' described by Hitler as 'God in the making'. This new being had overcome 'the terror of history' by declaring the historical process to be null and void while all aspects of its life were to unfold in that endless present rendered sacred by stalwart adherence to totemistic absurdities. For modern, political man, the merging of religion and politics in the sacred *Volksgemeinschaft* was an extraordinary, in many ways unprecedented, occurrence. What this led to had to have been ultimately monstrous. For, as Schneiderman has so eloquently put it, 'The more modern man has identified himself with his ancestral totem, the more terrible the sacrifice of himself and others that must result'.[28]

Notes

1. William L. Shirer, *Berlin Diary: The Journal of a Foreign Correspondent 1934–1941* (New York, Penguin Books, 1979), entry of 13 December 1939, p. 258.

2. Richard F. Hamilton, *Who Voted for Hitler?* (Princeton, New Jersey, Princeton University Press, 1982), p. 325. We will consider the question of National Socialist confrontation with 'established' religions in the Appendix.

3. Ibid., pp. 277, 285.

4. Ibid., p. 367.

5. Barrington Moore, *Injustice: The Social Base of Obedience and Revolt* (White Plains, New York, M.E. Sharpe, 1978), pp. 179–80.

6. For a fine description of this see Heilwig Schomerus, 'The Family Life-cycle: A Study of Factory Workers in Nineteenth Century Württemberg', in Richard J. Evans and W.R. Lee (eds.), *The German Family: Essays on the Social History of the Family in Nineteenth Century Germany* (New York, Barnes and Noble, 1981), pp. 177–81. Many of the workers who worked and lived in the larger cities also retained strong rural associations.

7. Moore, *Injustice*, p. 180.

8. Ibid., p. 209.

9. Michael Mitterauer and Reinhard Sieder, *The European Family: Patriarchy and Partnership from the Middle Ages to the Present*, translated by Karla Oosterveen and Manfred Hörzinger (Chicago, University of Chicago Press, 1982), pp. 24–44.

10. Ibid., p. 61; Robert Lee, 'Family and Modernization: The Peasant Family and Social Change in Nineteenth Century Bavaria', in Evans and Lee, *The German Family*, pp. 96–7.

11. Ibid., p. 95.

12. Mitterauer and Sieder, *The European Family*, p. 63.

13. Raphael Samuel, 'People's History', in Raphael Samuel (ed.), *People's History and Socialist Theory* (London, Routledge and Kegan Paul, 1981), p. xxii.

14. Mircea Eliade, *The Myth of the Eternal Return, or, Cosmos and History* (Princeton, New Jersey, Princeton University Press, 1974), p. 156.

15. William Sheridan Allen, as quoted in Hamilton, *Who Voted for Hitler?*, p. 377.

16. Mitterauer and Sieder, *The European Family*, pp. 25–6.

17. Eliade, *The Myth*, p. 157.

18. Ibid., pp. 160–2.

19. The best discussion of 'sacred space' is to be found in George L. Mosse, *The Nationalization of the Masses, Political Symbolism and Mass Movements in Germany from the Napoleonic Wars Through the Third Reich* (New York, Howard Fertig Inc., 1975), pp. 32, 63–5, 60–71, 73, 77, 208.

20. Leo Schneiderman, *The Psychology of Myth, Folklore, and Religion* (Chicago, Nelson-Hall, 1981), p. 103. Emphasis is Schneiderman's.

21. Ibid.

22. For a perceptive discussion of this, see Saul Friedländer, *Reflections of Nazism: An Essay on Kitsch and Death*, translated from the French by Thomas Weyr (New York, Harper and Row, 1984), pp. 38–40, 170–1. As I see it, a balance between bourgeois bathos and proclaimed 'eternal value' can easily be struck in a 'religion of nature'.

23. Jean-Pierre Sironneau, *Sécularisation et religions politiques* (The Hague, Paris, New York, Mouton, 1982), p. 565. In his posing of 'transcendence' *against* history, Sironneau is, of course, close to Eliade.

24. For an interesting treatment of the National Socialist anti-historical posture, see Fred Weinstein, *The Dynamics of Nazism: Leadership, Ideology, and the Holocaust* (New York, Academic Press, 1980), pp. 124–6, 137–8.

25. John T. Pawlikowski, 'Christian Perspectives and Moral Implications', in Henry

Friedlander and Sybil Milton (eds.), *The Holocaust: Ideology, Bureaucracy, and Genocide* (Millwood, New York, Kraus International Publications, 1980), p. 296.

26. Klaus Vondung, *Magie and Manipulation: Ideologischen Kult und politische Religion des Nationalsozialismus* (Göttingen, Vandenhoeck and Ruprecht, 1971), p. 199.

27. Shirer, *Berlin Diary*, p. 19.

28. Schneiderman, *The Psychology of Myth*, p. 105.

7 CONCLUSION

When Max Weber declared that, through increased rationalisation the world was becoming 'disenchanted', he must have assumed that he was stating the obvious. In any case, he was hardly alone in making what was in fact an assumption. Even — and perhaps especially — theologians came to share in this assumption, and not a few of them assumed that such a process would, in the end, be beneficial to what they perceived to be the most crucial elements of the Judaeo-Christian tradition. Disenchantment, secularisation of the world could, at least hypothetically, serve to elevate humankind, to emphasise the divinity embodied in it either as the gift of God's grace or due to more mundane, but none the less singular, evolutionary processes. Yet, as we have seen, disenchantment can be something extremely difficult for increasingly alienated, finite beings to accept.

Dr Richard Rubenstein had declared that the Judaeo-Christian tradition, through setting God 'apart' from His creation, has made the earth 'devoid of independent divine or magical forces which men had to appease'.[1] The removal of God from the world, a world over which man was allowed to reign supreme, effectively removed ethical content from it, and, in such an atmosphere, there could occur a 'merging of fact and value' which allowed for the coldest of attitudes towards human suffering.[2] The demystification of life, a product, however unintended, of the Judaeo-Christian tradition, led to a coldly rationalistic way of perceiving problems and solutions, something that in turn led to the death-factories of World War II. Indeed, he maintains, the 'Necropolis', Auschwitz, was the 'ultimate cry of Western Civilization'.[3] There will always be the danger, Rubenstein states, that 'Metropolis will become Necropolis', because the city 'is by nature anti-nature, antiphysis, and hence, anti-life.'[4] Among other things, National Socialism was the result of a process of disenchantment or demystification which, ironically enough, came out of that Judaeo-Christian tradition which it was seeking to extirpate.

It certainly might well be true that secularisation or disenchantment of the world could have had consequences which have to be described as 'anti-humanistic'. In any case, there can be little doubt that those who have rejoiced in this process have been overly optimistic, if not a trifle fatuous. Yet we have considered a movement, informed by religious

149

principle, which, in its efforts to reinform the world with its version of enchantment, was systematically, and conscientiously, anti-humanistic in ways almost unthinkable to previous generations.

There can be no question but that the Nazis were sincere in believing that the world had been deprived of mystery and enchantment by Judaeo-Christian dualism. In their religion of nature, a strikingly effective fusion of crude scientism and those mystical motifs generally associated with *Lebensphilosophie*, they thought that they had discovered a means of bridging the gap between human beings (at least *some* of them) and nature while at the same time providing for the extermination of those who had utilised vulgar 'modernity' to alienate man from his natural roots. The phrase '*Alles ist Leben*', which figured so prominently in the Bad Tölz SS handbook, provided a convenient means by which a necrophilic fascination with death could be absorbed into a putative religion of life which claimed to have brought enchantment back into the world.

Of course, one could argue that, in a religion of nature, it is not *necessary* to see some men as less 'natural' than others, or perhaps as being in a sort of border area between the animate, i.e. life-bound, and inanimate worlds. Should, however, the conception of man as being merely a slightly more intelligent — and hence less likeable — animal be applied within social and political contexts, then, in a world replete with tensions and hatreds, avoidance of drawing certain crudely-affirmed conclusions could become difficult, if not impossible. To be sure, pitiless massacre and rapine have accompanied the spread of religious movements which, hypothetically at least, accepted mankind's divinity. There was, however, at least an ethical or axiological counterbalance in the conception that human life was to be valued simply by virtue of its being human. The average German or French peasant at the time of the First Crusade — the sort of person who might become associated with the dreaded and thoroughly abominable Tafurs — was no doubt a much tougher and probably crueller *individual* than his counterpart (if such could be found) today. Nevertheless, murder as a part of public policy was not part of the Medieval vision, and the process of conversion precluded the racist concept of the permanently tainted soul.[5]

One can argue, of course, that the religion of nature which was central to National Socialism emerged from traditions generic to a politically and socially backward Central Europe. Furthermore, that tendency to reach for a *Lebensphilosophie*, towards that form of totalism in which biologism and mysticism become merged, was itelf a rather singular phenomenon; the produce of time-bound forces and conditions. Certainly, these are valid arguments and this book has demonstrated that the author believes that the National Socialist phenomenon was, in its most important aspects, singular. Yet, it would be naïve, perhaps dangerously so, to assume that a supposedly more politically mature Western tradition, presumably grounded in the humanistic aspects of the Judaeo-Christian tradition, is immune from being strongly influenced by elements identified as central to the National Socialist religion.

As we have noted earlier, rebellion against the rationalisation or disenchantment of the world has hardly been confined to Central Europe. Indeed, in the West, nature worship, varieties of occultism, psychedelic religiosity, adherence to perverted forms of Eastern mysticism and so on are stronger than ever.[6] Historical, cultural and social circumstances have determined that those who have reached out for such solutions to alienation have been largely middle or upper middle class — or at least the children of middle or upper middle class parents. Furthermore, the politics of such people has generally been liberal, or even, on occasion, left-wing. None the less, nature worship (as distinct from 'environmentalism'), occultism and related phenomena have to be either implicitly or explicitly anti-humanistic, and there is little to go against Wilhelm Reich's assertion that ultimately the political expression of mysticism has to be reactionary.[7] As yet, there has been no coherent political expression for such varieties of mysticism. Yet, in all of these phenomena we can see that yearning for 'return', and eagerness to abandon rationality on the way, that have been symptomatic of all bourgeois societies, under stress. Certainly, when one bears in mind the rape of planet Earth that has occurred as the most significant result of predatory capitalism, an overwhelming desire for return to the great, earth mother becomes understandable. Indeed, there appears to be a sort of ethical imperative attaching to it. Yet, in the end, this always has constituted withdrawal, a supposedly 'apolitical' decision that must be right-wing in nature. At the same time, the radical anti-humanism inherent in such withdrawals must constitute an evasion of ethical responsibility, both with regard to human beings and, ultimately, to the planet over which, like it or not, we have sovereignty. In the face of a hostile economic, social and cultural environment, some millions of desperate or discouraged folk have opted for a world view which, particularly in view of the crucial political decisions at hand, is self-serving in the most narrow sense of the term. The 'self' to be served is of course engaged in the seemingly ingenuous enterprise of securing a sacred space/time realm, impervious to cruel historical forces. Politicalisation of this enterprise, or, more precisely, the results of one variety of politicalisation, have been a major concern of this book.

Yet the 'movers and the shakers' in Western society, as well, of course, as the majority of the citizenry, are not 'mystics', except, perhaps, in their spare time. Furthermore, there has yet to arise a major political party which, in self-consciously espousing any variety of political mysticism, has come close to the National Socialists. Indeed, it is precisely this sort of nominalist attitude — often informed by a large dose of Calvinism — that has made it so difficult for Western thinkers to come to grips with the National Socialist phenomenon. While this writer believes that the Judaeo-Christian tradition, with its suspension of humankind between natural world and a divine order, has placed a tremendous burden upon painfully finite beings, most inhabitants of Western lands seem comfortable enough, at least consciously, with it. Self-conscious immersion in nature is still generally viewed as a somewhat esoteric enterprise, to be engaged in by environmental extremists, occultists and other aberrant sorts described earlier. None the less, while there would appear to be a good deal of at least conscious resistance to any kind of 'religion of nature' — certainly, in any case, one which would supplant traditional religious forms — certain elements crucial to this religion are prevalent today, even if cast in deceptively prosaic molds. These elements are: (1) a flight from history; (2) efforts to sanctify national life; and (3) belief in a 'natural order of things' within which varieties of human beings are perceived as being almost providentially condemned. What we will be talking about are elements, which, if not strictly speaking constitutive of a 'religion of nature', are none the less central to an ideology so widespread and so pervasive as to be almost unrecognisable as such. The author assumes that these elements are generic to the West as a whole, but will be devoting his remarks mainly to contemporary American life.

There is little question but that today's problems not only suggest but demand that nationalism's role in world affairs be severely limited or abolished altogether. At one point, 'the tribal mentality', of which, of course, nationalism is merely an extension, might have assured survival. 'However, this tribal mentality . . . is anachronistic in the age of mass killing and genocide.'[8] Yet appeals to nationalism are stronger than ever before, at least in recent years. It is no doubt true that, as Dr Johnson put it, 'Patriotism is the last refuge of a scoundrel', but those who make the most effective use of this 'refuge' generally are elected to public office. At the same time, of course, important social concerns are neglected in the name of 'the national interest'. Nationalistic sloganeering, in a nuclear, genocidal world, constitutes a 'flight from history', as real, and as least as dangerous, as that undertaken by those ingenuous souls who once sought refuge from the perils of transcendence in a *Volksgemeinschaft*. Indeed, in present-day America, there are probably more people who believe that they are participating in a chimera approximating this than there were in National Socialist Germany. As in the Germany of fifty years ago, people fear change, other than those technological advances perceived of as being immediately beneficial, and American politics today is infused by a longing for timeless *stasis*. Accompanying this we can perceive a sanctifying of national life which finds expression in appeals to the most jejune nationalistic atavisms imaginable. Probably the most poignantly naïve — and also dangerous — of these is the notion that a country indeed exists in some sort of sacred space/time continuum. President Ronald Reagan recently expressed this when he declared that he saw American values — if not the country itself — as 'eternal'. Perhaps, in a non-nuclear age, this remark could be taken as an ahistorical joke, albeit a bad one. Nowadays, it borders on the obscene. It is, of course, no more obscene than the remark made by a Soviet airforce general; to wit, that his airmen were justified in shooting down an obviously defenceless airliner because it had dared to transgress his country's 'sacred frontiers' (the phrase itself is most suggestive). I will however, leave it to other authors to consider the Soviet variant of nationalistic lunacy, which, of course, is supposedly informed by a 'sincere' search for some sort of *Marxist* sacred realm, but, in any case, is at least as much of a flight from history as its American equivalent.

Perhaps it is true that any form of nationalism, at any time, implicitly involves some sort of sanctification of national life. Nineteenth century variants of it, however, did not involve, in fact, could not have involved, a flight from history. Indeed, steeled by doctrines of social change and universal progress, however illusive these might have been, nationalists of that time saw themselves as being on the cutting edge of history; and indeed, they were often correct. World War I, however, demonstrated the bankruptcy, if not the moral rot, of nationalism in an age of mass slaughter. Yet, ironically enough, while the war did little, if anything, to stem the nationalist tide, it was almost precisely at that time when the wedding of totalitarian ideology to mechanised technique made it possible for claims to be made on the whole man, and a 'genuine' sanctification of national life thus made possible.

Concurrently, modern mass warfare demonstrated for all to see that nationalism could have no more 'progressive' claims to make; that the absolutising of national values had to involve a suspension of ethical responsibility which could only take place within the context of a flight from history; a flight into a sacred space within which hideous archaisms could be nurtured. Present day Western nationalisms, e.g., American nationalism, are not sustained and enforced by movements which proudly claim to have grasped 'the laws of life'. None the less, they have to involve flights from history and claims upon sacred spaces which, in the nuclear age, are as idolatrous as the more self-conscious and systematic National Socialist efforts to bring the world into conformity with its naturalistic fantasies.[9] At the time of writing, the American political leadership, to say nothing of the public which elected it, seems to have accepted the existence of a sacred, and hence, in the twentieth century context, ahistorical national community.

The 'sanctification of national life' which we can observe in the United States has been justified through appeal to presumably traditional Judaeo-Christian values. In this distinctly American claim, one which might well be traced to the Puritan 'City on the Hill' (a favourite phrase of the current President), we can observe an approach seemingly the opposite of that of the National Socialists, who were eager to dispense with this tradition altogether.[10] As has to be the case, though, if an ahistorical national community is to receive divine sanctification, the religious values emphasised must be ones which are magically congruent with those hallowed totemisms deemed vital to the life of this community. Richard Rubenstein has pointed out what these values are. They are those grounded in a concern for personal salvation and that earthly reward which testifies to this blessed state. They have either resulted in, or have served to rationalise, a 'dichotomising, possessive individualism' which, in turn, has informed American social thinking.[11] In this regard, Rubenstein has quoted H. Richard Niebuhr: 'in bourgeois religion the problem of personal salvation is far more important than that of social redemption'.[12] Thus, as Rubenstein has seen it, the rationalising, disenchanting (or demystifying) effects of the Judaeo-Christian tradition have been complemented by a coldly individualistic way of looking at the world which is also generic to this tradition. As has been obvious in the discussion up to now, the author has posed National Socialist emphasis upon its own variety of *re*enchantment of the world *against* elements of the Judaeo-Christian tradition that he views more positively. Nevertheless it would be very difficult to argue with Rubenstein's assertion that certain crucial elements of this self-same tradition have had extremely negative effects in so far as social consciousness is concerned. Furthermore, it would also be difficult to argue with his claim that emphasis upon salvation of a select few, prominent in the Judaeo-Christian tradition as a whole, but especially developed in Calvinism, helped prepare the way for a general acceptance of some of the crueller elements of

Darwinian thinking.[13] At the same time, however, it is my opinion that application of coldly individualistic, in the end, anti-social aspects of the Judaeo-Christian tradition to the world allowed for, if it did not cause, another *variety* of enchantment which found expression in sanctification of an assumed 'natural order of things'.

The sanctification of this natural order is something that had to result from emphasis upon individual salvation and a 'saved' community of the elect; earthly reward of course is the outward sign of such a condition. It is, however, crucial to point out that what allows for a sanctification of a natural order, i.e., of the 'given' is, a de-emphasising of transcendence. For individual gain to become sanctified through its being perceived as part and parcel of a 'natural order', emphasis could not be placed upon a 'world without end', but rather, upon one which effectively 'ended' in one's own time. Emphasis upon a purely individual salvation and upon that material gain seen as emblematic of it has to be purchased at the price of transcendence even if what we have in mind by it — as indeed we have throughout this book — is 'merely' historical change of a possibly radical nature. Concurrently, what must result is, what Marx has called, the 'fetishism of objects'. More than that, however, there emerges a fetishistic attitude towards, not merely 'objects' — i.e., manufactured goods and the money which both is generated by those and allows at least to some people to purchase them — but all institutions and symbols which are identified with stasis. The government, private enterprises, the military and the flag become charged with mystifying, or 'enchanting', values.[14] In turn, they are perceived, indeed, *must* be perceived, as part of a sanctified natural order. To be sure, Weber and Veblen were certainly correct when they maintained that modern, rationalising technique had served to deprive the world of that 'magic' identified with animistic or 'other-worldly' values or beliefs. Yet, if as a variety of commentators have claimed, human beings are always more religious than they or others think, then it follows that religiosity must find expression.[15] Belief, at times quite fanatical, in a sanctified natural order within which the most anti-humanistic and anti-transcendent values reign supreme, has been a form of expression congruent with the social, political and cultural circumstances prevalent in the West in general, and the United States in particular.

Naturally, belief in a natural order implies acceptance of inequities within it. There will always be those who cannot 'make it', those whom a conveniently bourgeois Providence has condemned to being 'drones'. At times, of course, when governments have been moved by more humanistic values, various programs on behalf of such people have been undertaken. If, however, fiscal problems, economic deficiencies and questions of the 'national interest', i.e., defence, are perceived as being paramount, then, as must be expected, the fate of those who cannot 'make it' on their own becomes of secondary importance. In contemporary America, there seems to be a *willingness* to accept the existence of a large body of permanently poor, unassimilable folks, while the current British government seems willing to accept a permanent level of fairly high unemployment.[16] Particularly in the United States, it would seem, the neglect of a large portion of its citizenry has been accompanied by frenetic declarations of faith in the old totemisms the relevance of which, in a nuclear age, is highly doubtful at best.

What we have been considering is not a 'religion' antipodal or dialectically related to, the National Socialist 'religion of nature'. At the very least, however, it is an ideology seemingly responsive to the needs of a post-industrial population fearful both of that alienation generic to the human condition and of historical change, transcendence, more than ever called for by the terrible exigencies of the nuclear age. Certain elements crucial to the National Socialist religion of nature are also central to this ideology. As we have seen these are: (1) the flight from history; (2) the sanctification of national life; and (3) belief in a 'natural order of things'. Perhaps because all of these elements have been informed by, indeed, are rooted in, certain aspects of the Judaeo-Christian tradition, the ideology is so pervasive that it is often not even recognised as being such. It is not characterised by, indeed, its bearers would largely reject, the now seemingly absurd bits of exotic symbolism representative of the National Socialist religion. It does not call for the extermination of any people. Indeed, it occasionally articulates itself in calls for 'brotherhood' of one sort or another. Obviously, a 'religion of nature' would be perceived as blasphemous by those who adhere, consciously or not, to the current ideology generic to the post-industrial West, or at least America. Yet, as was the case with National Socialism, this ideology represents a flight from history and search for some sort of sacred space/time realm. Also, although a good deal more subtly, it provides for a form of enchantment absolutely compatible with social stasis. It is fundamentally anti-transcendent and anti-humanistic. Certainly, the author is not claiming that this effort to deal — or really, *not* to deal — with the perennial questions of alienation, as well as those obviously pressing ones generic to our age, somehow, even unconsciously, 'stems from' or is a copy of, the National Socialist solution we have been considering throughout the book. What it points to, though, is the terribly human tendency to try and avoid facing disquieting issues which might well necessitate radical social, political or cultural change. 'Fear of transcendence'; 'flight from history'; the searching out for some sort of 'sacred space' immune from change, and efforts to sanctify a 'natural order', and, concurrently, national life — all of these are part and parcel of a broader effort to *re*enchant, or remystify, a world when 'times are out of joint'.

A particular constellation of historical circumstances and contemporary conditions assured that very basic human responses would assume the form they did (at least for some) in a National Socialist religion of nature opposed to the Judaeo-Christian tradition. Another constellation of circumstances and conditions has produced an *ideology* which, while vastly different in many ways, yet points to the same general underlying needs and responses. With regard to this ideology, it is of crucial importance to note again that it has drawn upon certain aspects of the Judaeo-Christian tradition. At the same time, though, it is equally important to note that other elements, of perhaps even greater importance, have been either played down or ignored. These, the same elements upon which the National Socialists focused most of their rage, are an emphasis upon the divinity of humankind, the idea of people being, as the psalmist put it, 'little lower than the angels', and the crucial role of transcendence. Deemphasising the two of them allows for a brutal freezing of reality which can be viewed as providentially-ordained. Humanity, however one might be repelled by various of its representatives, and transcendence necessarily go together. In truth, one of those factors which makes certain beings human is *precisely* this ability to perceive situations or conditions as they are and move beyond them. Perhaps, if one is to be thoroughly literal about it, neither the divinity of humankind or transcendence is 'real'. Yet, the example provided by National Socialist excursions into naturalism, and the desperate, pressing needs of today suggest that, if one must orient one's behaviour in terms of myths (and this more assuredly has proved the case thus far), it would serve humanity far better if one chose to believe in these. Humankind would most assuredly be better served if we acted as if it were ultimately responsible for its fate. The author realises that, strictly speaking, this is not exactly a 'logical' approach. In a world which must be without end inhabited by finite beings, it is, though, probably the only *rational* one.

In his *Life on the Mississippi*, Mark Twain included an essay entitled 'Enchantments and Enchanters'. It was largely devoted to attacking what he saw as the nefarious influence of the romanticism of Sir Walter Scott upon the American South, and obviously was concerned with the sources of that variety of enchantment which would eventually be manifested in National Socialism. After describing the progressive influences of the

French Revolution and Napoleon, Twain made the following observation:

> Then comes Sir Walter Scott with his enchantments, and by his single
> might checks this wave of progress, and even turns it back; sets the
> world in love with dreams and phantoms; even decayed and swinish
> forms of religion; with decayed and degraded systems of government;
> with the silliness and emptiness, sham grandeurs, sham gauds, and
> sham chivalries of a brainless and worthless long-vanished society.
> He did measureless harm; more real and lasting harm, perhaps, than
> any other individual that ever wrote.[17]

Of course, the author has included a lengthy quote from this essay
because, while recognising the hyperbolic character of Twain's attack
on the medieval period, he none the less thoroughly approves of the
general message conveyed. Twain was not, of course, attacking the right
of an individual to grasp for enchantment. He *was* saying, however, that
if such a desire comes to inform the character of a whole society, then
a disturbing if not dangerous situation can arise. The problem is, of
course, whether one is able to recognise that these personal efforts to
overcome that alienation characteristic of modern society — efforts which
almost always fail — which assume the several forms of enchantments,
are merely phantoms, fantasies by means of which brains tortured by
the agonies of modern life seek temporary relief. The back-to-nature fantasy is probably more of the most wide-spread in modern, Western
civilisation. So is the fantasy of avoiding transcendence through fleeing
history and seeking shelter in some sort of providential 'natural order'.
To be sure, they are both based on a fundamental truth, *viz.*, humans
are part of a natural order. However, they are fantasies to the extent
that they fail to recognise that humans — often nasty, brutish, thoroughly
unlovable — can neither go home again to those presumably ingenuous
pleasures associated with arboreal ancestors, or in the end, *survive*, if
they seek refuge in some sort of endless present.

    In National Socialism we see an example of what can occur when
the desire to achieve a virtually timeless state, to return to what could
be called, to use a Freudian analogy, a permanent state of 'oceanic feeling' (to a time in which that alienation made unavoidable by ego dif-
ferentiation has not yet appeared) becomes the guiding principle of public
life. In the immanency of the National Socialist *Weltanschauung* religion
and politics were one, and fantasy became reality through counter-
revolutionary praxis. Enchantment attained through the translation of
'laws of life' into reality quite naturally had to result in the elimination

of those beings who deaths were justified by their living outside life in the first place.

As Richard Rubenstein has pointed out so well, population pressures, food shortages and the like might well result in the application of Nazi-like solutions in the future.[18] Most certainly the existence of coldly efficient, depersonalised bureaucracies, to say nothing of computers (as Rubenstein has said, one can only marvel at what the Nazis were able to accomplish without them), have provided modern states and/or political movements with the means of carrying out such solutions. These mechanisms of modern life are certainly products of and contributors to, processes of rationalisation and secularisation. However, that which called for the most efficient of techniques to be applied to tasks of extermination was a form of religiosity seemingly congruent with modern needs. Most of these needs centre around the questions of alienation and fear of change. The unwillingness to deal realistically with these needs has been reflected in rigid adherence to a 'Western' ideology that, in certain crucial ways, however unintended, has replicated aspects of the National Socialist religion. In the end, it is hypothetically as dangerously utopian, and in practice perhaps equally dystopian, as its more obviously hideous predecessor. 'Utopia' literally *is* 'no place'; but the remains of the gas chambers and crematoria of Auschwitz can be seen today.

Notes

1. Richard L. Rubenstein, *The Cunning of History: Mass Death and the American Future* (New York, Harper and Row, 1975), p. 28.

2. Richard L. Rubenstein, *The Age of Triage, Fear and Hope in an Overcrowded World* (Boston, Beacon Press, 1983), p. 218.

3. Rubenstein, *The Cunning of History*, p. 94.

4. Ibid., p. 95. Although he views the city from a somewhat different perspective, Rubenstein's description of it bears a startling resemblance to those provided by representatives of the German right.

5. One could, of course, offer the notion of original sin, something that is part of the Christian, but not the Jewish, tradition. But this applied to all peoples, Christians included. While murder and annihilation as part of a conscientiously carried out policy rarely were undertaken in the West (one could perhaps suggest the Albigensian Crusade of the 13th century as an exception, but conversion had existed as a possibility until the undertaking of the crusade itself), it is instructive to note that such was *not* the case with regard to the Mongols, a people of course singularly removed from the Judaeo-Christian traditions. Estimates as to the lives taken in the Mongol massacre range up to 10 million, which demonstrates that what these people lacked in technology, they more than compensated for in enthusiasm.

6. Jean-Pierre Sironneau has seen this as a response to sensed inadequacies of the

major religions to deal with the question of secularisation. See *Sécularisation et religions politiques* (The Hague, Paris, New York, Mouton, 1982), p. 194.

7. Wilhelm Reich, *The Mass Psychology of Fascism*, translated from the German by Vincent R. Carfagno (New York, The Noontide Press, 1971), pp. xv, 5, 169, 344. The behaviour of the West German 'Green' Party has been somewhat ambivalent in this regard. For a good discussion of the contradictions in this party see Horst Mewes, 'The West German Green Party', in *New German Critique*, 1983, *28*, Winter. For a discussion of recent Green political behaviour in Hesse, see 'An die Tröge', in *Der Spiegel*, Nr. 18, 29 Jahrgang, 29 April 1985.

8. Dr. Helen Caldicott, *Missile Envy, The Arms Race and Nuclear War* (New York, William Morrow and Co., 1984), p. 289.

9. On the use of the term 'idolatry', in this context, see Sironneau, *Sécularisation et religions politiques*, p. 525. Paul Tillich declared idolatrous sanctification of an object 'without reference to the divine' to be 'demonic'. See Sironneau, p. 46. Also see Friedrich Gogarten (about whom more will be said later), *Despair and Hope for Our Time*, translated by Thomas Wieser (Philadelphia and Boston, Pilgrim Press, 1970), p. 108.

10. For an interesting, and somewhat sympathetic, treatment of the American tendency to sanctify at least political institutions, see Paul Johnson, 'The Almost Chosen People', in *Time & Tide: A Quarterly Review*, Spring 1985.

11. Rubenstein, *Triage*, p. 229.

12. Ibid.

13. Ibid.

14. A most interesting idea regarding the *origins* of flags has been advanced by Lloyd DeMause. They began as the actual placentas of pharaohs stuck on poles. This was 'the concrete prototype of all flags and standards to follow'. Lloyd DeMause, *Foundations of Psychohistory* (New York, Psychohistory Press, 1982), p. 289. The 'flag' thus resulted from efforts to utilise the 'life-giving powers of the king' in potentially dangerous situations. If memories of this origin subsist as unconscious residues of one sort or another, one can understand why flags, particularly in times of stress, become charged with emotional energy.

15. We have already considered the remarks of Leo Schneiderman. See also, Sironneau, *Sécularisation et religions politiques*, pp. 125, 560.

16. On the existence of such a group in America, see Rubenstein, *Triage*, p. 93.

17. Mark Twain, 'Enchantment and Enchanters', in Charles B. Shaw (ed.), *American Essays* (New York, New American Library, 1948), p. 67.

18. Rubenstein, *The Cunning of History*, pp. 83–5; *Triage*, p. 212.

APPENDIX: THE NATIONAL SOCIALIST RELIGION AND THE GERMAN PEOPLE

In Chapter 6, we were primarily concerned with what could be called the metaphysical, anti-historical appeal of National Socialism, and why such could exercise considerable drawing power in Germany. Yet the author was careful to point out that, in his opinion, it will always be difficult to determine just how many Germans were affected by this, or if so, to what degree. It is important to point out, however, that, in recent years, various investigators, making use of quantified approaches, have attempted to do this. One of these, Professor Richard Hamilton, was mentioned earlier. There have been others as well. Here, the pioneering work of Peter Merkl, cited from time to time throughout the text, must come to hand, as does that of William S. Allen who, while not strictly speaking a 'quantifier', applied something of a quantified approach to a now famous small German town.[1] Sarah Gordon, a student of Allen's, has published a work, *Hitler, Germans and the 'Jewish Question'*, in which the impact of probably the most crucial element, at least in historical terms, of the National Socialist religion upon the German populace has been studied at some length.[2]

In all of these works, one overriding conclusion has been drawn; namely, that while Hitler himself may have been influential as a speaker of immense power, the role of ideology *per se* — in Hamilton's case, an exception to this has been noted earlier — was not very great. This was so even, and perhaps especially, with regards to anti-Semitism. In fact, Gordon has gone so far as to question its role within the National Socialist Party itself.[3] In all events, she has maintained, anti-Semitism was not 'logically' necessary for the National Socialist movement to have attained power.[4] Obviously, particularly if we bear in mind the social origins and usages of ideology mentioned at the beginning of this work, the role of the Nazi ideology, to say nothing of the religiously-grounded *Weltanschauung* of which it was the expression, has been called into question. As a non-quantifier, Fred Weinstein, has emphasised in his work, it would seem that the reasons people supported National Socialism, even the reasons they joined the National Socialist Party, were so varied that any attempt to apply generalisations to the phenomenon must be seen as counter-productive.[5] Once again — though this was probably not the intention of any of the authors mentioned — the National

Socialist phenomenon seems to defy historical explanation of any kind. In at least one of the works, its excesses have been described as the result of one man's ability to impose his perverse will upon a nation-state cowed into submission by the coarse instrument of bureaucratised terror.[6] At the same time, as one might expect, the quantifiers considered hold little brief for broad 'psychohistorical' explanations; although, it must be noted that, on their parts, they show little understanding of what psychohistory is all about.

It is certainly true that quantification, as articulated in voting studies, measurements of opinion and evidence regarding individuals who aided Jews based on court records, has to be viewed as a useful guard against overly reductionist approaches to National Socialism. As we have seen, reductionism can lead to metahistorical or nihilistic explanations which are both, necessarily, anti-historical, even if the quantified approach can also tend in this direction. Furthermore, quantified studies have the virtue of not allowing historians of any kind to remain comfortable with 'truths' so well established as to be virtually bromidic in their effects; e.g., that National Socialism was *primarily* a lower middle class phenomenon.[7] Even if, in counterargument, evidence in support of one or the other particular 'truth' can be presented, the challenges posed by quantifiers are healthy ones. They serve to keep other varieties of historians on their toes, perhaps a bit humble, and, at times, refreshingly baffled. Yet I think that, particularly with regard to the roles of ideology and what we have called the 'National Socialist Religion', both within the movement itself and in relation to the German people, these methods do not tell us a great deal.

Certainly, we can learn much about those courageous individuals, inside the party or outside of it, who either offered opposition to the National Socialist regime or 'aid' of one sort or another to Jews. Sarah Gordon's study, based on the police records of Düsseldorf, tells us that such people tended to be 'males, older individuals, independents and white-collar workers'.[8] Here, Gordon, much like her mentor William Allen, has made much of the notion of abstract anti-Semitism.[9] Thus there is the clear impression that many, perhaps most, Germans harboured a certain dislike for Jews in a general, abstract sort of fashion. Yet they were not likely to participate in concrete anti-Semitic activity.[10] Indeed, during such 'actions' as *Kristallnacht*, in November 1938, they might even have offered assistance to Jews they knew. Certainly, there can be little doubt that the 'abstract' variety of anti-Semite was often shocked by the gross violence and, above all, illegal behaviour, undertaken against Jews, particularly those with whom they had been acquainted.[11] At the same time, however, the existence of an 'abstract' variety of anti-Semitism, something that all authors have widely acknowledged, is instructive. It points to the existence of a general set of beliefs and values more or less taken for granted in German society. The beliefs can, I think, be summed up by the term 'bourgeois group fantasy' and, while elements of this fantasy had been in existence for some time — certainly since Germany's emergence as a major industrial power — it became of immense political importance only after World War I. We have in part touched upon this in our earlier considerations of 'sacred time', i.e., the desire to flee from or freeze history that was so crucial to the National Socialist Religion. More important, though, in considering the relationship between this religion and the German population as a whole, was this generally held 'bourgeois group fantasy' the most important aspects of which were the following: persistent yearning for a super-political 'folk-community' (*Volksgemeinschaft*); a continuous unease with industrial society and, linked to this, a strong anti-urban bias; a tendency to extol the values of 'natural' and 'unpolitical' youth, an almost frenetic desire for strong leadership; and, finally, the *feeling* — for usually it was little more than that — that Jews, a foreign, apparently unnatural element, perhaps did not *belong* in Germany, even if it would be rather untoward to drive them from the country.[12]

Naturally, not every German, not even every middle-class German, believed in all aspects of the fantasy all the time. Also, there had to have been — and were — differences between 'liberals' and 'conservatives' as to the persistence and importance of the fantasy in day-to-day life. While, however, this could be crucial from time to time — and while 'working class' belief in this fantasy has never been determined with certainty — the existence of such belief is beyond question.[13] Naturally, not every bourgeois who believed in some parts, or even all, of this fantasy necessarily voted National Socialist. Furthermore, as Gordon has proved, not even seemingly convinced members of the party — individuals who accepted the bourgeois fantasy and, indeed, went well beyond it — had to accept the practical consequences of some of its more strident aspects. With regards to beliefs of a seemingly 'abstract' nature and, for many, anti-Semitism was more of an abstraction than, say, the *Volksgemeinschaft*, it is both difficult and dangerously misleading to draw some sort of line between thought — or 'fantasy' — and action.

It would, however, be equally misleading to assume that all of National Socialism, even the National Socialism that mattered — i.e., that of the leadership — was qualitatively removed from the pathetic musings of a bewildered citizenry. Indeed, as we have noted earlier, a veritable legion of authors has attempted to demonstrate how varieties of what can be called 'political romanticism' at least provided the background for the rise of National Socialism. At the same time, though, the much-discussed protean nature of the National Socialist ideology — as opposed to the religious core — allowed for a variety of groups and individuals to support the movement, and the recent quantitative studies under consideration have served simply to underscore this. Thus, an individual might *not be* an avowed political romantic, much less a consistent anti-Semite, to vote National Socialist, or even to lend the movement support beyond the voting booth. A large dose of anticommunism, anger at economic conditions, or a sudden, and understandable, outburst of resentment against Versailles might have sufficed. Yet whatever their opportunistic or agitational value might have been, *all* of these elements were crucial to National Socialists. The National Socialist Party for which millions of Germans voted and, in some cases, fought, stood, albeit in a more ruthless fashion, for what they believed. Thus, as has been pointed out earlier, it is questionable whether or not National Socialist anti-Semitism was indeed necessary for the party to have come to power. Yet one can make the point that some of the nastier elements of the National Socialist outlook, as known to the German public, did not *prevent* large numbers of this public from voting National Socialist.[14]

People voted National Socialist, or, beyond that, lent it support, because of the basic *acceptance* of certain assumptions, assumptions which were crucial to a fantasy world generic to at least German middle class life. From the perspective of National Socialist actions once the movement had attained power, the most important of these assumptions was the existence of 'The Jew' as a sort of unlovable 'other'.[15] The average German might not have wanted to hurt the Jews, much less exterminate them, and actions such as those of *Kristallnacht* might well have been offensive to his/her sense of propriety. None the less, in view of the surging dynamism of National Socialism, in its consistent representation of so many elements crucial to the 'bourgeois fantasy' — most important of which was the almost sacred notion of *Volksgemeinschaft* — the fate of Jews *as a group* really did not matter all that much.

Of course, once the National Socialists were in power, the *Volksgemeinschaft* proved to be most elusive, and every class had reasons to complain against some of the alternately ineffective or heavy-handed policies of the regime; policies which, none the less, sufficed to bring Germany out of the depression.[16] Furthermore, as mentioned earlier, the National Socialist regime never really succeeded in creating a 'totalitarian state' and there is some question whether such was actually envisaged in the first place. Also, efforts at ideological control in such areas as education and science were halting and inconsistent, despite the fact that various ideologues such as Ernst Krieck saw these as crucial. Besides, the average engineer, research scientist and physician was quite content to 'go along' with the regime so long as he was left alone in his particular bailiwick.[17]

It is of immense interest to note that, whenever various party zealots attempted to challenge either of the two important churches — in a word, whenever the National Socialist religion, inherently anti-Christian in nature, confronted the traditional religious groups — National Socialist enthusiasts were forced into hasty, embarrassing retreats. As we have seen, the churches, particularly the Catholic church, played a decisive role in the calling off of the euthanasia campaign. Earlier, in 1934, National Socialist attacks upon a popular Lutheran Bishop, Hans Meiser of Nuremberg, and their eventual efforts to replace him, aroused a storm of protest which resulted in a somewhat undignified withdrawal on the part of local ideologues.[18] National Socialists suffered a similar, perhaps even greater embarrassment in 1941 when, in the Catholic portions of mainly Catholic Bavaria, they tried to enforce an edict banning crucifixes from the public schools. After some months of bitter confrontation, the order was rescinded.[19] Particularly to those most adamantly concerned with the eventual overthrow of Judaeo-Christian usages, it became plain that, because the political victory of the movement was 'only the prerequisite for the beginning of the fulfilment of their real mission', challenges to established religious traditions, particularly if domestic tranquillity were to be preserved, had to be rather subtle.[20]

It is obvious that, in very real ways, the established churches had managed to retain a good deal of influence, perhaps even gaining some as vehicles of popular protest against unpopular aspects of National Socialist rule. All observers, however, are united in the observation that church protest of any kind against either the general course of National Socialist foreign policy or the regime's anti-Jewish measures was minimal.[21] To be sure, the Bishop of Münster attacked the paganism of Alfred Rosenberg, Cardinal Faulhaber defended the Old Testament of Christianity (he did not, however, defend 'modern' Jews), and various priests offered protests against the treatment of Jews and the general conception of 'Aryanism'.[22] Protestant leaders, such as the well-known Martin Niemöller and Dietrich Bonhoeffer did the same, and the latter paid with his life for his participation in the 20 July 1944 bomb plot. Pastor Heinrich Gruber set up a relief agency to help Jews to emigrate. He paid for his commitment to Christian principle by being tortured in a concentration camp, and many of those involved in his relief agency were killed there.[23] He at least survived. Helmut Hesse, another pastor who spoke out in defence of Jews, did not, dying in Dachau in 1943.[24] The courageous preaching and in some cases, actions of these and other clergymen point out the fact that, as might have been expected, various representatives of the Christian faith recognised the religious challenge of National Socialism for what it was.

As stated above, however, all who have commented on the role of the churches have had to report that these individuals were the exceptions; that, in fact, organised church opposition to Nazism, except when it challenged church authority *per se*, was virtually non-existent. This points to the extremely crucial role of the hyphen in the term Judaeo-Christian. Certainly, all orthodox Christians had to recognise that there was such a unified tradition. Yet, the traditional identification of the Jews of killers of Christ — as, in fact, having committed 'Deicide' — or, at the very least, as being stiff-necked apostates, had to have been influential in deciding just how far representatives of Christianity would be willing to go in defending a group of people whose traditional economic and social roles in German life seemed to suggest that an angry God had provided a pariah role for it.[25] As has been noted, Cardinal Faulhaber's somewhat attenuated 'defence' of Biblical Judaism did not necessitate — nor, it seems, would he have wanted it to — defence of those 'modern' Jews threatened by National Socialism, and even the courageous Dietrich Bonhoeffer thought that, in the future, greater pressure would have to be put upon the Jews to compel them to recognise Jesus Christ as Lord.[26]

The response of German Christian clergy to National Socialist persecution of the Jews had to have been vitiated by centuries of traditional anti-Semitism. This, combined with a general approval of the anti-Bolshevik stance of the Nazis, particularly after later ideological embarrassments had been resolved through the invasion of the Soviet Union, tended to make meaningful church opposition to the salient principles of National Socialism weak in the extreme.[27] Thus, representatives of the major Christian denominations could not offer real leadership, particularly once the war became 'serious', and, most significantly, particularly once persecution became transformed into extermination. Furthermore, as seen earlier, the 'moralistic' side of National Socialism — it emphases upon family life, the 'traditional' role of women, and the seeming commitment to the uplifting of national life in general — elicited initial support from some clergymen. Friedrich Gogarten, a Protestant theologian who, with Karl Barth, had at one time fought against the liberalising influences

in late nineteenth century theology, and, like Barth, had placed emphasis
upon the absolute contrast between God and man, was an early supporter
of National Socialism, eventually counting himself a 'German Christian'.
In a curious sort of way, he placed emphasis upon *both* the radical separation of the world of God and the mundane world and a newly sensed
role of divine guidance in the world to justify National Socialism. Thus,
on the one hand, the coming to power of Hitler had to be seen as a
demonstration of how God showed direction and leadership through
political events. On the other hand, the vicissitudes of that purely *human*
existence, provided for by the will of God, necessitated that a person
render obedience to the state because it was the expression of the will
of that *Volk* to which he belonged.[28] His one time friend and ally, Karl
Barth, who played a prominent role in the anti-Nazi 'Confessing Church'
(*'Bekennenden kirche'*) did sense something of a contradiction in this,
and the friendship soon died as a result. Yet it would be erroneous to
assume that simple opportunism was responsible for Gogarten's descent
into theological conundrum. National Socialism was correctly perceived as constituting an assault upon liberalism in *any* form. At the same
time, the total claim upon the earthly essence of humanity exerted by
National Socialism seemed to underline the relevance of a church which,
traditionally, had often rationalised its existence in terms of 'rendering
unto Caesar'.[29] In any case while drawing a line between the National
Socialist *Weltanschauung*, at least as he understood it, and the Christian
faith *per se*, Gogarten voiced strong approval of the anti-individualistic,
anti-liberal stance of the new regime. In this, of course, he was at one
with a great many clerics who had never accepted either the fall of the
monarchy, or that liberal abomination, the Weimar Republic.

The radical 'totalism' of the National Socialist movement greatly attracted Gogarten. He declared that since it came 'out of the core of human
life', it embraced the totality of at least earthly existence.[30] No doubt
bearing in mind the apparent anomic chaos of Weimar life, he went on
to state that any person unwilling to accept the fact that true human
freedom came only with the rule of a state governed by the National
Socialist movement was only an 'abstract individual'.[31] There can be
little doubt that, in its apparent total moral commitment to the German
people, National Socialism was perceived by Gogarten as being a
providentially-ordained bridge between the ontologically divided worlds
of God and man. In due course, he came to regret (at least partially)
his early, unfortunate evaluation of the saving power of National
Socialism and, after the war, became a leader in the 'secularisation'
movement of Protestantism, one which, even more than Gogarten had

done earlier, emphasised the radical separation between the world of God and the world of man. This time, there would be no room for political mediation.[32]

The conservative Protestant theologian, Wilhelm Stapel, also sought accommodation with the National Socialists and, in some ways, went even further than Gogarten. A strong believer in the *Volksgemeinschaft*, the rebirth of German military power and the *Führerprinzip*, he emphasised the 'cleansing' role that National Socialism would play regarding a perceived Jewish domination of German culture. In a strongly moralistic diatribe, which appeared in 1937, Stapel declared that it had been the 'Jewish Spirit' that had been responsible for the degenerating intrusions of 'psychology' and liberal values into literature.[33] Jewish emancipation which, thank God, was now being undone by the National Socialist movement, had been fearfully mistaken in considering the Jew as a human being when, in reality, he remained the same archetypal Jew 'that he was from the beginning'.[34] Stapel, who here came close to rejecting Christianity altogether in favour of racism, would later have cause to regret much of what he said, and became a critic of Hitler. Yet, particularly in his attacks on a perceived Jewish immorality, he represented a fairly substantial body of clerical opinion.

Thus, while one can point to a number of religious leaders who, for theological or simply ethical reasons, offered opposition to National Socialism, there were many more who either offered no opposition whatever (unless, of course, the religious claims of some National Socialists brought about jurisdictional disputes), or who sought accommodation with the new order, seeing within it a strong moral imperative. They (many of them 'German Christians'), as did of course no small number of lay people, saw little conflict between National Socialist goals *as they understood them* and the transcendental claims of Christianity. As a rule, the National Socialist leadership had no intention of disabusing these people, while those who did sense the tension between two *Weltanschauungen*, and perhaps acted on that basis, could be dealt with over time.

In all of this, it is important to bear in mind that 'true believers' such as Hitler, Himmler, Goebbels and others (here, Martin Bormann must be reckoned as being something of an exception) came to recognise that their own very real system of religious values had to be introduced to the German people 'in small doses'. To the extent that the average German adhered to 'traditional' religious values, these could not be attacked head-on. To the extent that the average German, while 'abstractly' anti-Semitic, still disapproved of the window-breaking, head-breaking violence of *Kristallnacht*, the far-reaching actions against Jews necessitated by their religion of nature could not be publicised. As mentioned earlier, the 'mission' of National Socialism necessitated caution. Like missionaries in a possibly hostile environment, National Socialist bearers of the religion of nature could not afford to discomfit the populace to an inordinate degree.

Nevertheless, there was enough 'overlap' at certain levels, and enough anti-Semitism, usually 'abstract', but sometimes more than that, and enough visceral enthusiasm generated by diplomatic and military successes, to assure a level of support, necessary for the National Socialists to undertake the first crucial steps in their own revolution.[35] Ironically enough, that 'traditional' anti-Semitism which in large measure flowed from Christianity, something which National Socialism supposedly would supplant, helped to assure a general level of support for 'moderate' anti-Semitic measures, e.g., the Nuremberg laws of 1935.[36] More ideological variants of anti-Semitism that had become generic to German cultural life certainly were of value in this regard, although how much so can probably never be established with certainty. Certainly, as we have seen, there were Germans who did not go along with all of this. As has been pointed out, there were even cases in which SS guards at concentration camps showed kindness to prisoners.[37] None the less, the fate of a generally disliked portion of the population could not excite the same sort of opposition as could threats to established and respected religious traditions. For most Germans, such opposition was not worth the risk to oneself or to one's family, and the persistent barrage of official anti-Semitic propaganda most assuredly had a strong influence, particularly with the younger generation.[38] For those who, quite simply, did not *want* to know what was happening, — and once the extermination programs began, this was crucial — quite simply, one did not *have* to know. All who have commented upon public opinion in National Socialist Germany have emphasised that, while there was much grumbling over such things as economic controls, food shortages, and the persistence of class privilege — itself a testimony to the chimerical nature of the *Volksgemeinschaft* — the 'Jewish Question' was not very important to most Germans.[39]

Thus, the degree to which major tenets of the National Socialist Religion affected the behaviour of the everyday German must remain elusive. Opinion polls, police records, and even specific examples of assistance to declared racial enemies cannot, in the end, measure the degree to which most Germans accepted even that which they were allowed to know about the guiding principles of National Socialism. With regard to the religious 'core', it is plain that the regime itself was, and had to be, extremely cautious. Outside those in the leading circles of the party or the SS, or those who listened attentively to lectures at SS training schools such as Bad Tölz, probably relatively few Germans were aware of the revolution in religious values, of which the 'Final Solution' was deemed a necessary first step.

Yet, even the *core* of the National Socialist religion of nature was not something utterly alien to Western/Central European cultural history in general, and that of Germany in particular. In part it was rooted in a general *malaise* that was a byproduct of material progress, a *malaise* which found articulation in 'the return to nature'. It received much of its specifically German centre from a 'group fantasy' that constituted a substantial portion of *at least* the bourgeois response to rapid economic growth, social displacement, military humiliation and cultural and political upheaval. Implicit in any fantasy is the guiding notion of freezing time, of a certain flight from historical reality. The sense of 'timelessness', or, as Eliade put it, of 'sacred time', is a crucial factor in determining the existence of fantasy *as fantasy*. In their efforts to assure the emergence and advancement of the 'new Aryan man', the bearers of National Socialist religiosity had to set the stage for a frozen, anti-transcendent world in which archetypal suppositions became truths grounded in 'nature's eternal laws'. Here, the National Socialists went beyond bourgeois fantasising in their determination to push matters through to a logical, if not rational, conclusion; in a word, to the point at which the literally *'fantastic'* became real. The vast mass of citizenry who, as German Europeans, had helped to construct a fantasy world which more ruthlessly consistent souls were attempting, with religious fervour, to transform into reality, bore witness to this process without, necessarily, being aware of implications.

From time to time, the fanfare of Liszt's 'Preludes' would blare forth from the radio, and this was inspiring, because it always preceded victory proclamations. From time to time, heavy-handed policies or oversights would arouse hostility on the part of one group or another of the population, and grumblings were dutifully recorded by members of the SS 'Security Service'. Perhaps citizens would read about, or even witness, an SS ceremony of some sort. No doubt it struck 'lay people' as interesting, perhaps a bit frightening, certainly a trifle bizarre. Occasionally, citizens would catch a glimpse of wizened, wax-faced wraiths in outsized pyjama-uniforms and hear rumours about where they were going and what was being done to them.[40] Eventually, there was aerial bombardment, military decline and, finally, disaster. In the end, a people embittered by party corruption and awash in a sea of contradictory or disturbing evidence best not reflected on, much less assimilated, had only an increasingly remote Führer in whom to believe. Almost until the end, most of the German people continued to put their faith in him, unaware that the guiding principles of his religion necessitated that he condemn them to destruction even as he prepared to take leave of a world unworthy of so singular a prophet.

Notes

1. William S. Allen's classical study, *The Nazi Seizure of Power*, has recently appeared in updated form as, *The Nazi Seizure of Power: The Experiences of a Single German Town, 1922–1945*, revised edition (New York, Franklin Watts, 1984).
2. Sarah Gordon, *Hitler, Germans and the 'Jewish Question'* (Princeton, New Jersey, Princeton University Press, 1984).
3. Differences of opinion as to the proper solution to the 'Jewish Question' are discussed in Chapters 2 and 4 of the above work.
4. Ibid., p. 311. See also, John Hiden and John Farquharson, *Explaining Hitler's Germany* (Totowa, New Jersey, Barnes and Noble, 1983), p. 31.
5. Fred Weinstein, *The Dynamics of Nazism: Leadership Ideology, and the Holocaust* (New York, Academic Press, 1980), pp. 59–60.
6. Gordon, *Hitler, Germans and the 'Jewish Question'*, pp. 312–6.
7. A challenge to the notion that the German lower middle class bore the greatest degree of responsibility for Hitler's coming to power has been posed by Richard F. Hamilton, *Who Voted for Hitler?* (Princeton, New Jersey, Princeton University Press, 1982). Michael H. Kater, *The Nazi Party: A Social Profile of Members and Leaders* (Cambridge, Mass., Harvard University Press, 1983), while not concerned with those who voted for the National Socialist Party, suggests that much of the membership of it was lower middle class, and that the party as a whole was dominated by lower middle class values.
8. Gordon, *Hitler, Germans, and the 'Jewish Question'*, p. 271. Gordon states that her research has revealed that women and blue-collar workers were least likely to offer assistance to Jews. Social, psychological and political reasons why this might have been the case have not been explored.
9. The existence of such is implied throughout Gordon's work. Allen uses the term on p. 84 of *The Nazi Seizure Power*.
10. Ian Kershaw, *Popular Opinion and Political Dissent in the Third Reich: Bavaria 1933–1945* (New York, Oxford University Press, 1983), pp. 266–8.
11. Ibid., pp. 232, 234–5, 273.
12. For a discussion of this 'fantasy' and its relationship to the National Socialist religion, see Robert A. Pois 'Jewish Treason against the Laws of Life: Nazi Religiosity and Bourgeois Fantasy', in Michael N. Dobkowski and Isidor Wallimann (eds.), *Towards the Holocaust: The Social and Economic Collapse of the Weimar Republic* (Westport, Connecticut, Greenwood Press, 1983). Also, the reader is referred to Peter Loewenberg, 'The Psychohistorical Origins of the Nazi Youth Cohort', in Peter Loewenberg, *Decoding the Past: The Psychohistorical Approach* (New York, Alfred Knopf, 1983); Rudolf Binion, *Hitler Among the Germans* (New York, Elsevier, 1976); Irving L. Janis, *Victims of Group Think: A Psychological Study of Foreign-Policy Decisions and Fiascoes* (Boston, Houghton Miflin, 1972). Lloyd DeMause developed the group fantasy concept to what could be considered its logical conclusion when he declared that all forms of human organisation, including the state, are really group fantasies. See his *Foundations of Psychohistory* (New York,

Psychohistory Press, 1982). For a review of the various uses made of this idea, see Peter Loewenberg, 'Psychohistory', in Michael Kammen (ed.), *The Past Before Us — Contemporary Historical Writing in the United States* (New York, Cornell University Press, 1980). A somewhat shortened version of this essay is in Loewenberg, *Decoding the Past*, pp. 14–41.

13. Working class musings about a sort of pre-industrial rural idyll, as discussed in Barrington Moore, *Injustice: The Social Bases of Obedience and Revolt* (White Plains, New York, M.E. Sharpe, 1978), have been considered earlier in this work. Whether or not the fuller articulation of this, the *Volksgemeinschaft* ideal was broadly represented in the working class is not known. Most workers, of course, continued to vote Social Democratic or Communist (although working class representation in the National Socialist Party was not insignificant), and the 'internationalism' of these two leftist parties certainly flew in the face of the *Volksgemeinschaft* idea.

14. For a discussion of the rather marginal role that concern for the Jews played in the political decision-making process of many Germans, see Weinstein, *The Dynamics of Nazism*, pp. 23–7. Also see Kershaw, *Popular Opinion and Political Dissent in the Third Reich*, pp. 276–7.

15. See Eugen Weber, 'Modern anti-Semitism', in Henry Friedlander and Sybil Milton (eds.), *The Holocaust: Ideology, Bureaucracy and Genocide* (Milwood, New York, Kraus International Publications, 1980), p. 44. Also, Arnold Paucker, *Der jüdische Abwehrkampf: gegen Antisemitismus und Nationalsozialismus in den letzen Jahren der Weimarer Republik* (Hamburg, Leibniz-Verlag, 1968), p. 146.

16. Complaints about the continued existence of class discrimination and class advantage were extremely common during the Hitler years. Ian Kershaw, in *Popular Opinion and Political Dissent in the Third Reich* has pointed out that farmers and businessmen (at least in Bavaria) apparently felt fairly free to voice complaints about various Nazi economic policies which seemed to — and did — favour well-established interests. Working class people even participated in an occasional strike. As Kershaw has stated, however, e.g., on p. 139, such complaints and protests were almost never political in nature.

17. See Gerth H. Brieger, 'The Medical Profession', Alan Beyerchen, 'The Physical Sciences', and Thomas D. Hughes, 'Technology', in Friedlander and Sybil, *The Holocaust*. Also, Reece C. Kelly, 'Die gescheiterte nationalsozialistische Personalpolitik und die misslungene Entwicklung der nationalsozialistischen Hochschulen', in Manfred Heinemann (Hrsg.), *Erziehung und Schulung im Dritten Reich*, Teil 2; *Hochschule, Erwachsenbildung* (Stuttgart, Klett-Cotta, 1980).

18. Kershaw, *Popular Opinion and Political Dissent in the Third Reich* (New York, Oxford University Press, 1983), pp. 163 ff. The 1934 Meiser dispute is also discussed in Ian Kershaw's earlier work, *Der Hitler-Mythos: Volksmeinung und Propaganda im Dritten Reich* (Stuttgart, Deutsche Verlag-Anstalt, 1980), pp. 98–102. Once the dispute was over, Meiser had no qualms about offering prayers thanking God for providing the German people with Hitler. See Kershaw, *Der Hitler-Mythos*, p. 93.

19. Kershaw, *Popular Opinion and Political Dissent in the Third Reich*, p. 341 ff. Kershaw, *Der Hitler-Mythos*, pp. 103 ff.

20. Kershaw, *Popular Opinion and Political Dissent in the Third Reich*, p. 1. In the church controversies of 1934 and 1941, Hitler's popularity as opposed to that of the party, increased, because he was perceived as being a moderate force, as indeed he was. He was ultimately responsible for at least slowing down the pace of anti-Christian activities. See Kershaw, *Der Hitler-Mythos*, p. 90 ff and p. 101 ff.

21. Indeed, with regard to bloodless victories, such as the *Anschluss* of Austria in March, 1938, the churches, particularly the Catholic church, assumed a very positive stance towards Hitler's foreign policy. See Kershaw, *Der Hitler-Mythos*, p. 97.

22. Gordon, *Hitler, Germans and the 'Jewish Question'*, p. 248. On Faulhaber's rather 'mixed message', see Kershaw, *Popular Opinion and Political Dissent*, pp. 247–8.

23. Kershaw, ibid., p. 255.

24. Ibid., p. 258.

25. David Winston, 'Pagan and Early Christian Anti-Semitism', in Friedlander and Milton, *The Holocaust*, pp. 23–4. In another essay in this volume, Gavin I. Langmuir has described a more 'popular' form of anti-Semitism which he has identified with Northern Europe. In his 'Medieval Anti-Semitism', he points to the following as characterising this version; '. . . repressed fantasies about crucifixion and cannibalism, repressed doubts about the real presence of Christ in the Eucharist, and unbearable fears of the bubonic bacillus that imperceptibly invaded peoples' bodies'. (Friedlander and Milton, p. 32.)

26. Gerald Fleming, *Hitler and the Final Solution*. With an Introduction by Saul Friedländer (Berkeley and Los Angeles, University of California Press, 1984), p. 12 fn.

27. On church support, particularly Catholic, of Hitler's war against Bolshevism, see Kershaw, *Popular Opinion and Political Dissent*, p. 340 ff.

28. Friedrich Gogarten, *Einheit von Evangelium und Volkstum* (Hamburg, Hanseatische Verlag, 1933), pp. 7–9.

29. John Conway has pointed out that while more conservative theologians, such as Barth, often offered resistance to National Socialism's claim upon the whole man, theologians who were somehow concerned with justifying the relevance of the church in an increasingly secular world usually either went along with the movement and its regime or capitulated to it altogether. See John S. Conway, 'The Churches', in Friedlander and Milton, *The Holocaust*, pp. 204–6.

30. Friedrich Gogarten, *Einheit von Evangelium and Volkstum*, pp. 10–11.

31. Ibid., p. 13.

32. For a consideration of Gogarten's role in the 'secularisation movement', one which approved of a demystifying of the world while exalting what its adherents saw as the 'true', Biblical notion of God and Christ, see Jean-Pierre Sironneau, *Secularisation et religions politiques* (The Hague, Paris, New York, Mouton, 1982), pp. 84–5. Considering his political decisions of the 1930s, it is perhaps ironic that, in his post-World War II writings, Gogarten expressed viewpoints which put him in a camp also occupied by Harvey Cox, Peter Berger and the late Dietrich Bohhoeffer.

33. Wilhelm Stapel, *Literartische Vorherrschafte der Juden in Deutschland: 1918 bis 1933* (Hamburg, Schriften d. Reichsinstitut für Geschichte d. Neuen Deutschland, 1937), p. 26, 41.

34. Ibid., p. 32. Stapel's 'critique' of Jewish influence in Germany, as well as his variant of racism, did not go far enough to please the National Socialists. For a good, general consideration of him and his career in National Socialist Germany, see Weinstein, *The Dynamics of Nazism*, pp. 11–12. In their efforts either to lend support to or come to an accommodation with, the National Socialist regime, few clergy went as far as Jesuit Hermann Muckermann, who praised a 'healthy racial stock' as a 'gift from heaven'. (Kershaw, *Popular Opinion and Political Dissent*, p. 250).

35. On Hitler's building upon, and then going beyond, 'traditional' German middle-class concerns, see Weinstein, *The Dynamics of Nazism*, pp. 24, 65–6.

36. Kershaw, *Public Opinion and Political Dissent*, pp. 269, 272–3. Gordon, *Hitler, Germans, and the 'Jewish Question'*, pp. 171–2. Of course, the Nuremberg Laws can be seen as 'moderate' only in comparison to what eventually happened. After all, they served to deprive the Jews of citizenship altogether and thus put them in a very precarious legal position.

37. George M. Kren and Leon Rappoport, *The Holocaust and the Crisis of Human Behavior* (New York, Holmes and Meier, 1980), p. 96.

38. On the role of propaganda in exacerbating anti-Semitism in German young people, see Gordon, *Hitler, Germans and the 'Jewish Question'*, p. 222.

39. Kershaw, *Public Opinion and Political Dissent*, pp. 360–1. Kershaw, *Der Hitler-Mythos*, pp. 132–3. Marlis G. Steinert, *Hitler's War and the German Public — Mood and Attitudes During the Second World War*, ed. and translated by Thomas E.J. de Witt (Athens, Ohio, Ohio University Press, 1977), pp. 151–3, 154.

40. While various authors talk about what the German people knew or did not know

about the slaughter of the Jews, probably the best discussion of this in English has been provided by Lawrence D. Stokes, 'The German People and the Destruction of the European Jews', in *Central European History*, 1973, *VI*, no. 2, June. See also Chapter I, 'Germany: A Wall of Silence?', in Walter Laqueur, *The Terrible Secret: Suppression of the Truth About Hitler's Final Solution* (Boston, Penguin Books, 1982).

BIBLIOGRAPHY

Archival Sources

Bundesarchiv, Koblenz: *Sammlung Schumacher*, Gruppe XIII, Gruppe XIV.
Institut für Zeitgeschichte, Munchen: Reels, MA 45, MA 138, MA 332, MA 558, MA
603, MA 608.
UCLA Library: *Völkischer Beobachter, 1938–1941, 1944–1945.*
Wiener Library, London: Files B2a, M3 (Books and Pamphlets).

Primary Sources

Darré, R. Walther, *Neuordnung unseres Denkens* (Goslar, Goslarev Volksbucherei, 1940).
Deutsche Kunstler und die SS (Berlin, n.p., 1944).
Domarus, Max, *Hitler: Reden und Proklamationen 1932-1945* (München, Suddeutsche
Verlag, 1965).
Dresler, Adolf, *Deutsche Kunst und entartete 'Kunst': Kunstwerk und Zerrbild als Spiegel
der Weltanschauung* (München, Deutschen Volksverlag, 1938).
Elbertzhagen, Alex, *Kampf um Gott in der religiösen Erziehung* (Leipzig, Armanen Verlag,
1934).
Fabricius, Cajus, *Positive Christianity in the Third Reich* (Dresden, H. Püschel, 1937).
Goebbels, Josef, *Final Entries 1945*, edited, introduced and annotated by Professor Hugh
Trevor-Roper; translated from the German by Richard Barry (New York, Putnam,
1978).
—— *The Goebbels Diaries 1939–1941*, Foreword by John Keegan; translated and edited
by Fred Taylor (New York, Penguin Books, 1984).
—— *The Goebbels Diaries*, translated and edited by Louis P. Lochner (New York, Lon-
don, Hamish Hamilton, 1948).
—— *Goebbels-Reden Band I: 1932–1939*, herausgegeben von Helmut Heiber (Düsseldorf,
Droste Verlag, 1971).
—— *Goebbels-Reden Band II: 1939–1945*, herausgegeben von Helmut Heiber (Düsseldorf,
Droste Verlag, 1972).
Gogarten, Friedrich, *Despair and Hope for our Time*, translated by Thomas Wieser
(Philadelphia and Boston, Pilgrim Press, 1970).
—— *Einhart von Evangelium und Volkstum* (Hamburg, Hanseatische Verlag, 1933).
Heiber, Helmut, and Kotze, Hildegard von, *Facsimile Querschnitt durch das Schwarze
Korps* (München, Scherz, 1968).
Himmler, Heinrich, *Himmler: Geheimreden!*, Einführung, Joachim C. Fest; herausgegeben
von Bradley F. Smith und Agnes F. Peterson (Frankfurt/M. and Berlin, Propyläen
Verlag, 1974).
—— *Reichsführer! Briefe an und von Himmler*, herausgegben von Helmut Heiber (Stutt-
gart, Deutsche Verlags-Anstalt, 1968).
Hitler, Adolf, *Hitler's Secret Conversations, 1941–1944*, with an introductory essay on
'The Mind of Adolf Hitler', by H.J.R. Trevor-Roper; translated from the German
by Norman Cameron and R.H. Stevens (New York, Farrar, Straus and Young, 1953).
—— *Secret Conversations with Hitler: The Two Newly-Discovered 1931 Interviews*, edited
by Edouard Calic, with a foreword by Golo Mann; translated from the German by
Richard Barry (New York, John Dayror, 1971).
—— *Mein Kampf*, translated by Ralph Manheim (Boston, Mass., Houghton Miflin, 1962).

Höss, Rudolf, *Commandant of Auschwitz*, translated from the German by Constantine Fitzgibbon (New York, Popular Library, 1959).

Jung, C.G., *Essays on Contemporary Events*, translated from the German by Elizabeth Welsh, Barbara Hannah and Mary Brines (London, K. Paul, 1947).

Kaiser, Fritz, (Hrsg.), *Entartete 'Kunst' Führer durch die Ausstellung* (Berlin, Kaiser, 1937).

Kersten, Felix, *The Kersten Memoirs 1940–1945*, with an introduction by H.R. Trevor-Roper; translated from the German by Constantine Fitzgibbon and James Oliver (New York, Macmillan, 1957).

Krieck, Ernst, 'Charakter und Weltanschauung', Rede zum 30 January 1938, *'Heidelberger Universitatsreden*, Neue Folge, Nr. 4 (Heidelberg, G. Winter Verlag, 1938).

—— 'Die Erneurerung der Universität', Rede zur Übergabe des Rektorats am 23. Mai 1933, Johann Wolfgang Goethe-Universitat, Frankfurter Akademische, Reden (Frankfurt/M, n.p., 1933).

—— 'Geschichte und Politik', Rede zum 30 January 1937, *Heidelberger Universitätsreden*, Neue Folge, Nr. 2 (Heidelberg, Carl Winter Verlag, 1937).

—— *Nationalpolitische Erziehung*, neunte und zehnte Auflage (Leipzig, Armanen Verlag, 1933).

—— *Völkische-Politische Anthropologie* Band I, *Die Wirklichkeit* (Leipzig, Armanen Verlag, 1938).

—— *Völkische-Politische Anthropologie*, Band II, *Das Handeln und die Ordnungen* (Leipzig, Armanen Verlag, 1937).

—— *Wissenschaft, Weltanschauung, Hochschulreform* (Leipzig, Armanen Verlag, 1934).

Lane, Barbara Miller and Rupp, Leila J. (eds.), *Nazi Ideology Before 1933: A Documentation*(Austin and London, University of Texas Press, 1978).

Meinecke, Friedrich, *Politische Schriften und Reden*, herausgegeben von Georg Kotowski (Darmstadt, Toeche-Mittler, 1958).

Mosse, George L. (ed.), *Nazi Culture* (New York, Grosset and Dunlap, 1965).

NSDAP Standartenkalender, 1937–1939 (München, Franz Eher Verlag, 1937–1939).

Rauschning, Herman, *Hitler Speaks: A Series of Political Conversations with Adolf Hitler on His Real Aims* (London, Heinemann, 1939).

—— *The Revolution of Nihilism: A Warning to the West* (New York, Longmans, Green and Co., 1939).

Remak, Joachim (ed.), *The Nazi Years: A Documentary History* (Englewood Cliffs, New Jersey, Prentice-Hall, 1969).

Rodens, Franz, *Vom Wesen deutschen Kunst* (Berlin, Franz Eher Verlag, 1941).

Rosenberg, Alfred, *Selected Writings*, edited and translated from the German by Robert A. Pois (London, Jonathan Cape, 1970).

Rust, Bernhard and Krieck, Ernst, 'Das Nationalsozialistische Deutschland und die Wissenschaft', *Heidelberger Reden* (Hamburg, Carl Winter Verlag, 1936).

Schultze-Naumburg, Paul, *Kunst aus Blut und Boden* (Leipzig, Verlag E.A. Seeman, 1934).

Shaw, Charles B. (ed.), *American Essays* (New York, New American Library, 1948).

Shirer, William L., *Berlin Diary: The Journal of a Foreign Correspondent 1934–1941* (New York, Penguin Books, 1941).

Speer, Albert, *Inside the Third Reich*, translated from the German by Richard and Clara Winston (New York, Macmillan, 1970).

Spelter, J. *Der Deutsche Erzieher als Lehrer der Rassenkunde* (Landsberg, Verlag Pfeiffer and Co., 1937).

Stapel, Wilhelm, *Literatische Vorherrschaft der Juden in Deutschland: 1918 bis 1933* (Hamburg, Schriften d. Reichsinstitut für Geschichte d. neuen Deutschlands, 1937).

Tröge, Walther, *Feuer und Farbe: 155 Bilder vom Kriege* (Wien, Wilhelm Frick Verlag, 1943).

Willrich, Wolfgang, *Des Reiches Soldaten* (Berlin, Verlag Grenze und Ausland, 1943).

Secondary Sources

Ackerman, Josef, *Heinrich Himmler als Ideologe* (Göttingen, Musterschmidt, 1970).
Adorno, Theodor *et al.*, *The Authoritarian Personality* (New York, Norton Library, 1950).
Allen, William S., *The Nazi Seizure of Power: the Experiences of a Single German Town 1922–1945*, revised edition (New York, Franklin Watts, 1984).
Altner, Günter, *Weltanschauliche Hintergründe der Rassenlehre des Dritten Reiches: Zum Problem einen Umfassenden Anthropologie* (Zurich, EVZ Verlag, 1968).
'An die Tröge', in *Der Spiegel*, Nr. 18, 39. Jahrgang, 29 April 1985.
Angebert, Jean Michel, *The Occult and the Third Reich*, translated by Lewis A.M. Sumberg (New York, Macmillan, 1974).
Arendt, Hannah, *Between Past and Future: Eight Exercises in Political Thought* (New York, Viking Press, 1977).
—— *Eichmann in Jerusalem: A Report on the Banality of Evil* (New York, Viking Press, 1963).
—— *The Origins of Totalitarianism* (New York, Harcourt, Brace Jovanovich, 1973).
Baird, Jay W., *The Mythical World of Nazi War Propaganda: 1939–1945* (Minneapolis, University of Minnesota Press, 1974).
Barnes, Hazel E., *An Existentialist Ethics* (New York, Alfred Knopf, 1967).
Berger, Peter L., *Facing Up to Modernity: Excursions in Society, Politics, and Religion* (New York, Basic Books, 1969).
—— *A Rumor of Angels: Modern Society and the Rediscovery of the Supernatural* (New York, Doubleday, 1969).
—— *The Sacred Canopy: Elements of a Sociological Theory of Religion* (New York, Doubleday, 1967).
Binion, Rudolf, *Hitler Among the Germans* (New York, Elsevier, 1976).
Bracher, Karl Dietrich, *The German Dictatorship*, translated from the German by Jean Steinberg (New York, Praeger, 1973).
Breitling, Rupert, *Die nationalsozialistische Rassenlehre: Ausbreitung, Nutzen und Schaden einer politischen Ideologie* (Meisenheim am Blan, A. Hain, 1971).
Brenner, Hildegard, *Die Kunstpolitik des Nationalsozialismus* (Hamburg, Rohwohlt, 1963).
Bridenthal, Renate, and Koonz, Claudia (eds.), *Becoming Visible: Women in European History* (Boston, Houghton Miflin, 1977).
Broszat, Martin, *German National Socialism 1919–1945*, translated from the German by Kurt Rosenbaum and Inge Pauli Boehm (Santa Barbara, California, Clio Press, 1966).
Buchheim, Hans, *et al.*, *Anatomie des SS-Staates*, Band I, Hans Buchheim, *Die SS-das Herrschaftsinstrument Befehl und Gehorsam* (München, Deutscher Taschenbuch Verlag, 1967).
—— *Totalitarian Rule: Its Nature and Characteristics*, translated from the German by Ruth Heim (Middletown, Connecticut, Wesleyan University Press, 1968).
Bullock, Alan, *Hitler: A Study in Tyranny* (New York, Harper and Row, 1964).
Caldicott, Dr. Helen, *Missile Envy: The Arms Race and Nuclear War* (New York, William Morrow and Co., 1984).
Carroll, Berenice A. (ed.), *Liberating Women's History: Theoretical and Critical Essays* (Urbana, Illinois, University of Illinois Press, 1971).
Cassirer, Ernst, *An Essay on Man: An Introduction to a Philosophy of Human Culture* (New York, Doubleday, 1953).
Cecil, Robert, *The Myth of the Master Race: Alfred Rosenberg and Nazi Ideology* (London, B.T. Batsford, 1972).
Cocks, Geoffrey, *The Göring Institute* (New York, Oxford University Press, 1984).
Cohn, Norman, *Pursuit of the Millenium* (New York Harper and Row, 1961).
Czichon, Eberhard, *Wer verhalf Hitler zum Macht? Am Anteil der deutschen Industrie an der Zerstörung der Weimarer Republik* (Köln, Paul-Rugenstein, 1967).

Damus, Martin, *Sozialistischer Realismus und Kunst im Nationalsozialismus* (Frankfurt/M Fischer Verlag, 1981).

Davidowicz, Lucy S., *The War Against the Jews 1933–1945* (New York, Holt, Rinehart and Winston, 1975).

DeMause, Lloyd, *Foundations of Psychohistory* (New York, Psychohistory Press, 1982).

Douglas, Mary, *Natural Symbols: Explorations in Cosmology* (New York, Pantheon Books, 1970).

Drescher, Seymour, Sabean, David and Sharlin, Allan, *Political Symbolism in Modern Europe* (New Brunswick, New Jersey, Transaction Press, 1982).

Eliade, Mircea, *The Myth of the Eternal Return, or, Cosmos and History* (Princeton, New Jersey, Princeton University Press, 1974).

Evans, Richard J. and Lee, W.R. (eds.), *The German Family: Essays on the Social History of the Family in Nineteenth and Twentieth Century Germany* (New York, Barnes and Noble, 1981).

Farquharson, J.E., *The Plough and the Swastika: The NSDAP and Agriculture in Germany 1928–1945* (London and Beverly Hills, Sage, 1976).

—— and Hiden, John, *Explaining Hitler's Germany* (Totowa, New Jersey, Barnes and Noble, 1983).

Fest, Joachim, C., *Hitler*, translated from the German by Richard and Clara Winston (New York, Vintage, 1975).

—— *The Face of the Third Reich: Portraits of the Nazi Leadership*, translated from the German by Michael Bullock (New York, Pantheon, 1970).

Fleck, Ludwick, *Genesis and Development of a Scientific Fact*, Foreword by Thomas S. Kuhn; translated by Fred Bradley and Thadeus J. Trenn (Chicago, University of Chicago Press, 1979).

Fleming, Gerald, *Hitler and the Final Solution*, with an Introduction by Saul Friedländer (Berkeley and Los Angeles, University of California Press, 1984).

Freud, Sigmund, 'Thoughts for the Times on War and Death', *Standard Edition of The Complete Psychological Works*, Volume XIV, edited by James Strachey (London, Hogarth Press, 1957).

Friedlander, Henry, and Milton, Sybil, *The Holocaust: Ideology, Bureaucracy, and Genocide* (Millwood, New York, Kraus International Publications, 1980).

Friedländer, Saul, *Reflections of Nazism: An Essay on Kitsch and Death*, translated from the French by Thomas Weyr (New York, Harper and Row, 1984).

Frischauer, Willi, *Himmler: The Evil Genius of the Third Reich* (Boston, Beacon Press, 1953).

Gasman, Daniel, *The Scientific Origins of National Socialism: Social Darwinism in Ernst Haeckel and the German Monist League* (New York and London, Macdonald and American Elsevier, 1971).

Geertz, Clifford (ed.), *Myth, Symbol, and Culture* (New York, Norton Library, 1972).

Gordon, Sarah, *Hitler, Germany, and the 'Jewish Question'* (Princeton, New Jersey, Princeton University Press, 1984).

Hallgarten, George, *Hitler, Reichswehr und Industrie: Zur Geschichte der Jahre 1918–1933* (Frankfurt/M. Europaische Verlagsanstalt, 1955).

Hamilton, Richard F., *Who Voted for Hitler?* (Princeton, New Jersey, Princeton University Press, 1982).

Heer, Friedrich, *Der Glaube des Adolf Hitler: Anatomie einer politischen Religiosität* (München, Bechtle, 1968).

Hinz, Berthold, *Art in the Third Reich*, translated from the German by Robert and Rita Kimber (New York, Pantheon, 1979).

Höhne, Heinz, *The order of the Death's Head*, translated from the German by Richard Barry (New York, Ballantine Books, 1970).

Jäckel, Eberhard, *Hitler's Welstanschauung* (Tübingen, R. Wunderlich, 1969).

Janis, Irving L., *Victims of Group Think: A Psychological Study of Foreign Policy Decisions and Fiascoes* (Boston, Houghton Miflin, 1972).

Johnson, Paul, 'The Almost Chosen People', in *Time & Tide: A Quarterly Review*, Spring 1985.

Kater, Michael H., *The Nazi Party: A Social Profile of Members and Leaders* (Cambridge, Massachusetts, Harvard University Press, 1983).

Kelly, Reece C., 'Die gescheiterte nationalsozialistische Personalpolitik und die misslungene Entwicklung der nationalsozialistichen Hochschulen' in Manfred Heinemann (Hrsg.), *Erziehung und Schulung im Dritten Reich*, Teil 2. *Hochschule, Erwachsenbildung* (Stuttgart, Klett-Cotta, 1980).

Kershaw, Ian, *Der Hitler-Mythos: Volksmeinung und Propaganda im Dritten Reich* (Stuttgart, Deutsche Verlagsanstalt, 1980).

—— *Popular Opinion and Political Dissent in the Third Reich: Bavaria 1933–1945* (New York, Oxford University Press, 1983).

Koenigsberg, Richard A., *Hitler's Ideology: A Study in Psychoanalytic Sociology* (New York, Library of Social Sciences, 1975).

Kohn, Hans, *The Mind of Germany* (New York, Harper and Row, 1960).

Kren, George M. and Rappoport, Leon, *The Holocaust and the Crisis of Human Behavior* (New York, Holmes and Meier, 1980).

Langer, Walter C., *The Mind of Adolf Hitler* (New York, Basic Books, 1973).

Laqueur, Walter, *The Terrible Secret: Suppression of the Truth About Hitler's 'Final Solution'* (Boston, Penguin Books, 1981).

—— *Young Germany* (New York, Basic Books, 1962).

Lehmann-Haupt, Hellmut, *Art Under a Dictatorship* (New York, Octagon, 1973).

Leiss, William, *The Domination Over Nature* (New York, G. Braziller, 1972).

Lifton, Robert Jay, *History and Human Survival* (New York, Random House, 1971).

Loewenberg, Peter, *Decoding the Past: The Psychohistorical Approach* (New York, Alfred Knopf, 1984).

Manvell, Roger and Fraenkel, Heinrich, *Heinrich Himmler* (London, New English Library, 1969).

Merkl, Peter H. *Political Violence under the Swastika: 581 Early Nazis* (Princeton, New Jersey, Princeton University Press, 1975).

Mewes, Horst, 'The West German Green Party', in *New German Critique*, 1983, *28*, Winter.

Mitterauer, Michael and Sieder, Reinhard, *The European Family: Patriarchy and Partnership from the Middle Ages to the Present*, translated from the German by Karla Oosterveen and Manfred Hörzinger (Chicago, University of Chicago Press, 1982).

Moore, Barrington, *Injustice: The Social Bases of Obedience and Revolt* (White Plains, New York, M.E. Sharpe, 1978).

Mosse, George L., *Nazism: A Historical and Comparative Analysis of National Socialism* (New Brunswick, New Jersey, Transaction Press, 1978).

—— *The Crisis of German Ideology: Intellectual Origins of the Third Reich* (New York, Grosset and Dunlop, 1964).

—— *The Nationalization of the Masses: Political Symbolism and Mass Movements in Germany from the Napoleonic Wars through the Third Reich* (New York, Howard Fertig Inc., 1975).

—— *Towards the Final Solution: A History of European Racism* (New York, Howard Fertig Inc., 1978).

Neumann, Franz, *Behemoth: The Structure and Practice of National Socialism* (New York, Harper and Row, 1942).

Nolte, Ernst, *Three Faces of Fascism*, translated from the German by Leila Vennewitz (New York, New American Library, 1969).

Norden, Albert, *Lehren deutscher Geschichte: Zur politischen Rolle des Finanazkapitals und der Junker* (Berlin, Dietz, 1947).

Paucker, Arnold, *Der jüdische Abwehrkampf gegen Antisemitismus und Nationalsozialismus in der letzen Jahren der Weimarer Republik* (Hamburg, Leibniz-Verlag, 1968).

Petsch, Joachim, *Kunst im Dritten Reich, Architektur, Plastic, Malerei* (Köln, Vista Point Verlag, 1968).

Pois, Robert, *Emil Nolde* (Lanham, Maryland, University Press of America, 1982).

—— *Friedrich Meinecke and German Politics in the Twentieth Century* (Berkeley and Los Angeles, University of California Press, 1972).

—— 'Jewish Treason Against the Laws of Life: Nazi Religiosity and Bourgeois Fantasy' in Michael Dobkowski and Isodor Walliman, *Towards the Holocaust, The Social and Economic Collapse of the Weimar Republic* (Westport, Connecticut, Greenwood Press, 1983).

Poliakov, Leon, *The Aryan Myth: A History of Racist and Nationalist Ideas in Europe*, translated from the French by Edmund Howard (New York, Basic Books, 1974).

Rabinbach, Anson G., 'Toward a Marxist Theory of Fascism and National Socialism: A Report on Developments in West Germany', in *New German Critique*, 1974, *3*, Winter.

—— 'The Aesthetics of Production in the Third Reich', *Journal of Contemporary History*, 1976, *11*, No. 4.

Rank, Otto, *The Myth of the Birth of the Hero and Other Writings*, ed. Philip Freund (New York, Vintage Books, 1959).

Read, Herbert, *The Philosophy of Modern Art* (New York, Meridian Books, 1959).

Reich, Wilhelm, *The Mass Psychology of Fascism*, translated from the German by Vincent R. Carfagno (New York, The Noonday Press, 1970).

Rhodes, James M., *The Hitler Movement: A Modern Millenarian Revolution* (Stanford, Stanford University Press, 1980).

Rubenstein, Richard L., *The Age of Triage, Fear and Hope in an Overcrowded World* (Boston, Beacon Press, 1983).

—— *The Cunning of History: Mass Death and the American Future* (New York, Harper and Row, 1975).

Rupp, Leila, *Mobilizing Women for War: German and American Propaganda 1939–1945* (Princeton, New Jersey, Princeton University Press, 1978).

Samuel, Raphael (ed.), *People's History and Socialist Theory* (London, Routledge and Kegan Paul, 1981).

Schapiro, Leonard, *Totalitarianism* (New York and London, Praeger, 1972).

Schneidermann, Leo, *The Psychology of Myth, Folklore and Religion* (Chicago, Nelson-Hall, 1981).

Schoenbaum, David, *Hitler's Social Revolution: Class and Status in Nazi Germany 1933–1939* (New York, Doubleday, Anchor Books, 1967).

Schweitzer, Arthur, *Big Business in the Third Reich* (Bloomington, Indiana, University of Indiana Press, 1964).

Simmel, Ernst (ed.), *Anti-Semitism: A Social Disease* (New York, International Universities Press, 1946).

Sironneau, Jean-Pierre, *Sécularisation et religions politiques* (The Hague, Paris and New York, Mouton, 1982).

Steinert, Merliss, G., *Hitler's War and the German Public: Moods and Attitudes During the Second World War*, edited and translated by Thomas E.J. de Witt (Athens, Ohio, Ohio University Press, 1977).

Stepan, Nancy, *The Idea of Race in Science, Great Britain 1800–1960* (Hamden, Connecticut, Archon Books, Inc., 1982).

Stephenson, Jill, *The Nazi Organization of Women* (London and Totowa, New Jersey, Croom Helm and Barnes and Noble, 1981).

—— *Women in Nazi Society* (New York, Barnes and Noble, 1975).

Stern, Fritz, *The Politics of Cultural Despair* (New York, Doubleday, Anchor Books, 1962).

Stern, J.P., *Hitler, The Führer and the People* (Berkeley and Los Angeles, University of California Press, 1974).

Stokes, Lawrence, D., 'The German People and the Destruction of the European Jews', in *Central European History*, 1973, *VI*, no. 2, June.

Thompson, Larry V., '*Lebensborn* and the Eugenics Policy of the *Reichsführer* SS' in *Central European History*, 1971, *IV*, no. 1, March.

Turner, Henry Ashby, Jr., *Big Business and the Rise of Hitler* (New York, Oxford University Press, 1985).

Unger, Aryeh L., *The Totalitarian Party: Party and People in Nazi Germany and Soviet Russia* (London, Cambridge University Press, 1974).

Veblen, Thorstein, *The Instinct of Workmanship and the State of the Industrial Arts* (New York, Macmillan, 1914).

Viereck, Peter, *Metapolitics: The Roots of the Nazi Mind* (New York, Capricorn Press, 1960).

Vondung, Klaus, *Magie und Manipulation, Ideologischer Kult und Politische Religion des Nationalsozialismus* (Göttingen, Vandenhoeck and Ruprecht, 1971).

Waite, Robert G., *The Psychopathic God: Adolf Hitler* (New York, Basic Books, 1977).

Weinstein, Fred, *The Dynamics of Nazism: Leadership, Ideology and the Holocaust* (New York, Academic Press, 1980).

INDEX